PÍO PICO

Portrait of Governor Pío Pico. Courtesy of the San Diego Historical Society.

PÍO PICO

The Last Governor of
Mexican California

Carlos Manuel Salomon

UNIVERSITY OF OKLAHOMA PRESS : NORMAN

Publication of this book is made possible through the generosity of Edith Kinney Gaylord.

Library of Congress Cataloging-in-Publication Data

Salomon, Carlos Manuel, 1967–
   Pío Pico : the last governor of Mexican California / Carlos Manuel Salomon.
      p.   cm.
   Includes bibliographical references and index.
   ISBN 978-0-8061-4090-2 (hardcover : alk. paper)
   1. Pico, Pío, 1801–1894. 2. Governors—California—Biography. 3. Mexican Americans—California—Biography. 4. Businessmen—California—Biography. 5. California—History—To 1846. 6. California—History—19th century. 7. California—Politics and government—19th century 8. Political leadership—California—History—19th century. 9. California—Ethnic relations. I. Title.
   F864.P45S25 2010
   979.4'04092—dc22
   [B]

                                                          2009020838

The paper in this book meets the guidelines for permanence and durability of the Committee on Production Guidelines for Book Longevity of the Council on Library Resources, Inc. ∞

1   2   3   4   5   6   7   8   9   10

To my beloved parents, Oscar and Mary Solomon

Contents

Illustrations

Acknowledgments

As a youth growing up in southern California, near San Pascual Valley, I often passed a landmark called "Mule Hill." It was dedicated to brave U.S. servicemen who had given their lives fighting for California. It wasn't until I went to college at San Francisco State University that I realized those men had died trying to rustle the land from its rightful owners. I learned that Andrés Pico had led the valiant Californios in a desperate battle to protect his homeland. As a young, impressionable man, this type of history came alive for me.

At SFSU, in Gordon Seely's seminar on California I produced a short paper on Pío Pico, brother of Andrés Pico. Professor Seely encouraged me to develop it further. I entered the doctoral program in history at the University of New Mexico and immediately found the mentorship I needed to develop my paper into a dissertation. UNM was a perfect place for me to study Latin American and borderlands history. The people, the food, and the history kept me alive during those years, and I began to realize how vitally connected borderland communities are. Robert Himmerick y Valencia immediately took me under his wing and encouraged me to continue my work on Pico. Linda Hall guided my graduate studies in Latin American history. A fine borderlands historian, Dr. Hall saw the potential in my project and helped me to envision it as a story grounded in the transition of two countries. Western historians Richard Etulain and Margaret Connell-Szasz gave generous support and time to the project. Professors Connell-Szasz, Linda Hall, Phillip B. Gonzales, and Sam Truett all read early versions of the entire manuscript and helped it to take shape. Sam Truett guided my research and he proved to be a valuable mentor and a source of constant support. I am indebted to the History Department at UNM, especially the *New Mexico Historical Review*, where I served as an assistant editor from 1996 to 1998. The department provided support and much needed funds. I am eternally grateful to Tobias Durán at the Center for Regional Studies (UNM) for essentially funding my entire doctoral program. I also received a fellowship from the Center for Regional Studies, which allowed me to conduct research in Mexico City.

Numerous people and foundations helped me in many different ways. I am grateful to the John Randolph Haynes Foundation for providing me a fellowship to study at the Huntington Library in southern California. While there I met Paul Gray, also a Pico researcher, who read an earlier version of the manuscript and shared his thoughts. At the Bancroft Library in Berkeley, Theresa Salazar was always kind and pointed me in directions I would never have thought about. At San Francisco State University, Abdiel Oñate, Nancy Mirabal, and Alejandro Murguia provided inspiration and support. At California State University, East Bay, I would like to thank Nicholas Baham, Barbara Paige, Noel Samaroo, Luz Calvo, and Colleen Fong for their engaging conversations and camaraderie. Others who have read sections and given invaluable comments are Merry Ovnick at California State University, Northridge, and my friend and colleague Andrae Marak at the California University of Pennsylvania. At the University of Oklahoma Press, Charles Rankin showed great patience while I made changes to the book. His initial comments helped transform the dissertation into a working biography, accessible to a wider readership. Matthew Bokovoy worked countless hours helping me to improve my writing and to broaden my interpretation. Our conversations on the phone were always helpful, and Matthew always seemed to go the extra distance to make sure this biography turned out the way it did. Also at the University of Oklahoma Press, I would like to thank Marlene Smith-Baranzini and Julie Shilling for their hard work and sharp eyes during the editorial process.

My greatest inspiration is my family. My wife, Dominica, experienced the trauma of living with an academic. She was always supportive and helped me to pursue my dreams. As a chef, her creative element inspired me to finish this book. My parents, Oscar and Mary Solomon, and my siblings Anna, Yolanda, Maria, Alma, and Oscar, Jr., helped me to finish my education and gave me the encouragement to enter graduate school. My father's life inspired me to write. As a storyteller, he gave us children his memories of the *frontera*, that unique piece of land along the United States-Mexico border, of our ancestors, of his life as a youth in Los Angeles and San Diego during the early 1940s, a fisherman, a veteran of World War Two, and a prisoner of war during the Korean War. My mother told us similar stories about her days as the queen of *las fiestas patrias*, or Independence Day celebrations, and as a cannery worker during World War Two. Her stories of life during the Depression were inspirational and kept me grounded in the history of my ancestors. Both of my parents have ancestry in Arizona and California that stretches back to the nineteenth century, and their knowledge of this landscape, of the people and culture of the borderlands, inspired me to become a historian.

PÍO PICO

Introduction

In January 1891, just months before his ninetieth birthday, Pío Pico fought to reclaim what little remained of his once vast empire. As he had done many times in his life, Pico again refused to admit defeat. A life of battles against political rivals and land-hungry swindlers had taught him a thing or two about resilience. After his ten-year legal battle against Los Angeles businessman Bernard Cohn, in which he lost his beloved *Ranchito* in Whittier, California, Pico pressed his lawyers for a third appeal. Concerned about receiving negative publicity that might influence his case, during the trial Pico turned down an offer to represent Mexico in an attempt to reclaim Catalina Island from the United States.

Pico's late-life decision to continue the fight for his home came at a time when many people believed that Mexican influence in California had been destroyed. By this time, most prominent Californios had passed away and many Anglo-Americans had forgotten their contributions to California history.[1] The story of how Mexican power and influence were usurped, however, tends to omit Californios' legal and economic agency. In other words, Californios decided their own fate and made their own decisions, often on their own terms.

In his youth, Pico was larger than life. He often played the role of hero and villain simultaneously and his presence stirred emotion everywhere. As the United States took possession of California, Pico's refusal to immediately accept U.S. hegemony made him a figure of vital concern to California officials. In a dramatic turn of events befitting the violent transition that swept California away from Mexico, Pico soon became one of the new state's wealthiest citizens. But the transformation of California was not going to stop for Pico. As each decade brought further dramatic changes, he faced increasingly complex challenges. After a long career filled with both success and failure, Pico was the last major Californio political figure to wield economic clout. His legal defeat in the second Cohn case was emblematic of California's transition from a Mexican to an Anglo-dominated society. Yet in the aftermath of the highly public trial, no one could imagine that the ninety-year-old Pico was preparing to fight on.

Pico's final economic struggle was characteristic of his extraordinary life. He succeeded in the face of incredible odds. The very longevity of his life, from 1801 to 1894, attests to his indomitable spirit. Yet the man who had such a broad and profound influence on California also had a reckless character. Pico never shied away from taking chances. In 1831, as we shall see, he led a territory-wide rebellion, made up of an informal militia, against the federally appointed governor of California, Manuel Victoria. Eventually, Victoria surrendered to Pico's forces on an arid, desolate battlefield just outside Los Angeles. As a result of his success, Pico was named governor, serving briefly, until he was officially replaced.

Pico's celebrated victory against Victoria made him an influential politician. As his prominence spread, he also acquired vast acreage and political prestige in California. During his second governorship, in 1846, Pico defended California against the invasion of the United States. He had accepted the appointment the previous year despite the belief among wealthy

Californios of an inevitable, imminent invasion by the United States, for which he knew California was not prepared. This bold move revealed Pico's insatiable appetite for power in the face of insurmountable odds.

Over the next forty years, after Mexico's defeat by the United States in 1848, Pico experienced the exhilaration of financial success—followed by bitter disappointment as he lost his assets in court. Many businessmen and land speculators viewed him as an undeserving foreigner controlling a vast empire. Beginning in the 1860s, legal challenges kept him in litigation almost for the rest of his life. Yet Pico was able to continue investing in real estate well into the 1870s. His survival as an important economic force following the U.S.-Mexican War, his centrality in the politics of early California, and his place among Californios help illuminate the larger political, economic, and racial transformation taking place in nineteenth-century California.

Pío Pico belongs to a portion of the American Southwest where the Mexican past has moved into the realm of fable. Unlike New Mexico and Texas, where marks of the early Mexican legacy are as vibrant as ever, California's Mexican past is often distorted, shrouded in museums, relegated to street names and old Spanish missions. Although California is home to more Mexicans than anywhere else in the United States, its massive population boom came after the heyday of the Californios. In Texas and New Mexico, the terms *Tejano* and *Nuevo Mexicano* still define a segment of the population whose culture developed during the Spanish and Mexican colonial periods and remains vibrant today. Massive immigration from all parts of the world, however, changed what was unique about Californio culture. Who were the Californios, what were they like, and why was their early presence important to this story?

The Californios, like the Tejanos and Nuevo Mexicanos, saw themselves as unique from their Mexican relatives. In fact, the Californios referred to themselves proudly as *hijos del país,* or sons of the country—their country, of course, being California. They were the offspring of settlers, mestizos, mulattoes, blacks, Indians, and some whites, who made the cumbersome journey north from places like Sinaloa, Sonora, and Baja California. They often saw later arriving Mexicans as intruders and referred to them as *de la otra banda,* that is, from the other branch of the Mexican nation. The hijos felt they had earned this distinction, settling the land and building towns with intermittent help from the Spanish and Mexican governments. They had roughed it in the wilderness, survived the continual lack of supplies from Mexico City, and rustled the land from the indigenous population. Their antagonism toward Mexico helps explain Pío Pico's often adversarial relationship with Anglo officials who came into power after the U.S.-Mexican War. Although Pico made peace with the newcomers, the Americanos often represented a group that wanted to displace the Californios from what they perceived as their rightful place on the land.

Land itself is a major theme in this history. As elsewhere in past centuries, land ownership in early California became the measure of one's fortune. Desire for land drove the young Pico to enter politics and business. For anyone born without inheritance, however, becoming an influential citizen proved nearly impossible, making Pico's success extraordinary. As a man of mixed African ancestry, Pico also overcame racial prejudice, especially during the U.S. period of California history. Mexican Californios placed far less importance on race than did people from other regions in Mexico, although they still recognized racial and class distinctions. Many military officers, political officials, and major landowners in California boasted of Spanish ancestry. But the distinction rarely affected Pico.

In California's late Spanish period Pico succeeded in opening a business. He purchased a small house in San Diego, and as Mexican independence settled in, he entered politics. As he matured politically, Pico focused on secularization issues, including the task of redistributing mission lands. The missionaries had held the prime real estate in California, and Pico became the chief proponent of a plan to divest the Church of its land. Secularization, which Pico finally completed in 1845, had a major impact on land tenure in California both before and after the U.S.-Mexican War. Had the Church been able to keep its land, the cities and counties in California might look entirely different today. But as the missions faced their slow transition to ruin, Pico began to distribute hundreds of land grants, equaling tens of thousands of acres, particularly to his friends and family.

Pico's land policies, which favored Californios, helped bring about the California Land Act of 1851. This reactionary law eventually destroyed the Californio power base and helped land speculators break up the larger ranches and shape the towns, cities, and counties of today. But Pico survived the initial attack, increased his empire, and became one of California's major cattle barons. He began to dabble in real estate in 1870, building and operating the Pico House in Los Angeles, for many years one of California's most luxurious hotels. He was incensed by the injustices against Californio land owners and many times served as a witness for them in court. He set up funds, wrote letters, and lent money to less fortunate Californios after the war.

Although Pico eventually lost his empire, he should not be seen as a victim of injustice. It can rightly be argued that he became the most litigious Californio of his time, and his utilization of the legal process demonstrates his enthusiasm for facing change. Pico marched headfirst into hostile terrain as a shrewd businessman. His bold personality enabled him to compete in a cutthroat business environment even after the United States had acquired California. Pío Pico's life brings into question the prevailing theory that accounts for the Californios' decline.[2] The traditional view is that with Mexico's defeat in 1848, U.S. institutions, culture, and prejudice began to erode the Californio power structure, eventually overwhelming it.

Pico's life experience demands an approach that is not confined to the idea of steady political and economic degeneration at the hands of overpowering enemies. The idea of economic decline cannot account for Pico's fluctuating success as a businessman. And unlike earlier investigations of hapless Californios and their property losses, a study of Pico's life reveals him as a man fully engaged in the American legal system. He made lasting alliances with white Americans, celebrated the U.S. political system through his active participation in the Republican Party, and attempted to reconcile Anglo and Mexican differences. Anglo-American avarice and greed was not the underlying factor in Pico's demise. He and his Californio counterparts were often fiercely independent and dictated their own fates.

Pico discovered his particular independence during his youth, when the young Californio became enmeshed in the politics of early republican Mexico. California played a more integral role in Mexican politics than many historians recognize. The political and physical battles Californios waged against the ruling Mexican government in the first half of the nineteenth century prepared them for the coming onslaught of American institutions. Pico played a central role in the troublesome relationship between California and the federal government of Mexico. Far from fearing ruination, the Californios looked toward the future with intense enthusiasm.

The biography of one man cannot hope to change the view of a people's predetermined economic and political decline (a reality for many Californios). More research on legal and economic agency is needed. Clearly Pío Pico was in a position to defend himself, unlike many Californios. Even so, an analysis of Pico's actions demands a retelling of the California narrative. While Pico ultimately fell victim to fraud, it was his own reckless behavior that undermined him. He controlled his own fate. He met his enemies with fierce legal opposition. He challenged notions of racial superiority, policies from Mexico City, U.S. aggression toward Californios, and the unrelenting attempt of Americans to disenfranchise the established population. He did these things not because of his economic decline but because of his desire to live life to its fullest. The fierce battles Californios waged in the late-nineteenth century presaged the battles Mexican Americans faced in the twentieth century. And like Pico's battles, they were not fought for survival, but for recognition and prosperity.

CHAPTER 1

A California Family

Historians have written that Pío de Jesús Pico (1801–1894) made his name as a revolutionary leader.[1] The popular image of Pico is as a young man on horseback, blazing trails in the arid southern California sun and confronting his opponents against impossible odds. While some truth can be found in these stories, Pico's true obsession concerned the forging of a new society. He was a politician, after all, and came of age during the formative period of California history. Californio politicians cherished their independence above all else. But as in any region destined to make up a borderland, competing forces pulled in contrasting directions. California was an immensely contentious region during the nineteenth century. Although it was part of Mexico, the government struggled to win the respect of California citizens as fiercely as the United States determined to conquer it. Borders are formed in such ways and are often the result of generations of cultural and political contention. No single episode can determine their nature or their outcome. The narrative of Pico's early life, however, evokes the transformative spirit of the Californios and reveals how enthusiastically they participated in the evolution of their homeland.

California was formed between two worlds at the decline of the Spanish empire and the dawn of an emerging United States. As the Anglo-American colonists prepared for revolution against England, Spanish California remained a largely unknown landscape to all but the indigenous population. By 1769 the Spanish government began to settle California. Roughly fifty years later, some of the first English-speaking sojourners marveled at the peaceful coexistence of its inhabitants and at the beautiful and bountiful land. Alfred Robinson, who arrived in 1829 as a clerk for the Boston firm of Bryant, Sturgis & Company, saw Monterey as "situated on the declivity of a beautiful rising ground, the top of which is crowned with stately pines. . . . There are many pleasant locations in the vicinity where the natives frequently resort to celebrate their festivities. . . ."[2] Although Robinson adapted to Californio life, converted to Catholicism, and married Ana María de la Guerra, a daughter of one of California's most illustrious families, his description of his new homeland foreshadows the menacing interest Anglo-Americans had in California land. The American westward movement was already in progress as Robinson's ship anchored in Monterey Bay. His employer, Bryant, Sturgis & Company, among others, helped to intensify the hide-and-tallow trade in California, dominated by U.S. firms, which brought Mexican California closer to the economic sphere of an emerging global market. Such seemingly innocent trade relations helped to create wealthy families like the Picos.

There is some truth to Robinson's descriptions of California, however flawed and romanticized his views may have been. When he arrived, California had an extremely diverse Indian population, living in hundreds of small villages and thinly populated settlements. In southern California the land was arid, yet suitable for sustaining life and ideal for ranching. As the first Spanish explorers recognized, California had profound geographic contrasts, where deserts gave way to bountiful

forests, and pine-covered coastal ranges dropped suddenly
into the expansive ocean. The settlers pushed forward to forge
a new society, brutally conquering lands and people that stood
in their way. The continuous construction of presidios,
missions, and pueblos allowed the Californios to create an
isolated and far-removed outpost of the Mexican nation.
Naming them as they trudged north, San Diego de Alcalá,
Los Angeles, San José, and Santa Barbara were but a few of the
sites they selected as settlements. Spain's imperial dreams laid
the ground work for a new land, literally on the cultural and
geographic fringe of Mexican society.

From the Spanish period forward, California attracted a
small but wide variety of people, mostly poor *pobladores*, or
townspeople. They were a racially diverse group who, as many
later settlers also would, saw California as an economic opportunity. Many families, like the Picos, were of African descent.
Twenty-six of the original forty-four founders of Los Angeles,
for example, were of Afro-Mexican origin. Also present were
Indians, mestizos, a few Spaniards, and a variety of mixed
racial castes. For the most part, early California settlers did
not fit the profile of the land owning classes living in the interior
of New Spain, who tended to be of pure Spanish descent.
The opportunity for land and a new start attracted them
from the beginning. As the years went by they began to take
root in their new homeland and a distinct culture emerged.
Like other communities on the borderlands, cultural contact
between settlers and the surrounding Indian population produced a convergence of ideas and identities.[3] Indian and
colonizer together created a hybrid culture in a land removed
from the cities of New Spain.

Like most early Alta California settlers, the Pico family had
few economic resources. Pío's grandfather, Santiago de la Cruz
Pico, came from Sinaloa, some six or seven hundred miles
northwest of Mexico City, and had accompanied Juan Bautista
de Anza to California in 1775 as a soldier. The colonial Spanish

government had commissioned Anza in 1774 to open a land route from Sonora to the California coast. With the success of his first journey, Anza recruited two hundred forty settlers for the next, including many soldiers, to found a settlement on the shores of the San Francisco Bay. These soldiers and their families mostly came from the states of Sinaloa and Sonora. The route north was dangerous, primarily because of the scarcity of water and the constant fear of Indian aggression. Father Pedro Font, who accompanied Anza on the second journey, presaged the urgency attached to the spiritual conquest of California as he observed indigenous communities along the way. "Shall we think that God created these men merely to condemn them to Inferno, after passing in this world a life so miserable as that which they live? By no means!"[4] For Santiago Pico and his sons, Font's words had a prophetic reality. Some, including Pico's father, would become mission guards.

The military personnel who settled in California were part of New Spain's strategic plan to protect California from the threat of foreign invasion and the reprisals of Indian converts.[5] Life in the military had few rewards. Charged with exploring California's vast terrain, soldiers had to protect against foreign invasions at the newly established presidios, guard settlements, and protect the missions against Indian attacks. But they also had the often brutal task of putting runaway Indian converts into irons. These frontier soldiers had the thankless undertaking of imposing colonialism on native inhabitants, even if it was an incomplete conquest. Although this imposition resulted in a hybrid culture because of the resiliency of native people and their methods of survival, the frontier military drastically altered the life of California Indians who lived near the Pacific coast.[6]

Santiago Pico's son, José María, found a constant source of employment as a guard in the mission communities. He eventually started a family, and in 1801 Pío Pico was born at Mission San Gabriel. Santiago often moved from mission to mission as duty called, and it was outside the tiny settlement of Mission San Diego that Pico spent his childhood.

San Diego was not a bad place to live in the early days of California. The region's first permanent settlement, it had the advantage of including both a mission and a presidio, similar to the settlements of Santa Barbara, Monterey, and San Francisco. Although not considered a civilian town like San José or Los Angeles, abundant opportunity for regional trade and travel existed. Young Pico received a modest education there, as well as any boy from his class could expect, and often read from the Bible at Mass. Years later he recalled, "I knew all Ripalda's catechism from beginning to end."[7] Although not profoundly religious, Pico and others in San Diego felt the immense presence of the Church, especially since the mission dominated the economy.

Life in San Diego also had its limits. Young men usually took an interest in the military or the Church since relatively few other work options existed. Pío became interested in his father's profession and in 1815 local officials temporarily left him in charge of the mission guards in his father's absence. By this time his family had established its reputation in the military and among leading politicians. Because of its limited population, San Diego allowed any eager youth the ability to make connections with high-ranking officials. With only a handful of families in residence, its military and religious foundation formed a shared landscape with a close-knit community. The French merchant Auguste Bernard Duhaut-Cilly visited San Diego in 1827 and estimated there were only thirty to forty houses in the community. Another visitor, the Bostonian Alfred Robinson, estimated just thirty houses in 1829.[8] In this relatively intimate location, Pico befriended priests, officers, and merchants. San Diego was the perfect location for a man of Pico's limited means to advance his situation.

In many areas of New Spain a man of Pico's racially mixed heritage had few options to advance himself. A rigid racial hierarchy existed throughout colonial Latin American society. The caste system insured that Spaniards and their American-born children held the highest social rank in society. But the atmosphere in California was much different, and the rigidity of racial purity was not as important there. This fact helps explain how California's prime location became a meeting place for intersecting cultures. As Mexico won its independence, many Anglos entered the region to take advantage of the newly opened commercial markets. Politicians hurled proclamations declaring the "liberation" of the Indians from the care of the friars, and more new settlers began to enter from Mexico. Although some hoped to maintain racial purity, it was not always possible in California. For example, Pío Pico's lineage included Indian, Spanish, and African ancestry, which together placed him near the bottom of the caste system. His great-grandfather, the Spanish-born Pío Pico III, had likely come to Mexico in the first or second decade of the eighteenth century, according to one source.[9] Pío Pico's mestizo grand-father, Santiago de la Cruz Pico, married María Jacinta Vastida, listed as *mulata* in the 1790 census.[10] An interesting fact about José María Pico is that the 1790 census listed him as a Spaniard but listed his brothers as mulattoes.[11] He was on his way, so he thought, to a promising military career. He may have won the "privilege" of listing himself as a Spaniard, or he may have simply used trickery, such as purchasing a certifi-cate that supported his claim. He also married an española, María Eustaquia Gutiérrez, which may have given his family certain privileges in late colonial California.[12]

However, Californios began to break away from such arbi-trary racial categories even before Mexican independence paved the way for the abolition of the caste system. Although many Californio officials and landowners could boast of Spanish lineage, mestizos and mulattoes often received grants of land and took on important political roles, especially after Mexican independence.[13] It was Pico's poverty that generated the

greatest obstacle to his mobility. Pico recalled that, because
of lack of housing at Mission San Gabriel, he was born in a
shack made of branches.[14] With a family of ten children, the
Picos found it difficult to support themselves.[15] Although a
hardworking, industrious man, José María Pico pursued an
elusive quest to gain land and become an officer in the
Spanish military.

Californios were impoverished for various reasons. Mexico
City's inability to continuously supply the distant colony,
especially during the wars of independence, left California
constantly undersupplied. Settlers complained about the
mission's near-monopoly of valuable coastal lands. Although
offering little aid to the settlers, Spain enthusiastically populated California with individuals like Santiago de la Cruz Pico.
He had five sons, two of whom, José María and José Dolores,
firmly established the Pico family in both southern and northern California. Despite their poverty, the Pico brothers had
distinguished themselves in the military. Californios often relied
on their own vision to shape California because of the Spanish
Crown's lack of involvement. For example, California Governor
Vicente Solá wrote to Mexico City in 1817 to report that the
soldiers hadn't been paid in months, often went hungry, and
suffered from lack of clothing.[16] It is no wonder the soldiers
soon came to envy the priests, whom they believed lived in
immaculate and fully stocked mission buildings. The priests
had the advantage of a free Indian labor pool, which dramatically increased the wealth of the missions.[17] Even so, the priests
often suffered from the same lack of supplies. The California
economy was heavily dependent on the missions because of
their ability to produce goods and trade. Despite some antagonism, there existed a mutual commercial relationship between
the missions and the government, while military personnel
often went poor.[18]

Certain members of the Pico family distinguished themselves, however, and are among a handful of enlisted families

who received grants of land during the colonial period. During the 1775 Anza expedition, Santiago de la Cruz Pico followed the colonizer to San Francisco where he intended to stay. In 1777 he transferred to San Diego and thereafter retired to the pueblo of Los Angeles.[19] His sons all joined the military, and like José María, distinguished themselves in duty. In 1795 Governor Diego de Borica granted José María's brothers, Javier, Miguel, and Patricio, along with their father, Santiago, the Rancho San José de García de Simí near Ventura and Los Angeles counties.[20] José Dolores, perhaps the most successful of the brothers, served in the Santa Barbara and later the Monterey military companies. He made a good name for himself as a soldier and Indian fighter and received the recognition of his superiors. José Dolores and his wife, Gertrudis Amezquita, raised their family in Monterey and later the government granted him the Bolsa de San Cayetano Rancho in 1819.[21] Government officials granted pueblo settlers plots of land for a house and a small claim of agricultural land on the pueblo outskirts. These small plots were the incentives for recruiting soldiers. But the largest grants were scarce during this period. The Spanish government gave a few of these ranchos to the most deserving petitioners.

Pío Pico's father, José María, never experienced such luck. He enlisted with the San Diego Company in 1782 and a few years later served as a guard at Mission San Gabriel.[22] From 1780 to 1790 José María Pico advanced as one of the most prominent enlisted men in southern California. By 1785 he seemed to be heading toward a promising future. That year military officials celebrated José María's skills when he uncovered a planned Indian uprising at Mission San Gabriel.

The Gabrieleño Indians' complaint was that the missionaries deprived the Indians of their culture and freedom. The Indians, once baptized, had to learn Christianity, reject their traditional religion, and work for the benefit of the mission community.[23] Work was regarded as a necessary step in the process of civilizing them. This atmosphere produced continuous Indian rebellions that took on various forms throughout the missions. Indians frequently attempted to escape from the padres. At Mission San Gabriel, the rebels prepared for a full scale attack.

Their plot was a single episode in the unending struggle of Indians against the California mission system. Unfortunately for the rebels, the plan failed. José María apparently could speak the native language of the Gabrieleños, or Tongva, as they called themselves. Somewhere in the vicinity of the mission, he overheard the rebels speaking of a plot to attack the mission.[24] José María hurried back to report the news to Corporal José María Verdugo.

Plans for the rebellion developed around a group of escaped neophytes, in particular, the so-called renegade Nicolas José. The rebels targeted Verdugo, the soldiers, and the padres alike. Apparently José made plans with a local chief to attack the mission, and in the process, begin a massive rebellion to repel the Spanish from southern California entirely. Pico informed Verdugo that the rebels depended upon the magic of a power-ful woman named Toypurina. Reportedly, Toypurina had convinced Nicolas José and Chief Temejasaquichi that she could place a spell on the priests and soldiers, putting them into a deep sleep while Tongva warriors went in for the easy kill. Pico must have been fluent in the Tongva language. He reported detailed information, including the time and place of the attack. With this knowledge, Pico spoiled the uprising and the leaders were apprehended.

The story of Toypurina, the female Indian leader, the neo-phyte Nicolas José, and the Tongva community is an important example of resistance against the colonial order in California.[25] It also reveals a great deal about power, land, and mobility in early California, especially if we look at Pico's life in the years following the event.

The uprising underscores the racial complexity in a religious and political system that perpetuated colonialism.

Although Pico had both Indian and black ancestry, he and all other soldiers sided with the Spanish. Indians were seen as a highly uncivilized group who could be "corrected" with careful instruction. Perhaps it is because of Pico's extraordinary service in foiling the plot that the 1790 census listed him as a Spaniard instead of a mulatto like his brothers. This constructed identity, along with the desire for upward mobility, is important in understanding why a landless soldier would perform his duties with such enthusiasm.[26] With the rebellion prevented for the time being, Corporal Verdugo distributed an official military report to high-level Spanish officials.[27] They took the matter so seriously that Governor Don Pedro Fages became directly involved. After Fages, Verdugo, and Pico completed an extensive interrogation, Governor Fages labeled José María "a Spaniard of implicit trust. . . ."[28] In reality, the San Gabriel rebellion initiated a troubled relationship between Hispanics and California Indians. The pervasiveness of Indian rebellion in California kept men like Pico employed in mission defense, even if it was a job that often failed to bring financial success.

Although Governor Fages praised Pico, he remained a soldier and never rose to the rank of officer. From time to time he may have wondered why he chose to remain on the distant California frontier. For many soldiers, duty in California kept them isolated from Spanish society, commercial markets, and accessibility to other conveniences found in the cities of New Spain. In fact, New Spain and Mexico often used California as a penal colony for felons. Some citizens, like Miguel Cuevas, who lived in the Mexican interior, asked the government for permission to send his son on military duty to California as a punishment for disobedience; Cuevas agreed to pay all his son's expenses.[29] José María Pico believed that his efforts would lead to a secure retirement and a grant of land, a *merced*. His long service to the Spanish military was certainly worthy of a land grant. He held many posts later in his life and in the early 1800s became sergeant of the San Diego Presidio, and Commander of the Guard at San Gabriel.

By 1810 the movement for Mexican independence began to escalate. California, although removed from the centers of industry and commerce, received news of the mounting problems from the beginning. José Antonio de la Guerra y Noriega, a Spanish lieutenant at the Santa Barbara Presidio, learned in 1809 of Napoleon's seizure of the Spanish throne.[30] Although most top officials in California rejected the idea of independence from Spain, many individuals heard rumors of tremendous battles being waged in the mainland, where ordinary men of mixed racial background made heroes of themselves. The national leader of the insurgents, mestizo priest José María Morelos, eventually called for the abolition of slavery and of all caste systems.[31] Spaniards everywhere became suspect, and in 1815 Mexican insurgents captured Guerra y Noriega along with a group of Europeans in San Blas.[32]

The motive that impelled José María Pico to join the Mexican cause is unclear; perhaps he agreed with the complaints of leading insurgents throughout Mexico. His support for Mexican independence did not help his chances of receiving a land grant for his earlier good deeds. At San Diego in 1811, military officials charged the local troops with conspiracy to side with the movement for independence. They accused José María of rebellion and incarcerated him. As sergeant of the troops at the time, Pico was imprisoned for conspiracy, along with at least sixty soldiers at the San Diego Presidio. Through the influence of local priests, Spanish officials set Pico free, yet they incarcerated his cohort, artilleryman Ignacio Zúñiga, who, according to Pico, was put "in chains until independence was achieved."[33] Colonial authorities marked José María as a conspirator in a movement that never gained much popular support in California.

Perhaps having lost faith in the virtues of a military career, José María Pico died at Mission San Gabriel in September

1819. He was not granted the honor of an early retirement nor given even a patch of land or money to leave his family. Never able to enjoy the prosperity that Mexican independence brought his children, José María died during the last gasp of Spanish colonialism. In the end he died at a relatively young age, failing to accomplish his goals.

At the death of their father, and with the eldest brother serving in northern California, the grieving Pío de Jesús Pico inherited the care of an enormous family. He recalled that "nothing was left us—even an inch of ground."[34] He had to somehow manage without the advantage of owning land, which, even after Mexican independence, remained a requirement for entering politics.

CHAPTER 2

California Rebel

Reexamining Pico's Role in California Politics, 1828–1835

Pío Pico was not born to be a politician. Yet more than any other single aspect of his life, his political career brought him power and sealed his place in the history of California. His success as a politician eclipsed that of any other Californio, with the possible exception of his *compadre* Juan Bautista Alvarado.[1] Pico's political life lasted only nineteen years, from 1828 to 1847, of a ninety-three-year lifespan (1801–94).[2] He came into politics with little more than his youthful idealism; often made drastic, even hasty, decisions; was jealous and capricious; and was one of the most ambitious individuals in early California politics.

Although Pico often used his power to accommodate the landed classes, he had what many politicians lacked: a flair for controversy. He was skilled at placing himself in the center of conflict and coming out ahead. He was not afraid to oppose direct orders from Mexico City, a quality that won him the enthusiastic support of many who believed the federal government encroached on their liberties. In fact it was this antagonistic feud with Mexico City that helped to forge the unique political space California held within the Republic of Mexico. Pico's early political life exemplifies a frenzied pattern of rivalry and reveals a political atmosphere in California intimately linked to government affairs in Mexico City.

The Californios were an industrious and calculating people intent on creating a new and unique society. They saw themselves as distinct from other Mexicans and adapted the government's liberal political doctrines to fit their new realities.[3] The result was the creation of a regional movement, one whose intention was to force the federal government to yield a degree of sovereignty to California.[4] Although the Californios' fight for sovereignty ultimately allowed wealthy families to dominate the distribution of land, their movement reveals a developing ideology associated with California's geopolitical situation. They were not a "static" people in any sense of the word, and California was not a region in decline. They managed an erratic political climate with strategic plans and with the distinct hope that their actions would create a bright future for themselves and their offspring. Political transition in California was constant during the nineteenth century, allowing politicians there to take immediate action as Spanish authority began to wane.

Nearly a decade before Mexico won independence in 1821, California's political structure had drastically changed. In 1812, with the passage of the Spanish constitution, representative government swept through the Spanish colonial world.[5] For the first time, town councils, or *ayuntamientos,* formed, as did *diputaciones,* or state and territorial legislative bodies. Although Mexican independence did little to change the form and function of these political bodies, the constitution of 1824 finally allowed local citizens to participate in key positions of power.[6] Despite California having been relegated to the status of a territory, Californios eventually organized their own ayuntamientos and a diputación.[7] Politicians scrambled to win seats in local government posts. Nevertheless, these territorial political bodies had limited power and waited for the federal government to approve many of their actions, including the appointment of California's governor. Lack of representation kept the territories of California and New Mexico under the control of the federal government, a fact that bred resentment in the population. Locally, *liberalismo,* or representative democracy, allowed Californios like Pío Pico to act independently of Mexico City.

Although Mexicans generally agreed that independence from Spain was necessary, citizens did not all agree politically. Some scholars question whether Mexico had a national identity at the time of independence. Did, in fact, the concept of nationhood exist?[8] At first, Californios had little concept of themselves as Mexicans, and their political identity did not emerge until they were forced to deal with national realities.[9] This may have been because of California's location on the geographic periphery. Most of those who settled there before 1830 had come from other frontier regions far removed from Mexico City. Thus the new republic inherited a region with fragmented links to the capital. Like all countries that evolve from colonies to independent nations, Mexico's process of nation building was painful, and the country as a whole may not have been prepared for such drastic change. With independence, leaders scrambled to create a new government. Although the political development of postindependent Mexico seems far removed from matters in the distant lands of California, events in the capital had a far-reaching impact on outlying regions. Most notably, California had to prepare for its role within the new country.

Mexican independence began with Agustín Iturbide's *Plan de Iguala,* the treaty that negotiated the end of hostilities between Mexico and Spain and established a constitutional monarchy, under which Iturbide took the name Agustín I. Iturbide was an elite officer who had defected from the Spanish army. The Plan de Iguala was in some ways a compromise between conservative *criollos,* those born in America of Spanish

descent, who fought to preserve Spanish rule, and the insurgents, who rallied for self-government.[10] The plan turned many
former royalists to the side of independence, especially because
it promoted conservative ideals and protected the rights of
Spaniards and criollos. Iturbide himself was a Mexican who
had originally fought to maintain Spanish colonialism. In fact,
six former royalists who ultimately turned to the side of the
insurgency would govern Mexico before the rise of Benito Juarez
at mid-nineteenth century.[11] The plan upheld Catholicism as
the official religion and required the appointment of a European prince or another suitable figure to govern Mexico. For
their part, the insurgents were satisfied with gaining independence. Unlike the victorious armies of Simón Bolivar in
South America, the Mexican insurgents had been defeated
on more than one occasion, despite making advancements.

Agustín Iturbide became emperor in 1822.[12] During the
revolution he had won a series of battles against the insurgents
and had come to understand that Spain could not impel the
rebels, who fought under the leadership of Vicente Guerrero
and Guadalupe Victoria, to surrender. The rebels' guerilla
warfare tactics eroded the confidence of the Spanish army.
Moreover, the king of Spain had been forced to accept the
liberal 1812 Constitution, which conservative criollos detested
for its anti-Church sentiment. This made their decision to
abandon the royalist cause an easy one.

After the war, Iturbide sought to impose conservative ideals
in Mexico. During his short reign, he empowered the Mexican
elite, dissolved Congress, and ignored the demands of former
insurgents. The insurgents, most of whom were liberals, wanted
a federalist government with a degree of sovereignty for the
states. By 1823 Iturbide was forced to abdicate because of
the constant protests of liberals, including the insurrection
of General Antonio López de Santa Anna, who in 1822 issued
the *Plan de Veracruz* calling for the overthrow of Iturbide and
the formation of a new congress.[13] In the ashes of Iturbide's

empire a fragile federal republic arose in Mexico, one in which explosive political debates had serious repercussions for California.

The primary political debate that ensued generally came from two factions: the centralists and the liberals. Centralists tended to favor a strong central government that dictated policy for the states. In their opinion, only men of status should govern; therefore, the elites would hold enormous power over the country. Centralists believed their ideas created stability as decisions would be made in a single locale, Mexico City, rather than among states sharing power. Centralists also believed in maintaining the overwhelming influence of the Church. In some instances, they even called for a return of racial distinctions, favoring those with Spanish ancestry.[14] Liberals, on the other hand, wanted a federal government that shared power with the states. They also believed in secular education apart from the influence of the Church. They viewed corporate property, such as that held by the Church, as detrimental to the rights of the citizens, and so they also favored the breakdown of ecclesiastical privilege. Liberals believed in liberty and the ability of the general populace to determine its own future.[15] Because Mexico adopted a federal government under the Constitution of 1824, it is safe to say that liberalism dominated the political imagination of most citizens.

The majority of Californios likewise supported liberalism. California had long ago developed a political culture separate from Mexico City, and many did not want the central government to interfere with their affairs.[16] Liberalismo influenced a handful of ambitious, young Californios to vie for top political posts. They had never tasted political power and, coming of age after Mexico's independence, they quickly became energized by the new political philosophies emerging in Europe and Mexico. One of theses Californios, Juan Bautista Alvarado, wrote that he, his uncle Mariano Guadalupe Vallejo, and his cousin José Castro were nearly excommunicated from the Church for secretly possessing the works of Voltaire and Rousseau.[17] These liberal ideas, which had consumed political thought in Mexico, sparked the imagination of many Californios. They lashed out against centralist ideas, the privilege and authority of the Church, and the judicial authority the military held over civilians. A generation of like-minded Californio youth seized the ideals of liberalism emanating from Mexico and championed the liberal cause.

In his *Narración Histórica*, which he recounted in 1877, Pío Pico described how dramatically liberalism influenced him.[18] He spoke of a merchant named Luis Bringas who came to California with a consignment of goods from the Mexican government. In 1827, when Captain Pablo de la Portilla brought charges against Bringas for misappropriation of funds, the merchant bitterly protested. Portilla, who had appointed Pico as his secretary, brought Bringas before a military tribunal. Pico watched in disbelief as Bringas proclaimed that "the civilians were the sacred core of the nation and that the military were nothing more than servants."[19] The merchant's response had a profound affect on Pico's developing beliefs. The event so affected Pico that he broke from the line of command and sided with Bringas. In the process he ended up in jail for refusing to comply with military orders. The incident marks the first time that Pico appears on record in a political capacity.

In the 1820s, California underwent a revolutionary shift in the political character of its citizens. With the arrival of Governor José María de Echeandía in 1825, California gained its first distinguished partisan of Mexican liberalism. Echeandía immediately began to attack long-standing conservative policies. Like many liberal politicians all across Mexico, Echeandía attacked the mission system. He favored secularization, which would allow the government to free mission Indians from the control of the padres, distribute the lands to them, and turn the missions into parish churches. Excess land was ordinarily auctioned off to the highest bidder. As secularization became such an important liberal policy, the missionaries took a defensive stance against it almost immediately. California officials countered, demanding the ecclesiastical hierarchy take an oath of allegiance to the Mexican nation.[20] Father President Vicente Francisco de Sarría refused to take the oath because, as he said in his defense, he had sworn an oath to the King of Spain.[21] When authorities in Mexico City learned of Sarría's resistance, they ordered him to report immediately to the capital.

Governor Echeandía instigated such unrest. With land as a prize he could award, he had no problem winning over young and impressionable politicians like Vallejo, Alvarado, and Pico. These young liberals made their marks in various ways. Mariano Guadalupe Vallejo became a skilled military officer known for brokering peace with Indians.[22] He went on to become the leading military figure in California. His nephew, Juan Bautista Alvarado, entered politics as the secretary of the diputación, and later served as governor from 1836 to 1842.[23] Both Vallejo and Alvarado became prominent land barons and, like Pico, were among California's wealthiest citizens. Alvarado, Vallejo, and Pico belonged to the same generation of ambitious, young politicians whose liberal ideas controlled California's political system and land base during the formative years of the Mexican republic.

Despite the influence of liberal politics in Mexico, liberalismo did not go unchallenged. Conservative politicians and theorists were adamantly opposed to modeling Mexico after the political values of the United States. Mexico had Spanish and Mesoamerican roots, unlike the Anglo North Americans.[24] Leaders argued that increased power for the states would create regional strife and perhaps even calls for separation from the central government. Nevertheless, both liberals and conservatives influenced the Mexican Constitution of 1824. Ratified on October 4, the Constitution created a federalist state with separation of powers. However, it also continued Catholicism as the only religion tolerated, and it continued the practice of military and ecclesiastical privileges for those groups.[25] Successful political theorists like José María Luis Mora felt that the distant territory of California, because of its isolation and seemingly uncorrupt officials, was a perfect testing ground for liberal reforms like secularization. At the same time, conservatives believed California was a perfect region in which to maintain Church authority.[26] California seemed destined to become a battleground for the two major political factions.

California politicians generally accepted the territory's role within the republic, unless of course the federal government tried to impose restrictions on them. Many complaints mounted against the federal government. For example, the fact that the government sent criminals to California to serve as soldiers became a major concern, and many Californios came to resent the federal government. Juan B. Alvarado, writing of an incident that occurred in the first years after independence, proclaimed that a "shipment of criminals was the first proof offered to the Californians that the general government had not forgotten them."[27] Although Californio politicians followed orders from Mexico City and often asked for various kinds of assistance, they grew more distant as centralists gained power in Mexico City. Soon frontier politicians in California began to feel that they lacked the autonomy other Mexicans enjoyed. Taking control of local politics could alleviate this situation, an endeavor that greatly inspired Pico and his colleagues.

Pico's success in California can also be attributed to family unions. He had seven sisters who married into some of the most important families in California. But unlike the marriages and unions forged among ranchero families, the Pico sisters most likely married for love. With little to give in terms of a dowry, the sisters were not from a family that bachelors targeted to increase their wealth. But San Diego's small and isolated population meant that couples often fell in love despite their financial situation. The marriages of Pico's sisters, Concepción to Domingo Carrillo in 1810, María Casimira to José Joaquín Ortega in 1821, and Estéfana to José Antonio Carrillo in 1823, gave the family its first taste of material security.[28] Carlos Carrillo, the son of Captain Raimundo Carrillo, would serve as California's representative to the Mexican Congress. Carlos's younger brother, José Antonio, had an impressive political career and would eventually become one of eight Californio representatives at the state Constitutional Convention in 1849. Earlier in his life he ran a school at the San Diego Presidio, where he taught Pío Pico.[29] This education would prove vital to Pico's future in the Mexican Republic, since the government required elected officers to be literate. Although it is difficult to determine, it is likely that his older and established brother-in-law José Antonio Carillo influenced Pico's political rise. Carrillo was certainly the greatest influence of Pico's youth.

Similar family unions created a network that would eventually dominate Californio politics. Pico became intimately involved with the families his sisters married into. These connections helped propel him to a new level of prominence, and by 1826 the twenty-five-year-old Pico had become a highly successful political figure in Alta California, winning elections in San Diego's town council and later as a member of the California-wide diputación in 1828. By 1830 a small group of military families that forged ties through marriage and *compadrazgo*, that is, godfathering, had managed to take complete control over territorial politics. In 1831, the California legislature consisted of the following individuals: Pico, Alvarado, Vallejo, Ortega, Argüello, Osío, Bandini, and Yorba, who were interrelated in one way or another.[30]

Emulating California's prominent families, Pico began to take advantage of his family's good name. Although without large estates, herds of cattle, or other significant assets, Pico capitalized on the well-placed marriages of his sisters. With his business skills and his knack for interjecting his voice into the center of sensitive political situations, Pico emerged as a highly successful politician.

By 1829 Pico had maneuvered himself into an influential political position in California. That year, Governor Echeandía granted him Rancho Jamul, Pico's first large ranch. Situated about thirty miles east of San Diego, Rancho Jamul brought Pico wealth and prestige. Pico fought to win a place as a member of the landowning class. With an economy partially based on cattle, property owners commanded the greatest amount of respect in Californio society. Similar land grants went to other California politicians during this time, as many began to accumulate wealth through government favors. In the north, for example, Mariano Vallejo received the 66,622-acre Rancho Petaluma in 1834.[31] The much smaller 8,926 acres of Jamul proved suitable for ranching, and Pico began stocking it with cattle and horses almost as soon as he received the grant.[32] Soon after, he had an adobe house built close to Jamul Creek. He hired *vaqueros*; a *mayordomo*, or manager, named Juan Leiva; and began to cultivate a cattle empire.[33] Although he had become a rancher, Pico remained actively involved in politics.

By the late 1820s the liberal party seemed to be crumbling from within. Although they had elected a president in Guadalupe Victoria and had taken political control of most state governments, factions begin to brew among them.[34] Encouraged by popular support for their vision, and especially their leaders, the federalists also gained momentum. Their popularity especially spread through the Masonic lodges, most notably the Yorkinos, who advocated a radical separation from Spanish colonial policies, including the expulsion of Spanish residents.[35] Leaders of the federalist persuasion found their way to all corners of Mexico, including California. The liberal ideology inspired a form of nationalism among the young politicians of Pico's generation. In liberalism they found paths to self-empowerment and a solution to their frustrations over California's isolation.

The federalists, however, were not unopposed. By 1829 the economy had faltered, and some blamed it on the expulsion of the Spaniards, who were, not surprisingly, among the country's most prominent financiers. To bolster the economy, liberal president Vicente Guerrero imposed a direct tax, which alarmed many and aroused anger even among supporters of the federation. Guerrero had actually risen to power as a result of a revolution waged on his behalf. After losing the election of 1828 to the moderate Manuel Gómez Pedraza, the pro-liberal general Santa Anna raised an army. Soon after, troops at the armory of Acordada, on the outskirts of Mexico City, declared themselves in open rebellion against Pedraza. Guerrero joined the rebellion, and Pedraza fled to England. Guerrero was named president after Pedraza's election was annulled. Although Guerrero was a national hero from the wars of independence, he entered office with scant support. Simón Bolívar, hero of independence in South America, saw the actions of Guerrero and Santa Anna as a death sentence to the federation, perpetuated by a "barbarian" (Guerrero), and other "demagogues" who took the presidency when unable to win through election, "in order to gain possession of the provinces."[36]

Nevertheless, Guerrero began to govern as if it *were* his right. In anticipation of a Spanish invasion in 1829, Congress reluctantly voted to grant Guerrero special war powers to rule by decree. Although Santa Anna crushed the Spanish, allowing Guerrero a moment of respite after his questionable rise to power, his enemies accused him of despotism. Ironically, the man once seen as the greatest defender of federalism was now accused of tyranny.[37] Interestingly, one of Guerrero's decrees was to abolish slavery on September 15, 1829, just after the capitulation of the Spanish forces. Even so, a movement mounted against him. With his liberal defenders unwilling to offer him support, the conservatives easily fomented a rebellion. Announced through their Plan de Jalapa, circulated in late 1829, the rebellion moved swiftly. Without defenders, Guerrero fled the capital. Guerrero's vice president, Anastacio Bustamante, became the new president, but he named arch-conservative and centralist Lucas Alamán to head the cabinet. The repercussions for California were felt almost immediately as Alamán sent a new governor to replace the radical Yorkino José María de Echeandía.[38]

Alamán set out immediately to purge the federal and state governments of liberal opposition leaders. In early January 1830 Congress ratified the Plan de Jalapa. Article four of the plan allowed negative public opinion to dictate the removal of elected or appointed officials. The Jalapistas, the name give to the promoters of the Plan de Jalapa, authorized themselves to determine the severity of the charges. Both the Church and conservative citizens naturally lodged complaints against federalists, especially those tied to the Yorkinos. Oftentimes the complaints were circumstantial. Around the country, in states such as Querétaro, Chiapas, San Luis Potosí, and Oaxaca, legislatures were replaced, governors forced to resign, and prominent Yorkinos arrested.[39] It was only a matter of time before the sweeping changes affected California.

Despite his influence on young Californio politicians, Governor Echeandía had plenty of detractors in California, especially among friars and foreign merchants. The missionaries despised him because of his ardent support of secularization. The merchants detested him because their prosperity depended on the missions' continuous material production.[40] A German merchant, Heinrich Virmond, who had tremendous influence with Bustamante and Alamán, wrote that Echeandía reacted bitterly when he learned he was to be replaced.[41] His successor, General Manuel Victoria, arrived in California in 1830 with a joint appointment as *jefe político,* that is, governor, and *comandante general,* or commander general, of California.[42]

Prior to the new governor's arrival, a defiant Echeandía issued several secularization decrees in an attempt to fully destroy the mission system in California, a move he knew the pro-mission Victoria would oppose.[43] Pico and many other liberal Californios approved of Echeandía's policy, however, making it the immediate cause of friction between the new governor and the Californios—a point of contention that Pico almost immediately attached himself to.

In California, the conservative vs. liberal struggle encouraged ambitious Californios to assert their political strength and challenge the policies emanating from Mexico City after the fall of Guerrero. In a country where rebellion often settled political turmoil, however briefly, many Californio politicians hungered for bold and radical leadership. Victoria, on the other hand, simply wanted the Californios to conform to federal authority. He began to ignore the influence of the diputación when it made demands. By 1831 Pico was the *primer vocal,* the senior member of the diputación, and wrote to the governor, demanding a meeting with him. Victoria considered Pico's letter a personal attack.[44] The governor sent back a stern rebuff, telling Pico not to concern himself with matters of the diputación, and stating that the governor alone would decide when that body should meet. In a circular dated September 21, 1831, Victoria accused members of the diputación of having "criminal objectives," and he promised to put an end to Echeandía's secularization policy.[45] In the circular, Victoria also accused the diputados of having been illegally elected to their posts. As a result, he would soon suspend the diputación entirely.[46]

This political conflict set the stage for Pico and other leading Californios to take the first big gamble of their lives— launching a revolt against a federally appointed governor. Although Pico took every precaution to place the blame on Victoria, he realized that he might face charges of treason. He took an enormous risk, even with Mexico City far away.

However, to Pico and other Californio leaders, Victoria's actions directly violated the principles of federalism, especially now that Victoria had in fact suspended the diputación. According to the federalists, the governor had no right to dismiss the authority of territorial officials. Nevertheless, it became clear that Victoria planned to abolish all town councils and replace civilian government with military rule.[47] This plan accorded with other political upheavals Lucas Alamán had instigated throughout the nation. The disruption of the diputación meant that local officials could no longer make policy decisions, a threatening situation for California's prominent families. By refusing to convene the diputación, plans for mission secularization could not take place, and the granting of public land to families or individuals could not proceed.

Many Californios also became resentful when the governor banished several prominent citizens for speaking out, namely José Antonio Carrillo, José María Padrés, and Abel Stearns, a U.S. immigrant who had married into the powerful Bandini family. By doing so, the governor unwisely humiliated California's top families.

In late September, from San Diego, Pico wrote a scathing response, a *contestacíon*, to Victoria's circular.[48] In it Pico argued that the diputación had the legal right to rebel against the governor. As the highest-ranking native California official, Pico believed he had the moral support to initiate a rebellion. Calling the expulsion of Stearns and Carrillo illegal and unjust, he protested against what he believed was the governor's debasement of federal laws and his interference with territorial commerce. He also argued that Victoria had no legal right to have nullified the election of the territorial diputados and that in doing so he had acted as a despot.[49] However, Pico, at least on paper, did not imply he might become a revolutionary but presented himself as a patriot protecting Mexican law.[50] In fiery *bandos*, pronouncements posted on public buildings, Pico painted himself as a man who fought for the liberty of common citizens. Pico complained, "How can he [Victoria] believe that it is his right to take measures so contrary to our federal system[?]"[51] Clearly Pico reacted to what he perceived as a violation of the 1824 Constitution.

As the primer vocal, Pico's public manifesto carried some weight among the inhabitants of California. He circulated the document among California's ayuntamientos and had it posted on public buildings. In Monterey, the ayuntamiento ignored Victoria's order to have it removed. The angry governor then sent a force of twenty-five men to tear it down.[52] Meanwhile, Alcalde Vicente Sánchez refused to publicize the manifesto in Los Angeles. Pío then asked his younger brother Andrés to post the document.[53] When Sánchez demanded the document, Andrés refused it, and Sánchez immediately threw him in jail.[54]

Nevertheless, Pico had an easy time justifying his actions to the citizens of California. The prominent rancheros had come to view Victoria as a despot, or so they claimed in their own manifestos and in defense of their actions. As a military man first and a politician second, Victoria was at odds with many California citizens.[55] He ruled as if their voices didn't matter. His actions left many Californios without their customary privileged access to local government. His suspension of the diputación mirrored practices occurring across the republic. He may have had a legal precedent to suspend Echeandía's movements against the missions, but his decision to do so without convening the territorial diputación was a fatal mistake. Soon, Victoria's only friends were in his small army, among some conservative settlers, and others, of course, in the Church. Recognizing the makeup of his small group of loyalist supporters inflamed Californio politicians and landowners. President of the missions, Fray Narciso Durán, wrote that members of the diputación resented the meddling governor for disrupting their plans: "Never had they [the Californios] pardoned this just chief for having rescued the booty already within their grasp."[56] According to Durán, the young Californios held secret meetings, conspired against Victoria, and tried to force him to reconvene the diputación.[57] When the governor refused to do so, the Californios came out in open rebellion against him. Although Victoria's pro-mission position influenced Durán's perspective, the priest made some revealing observations. Victoria's threat to stop the distribution of mission lands served to bring a tightly related network of rancheros together for a common cause.

Pío Pico's manifesto, particularly, created a rebellious atmosphere among the *sureños*, residents of southern California. It also gained support in the north, although *norteños* had already begun organizing against Victoria. According to Pico, Victoria intended to lead a force into southern California to have him and Juan Bandini hanged.[58] Pico learned this from his brother-in-law José Joaquín Ortega, also a *vocal* of the diputación. Ortega had come from Monterey to inform Pico of Victoria's plans. At the same time, the governor infuriated Bandini by dismissing him from his political post.

Pico responded quickly to Victoria's actions and put together a powerful opposition force that included the most influential men in southern California. Because this group had similar interests at stake, they organized their rebellion with relative ease. José Antonio Carrillo, Abel Stearns, Juan Bandini, Juan Osuna, and other important men joined Pico. Prior to their pronouncement against the government, Carrillo, Pico, and Bandini plotted their moves at Pico's secluded Rancho Jamul, southeast of San Diego. There they gathered information about Victoria's forces and made plans for an armed revolt.

While the rebellion was quietly being organized, Governor Victoria informed the federal government that he had suspended the California diputación and that he planned to enforce military rule in his territory.[59] The diputación, no longer recognized by the governor or the central government, acted clandestinely, deciding that Pico should journey to Los Angeles to gain support for their cause among important individuals of that city.

When he arrived there, he learned that Alcalde Sánchez had locked up most of those he hoped to talk with, including José María Ávila, several members of the Domínguez family, and Francisco Sepúlveda, all of them substantial ranchers and respected politicians.[60] Not to be dissuaded, Pico attempted to get the imprisoned José María Ávila to support the plan for revolt. Outside Ávila's cell, Pico cautiously explained the plan, asking him to generate support among other prominent Angeleños. Ávila, however, felt that the Angeleños should wait for Victoria to arrive, release the jailed men, and condemn the alcalde's actions.[61] Although he was disappointed, Pico found other support for the *pronunciamiento*.

On November 29, 1831, Pico, Bandini, and Carrillo issued their Plan de San Diego, a formal declaration opposing Victoria's authority, which officially put them in rebellion against the governor. The Californios detested "all-powerful" individuals like Victoria, and with their overthrow they planned to separate military from civil authority. Like Pico's contestación, the pronunciamiento accused Victoria of abusing his powers by banishing Carrillo and Stearns without trial. It also charged the governor with promoting illegal arrests in Los Angeles. As a result of the governor's actions, the pronunciamiento announced, it was suspending Victoria as jefe político and comandante general and calling for the election of an interim officer to run the government and military as prescribed by law.[62] Again in the document, Pico carefully stated that his actions merely protected the constitutional rights of the citizens and upheld Mexican law.

After less than two months of organizing, the rebels decided to strike on November 30, 1831. The events in December seem astounding if we consider that only a few prominent Californios succeeded in overthrowing a federally appointed governor.

Nevertheless, taking into consideration the unity of these families and the fact that they fought for the same interests and were threatened with forced exile, it seems reasonable that the plan came together as swiftly as it did.

Thus, on the last day of November, fifteen armed men, including Pico, Carrillo, Bandini, and Stearns, marched into San Diego and surprised the garrison. Pico, with some regret and embarrassment, placed his friend Captain Santiago Argüello under arrest, along with Ensign Ignacio del Valle. The surprised Argüello agreed to go peacefully with Pico. The three men went to the home of Pablo de la Portilla, who had been taken prisoner by Juan Bandini, and there the insurgents informed Argüello, Portilla, and del Valle of the plot to overthrow Victoria. Pico and Bandini encouraged the officers to join them, but they refused. Instead, Pico recalled, "They pledged themselves, under protest, not to take any steps against us until the conclusion of the affair."[63]

With that assurance, the rebels released Argüello, del Valle, and Portilla, who then allowed Pico and Bandini to take the artillery pieces from the barracks. Soon, various soldiers at the garrison began to join the side of the rebels. In Los Angeles they stormed the prison, released the prisoners, and put Alcalde Sánchez in irons.[64]

The rebellion gained wide public support, and it seemed that Pico's opposition to the governor had paid off. The early success of the movement encouraged Portilla and Argüello to join, although they only agreed to do so if Comandante General Echeandía led the rebellion.[65] Juan Bandini left and quickly returned with the former governor. Pico later recalled that "Echeandía took the chair as president of the junta, and manifested his consent to the desires of the officials. Having accepted the command, we rebels placed ourselves under his orders."[66]

Although Echeandía had had little involvement in the rebellion up to this point, he accepted the leadership in hope of deposing the conservative Victoria. He also hoped to continue his political career in California. Echeandía felt at home in California, and its leading families had already been won over by his liberal ideals. Now, as a leader of the California rebellion, his command legitimized the movement and persuaded other officers to join the cause. After the officers signed their names on the pronunciamiento, the soldiers followed their lead.

In early December Portilla led a force of about fifty men from San Diego to Los Angeles. The war parties met at Cahuenga, with Victoria's forces greatly outnumbered. Despite the death of two men, the sides fought more with words and nerves than with ammunition.[67] Recalling the event, Antonio María Osio reported that Portilla and Carrillo, who apparently fled the scene, acted with great cowardice. Osio wrote, "When Don José Antonio Carrillo and Don Pablo de la Portilla saw first Pacheco and then Ávila fall dead, and that the thirty *mazatecos* [soldiers from Mazatlán] were soldiers under the command of a good leader, they realized that their insurrection involved more than easily written words."[68] Even so, the rebels eventually gained the upper hand. Victoria himself received critical wounds and soon retreated. The following day he formally surrendered. On December 9, Victoria met with Echeandía and made plans to abdicate his authority and leave for Mexico.

Pico, Bandini, Echeandía, and others rejoiced at the outcome of their coup despite what the central government would call their "treasonous" actions. Yet the Californios were well aware of Mexico's lackluster involvement with the territory. They knew that if the federal government could not regularly supply goods to California, it also lacked the ability to send a force to punish them, especially with political instability growing throughout the country. The Californios craved equal representation within the republic, and the rebellion against Victoria represented a bold step toward this end. Soon the north also adhered to the *Plan de San Diego*. Mariano Guadalupe Vallejo, whose home during this period was in present-day Sonoma County, signed the plan, followed by the ayuntamientos of San José and Monterey, bolstering Pico's political clout.[69]

On January 10, 1832, the restored diputación, consisting of Pico, Vallejo, Antonio María Osio, Joaquín Ortega, Santiago Argüello, Tomás Yorba, and Juan Bautista Alvarado, met at Los Angeles.[70] These tightly related individuals could now continue their plans for California. Naturally, with Victoria out of the way, they could proceed with the granting of land, secularization of the missions, and the general governing of the territory. For the time being, they put aside their differences in order to pass the office of jefe político to another Californio.[71] A law dating back to 1822 entitled Pío Pico, as primer vocal, to hold this position. Pico later remembered that taking the oath of office required certain religious objects, all of which were locked in the church.[72] Apparently the padres had refused to let the rebels enter, so Juan Bautista Alvarado had broken in and taken the necessary objects. In an act that represented the Californios' first major victory and their imminent rise to power, the deputies gathered in Los Angeles, where Mariano Guadalupe Vallejo administered the traditional oath, making Pío Pico governor of California.[73]

Unfortunately, in less than a month, Pico's claim to the governorship came under fire, which Echeandía seems to have instigated. On February 1, Echeandía wrote to Pico of his concern with the legitimacy of the election.[74] When Pico failed to reply, Echeandía wrote to Manuel Domínguez, the new alcalde of Los Angeles, admitting that the diputación had appointed Pico governor, following legal procedures. However, Echeandía also made it clear that he opposed it, based on the circumstances of the recent rebellion.[75] Domínguez, perhaps after speaking with Echeandía, refused to accept Pico as provisional jefe político. To make matters worse, it was said that Victoria had passed the office of governor over to Echeandía before his departure.[76] This action, Echeandía believed, gave him the right to serve as governor.

Bolstered by his presumed authority, on February 16 Echeandía gave Pico an ultimatum: if he didn't step down, Echeandía would hold him and the entire diputación responsible to the nation for their actions against Victoria.[77] Because Echeandía had accepted a leadership role in the rebellion, his goal of reclaiming the governorship can only be interpreted as an act of personal ambition. Nevertheless, Pico and the diputación seem to have placated Echeandía's desires, and Pico's term as governor came to an abrupt end.

Pico and the diputación had other problems in addition to those created by Echeandía. Within days, Victoria's secretary, Agustín Zamorano, organized a revolution in the north and declared himself in open revolt against the southern California rebellion. He enlisted many foreigners for his cause and appointed William E. P. Hartnell, a prominent merchant, as leader. Zamorano and his northern followers declared against the Plan de San Diego and refused to accept the actions of the diputación. In their *Pronunciamiento de Monterey contra el Plan de San Diego* they also refused to accept the authority of Echeandía.

By March 22, 1832, the diputación seemed to have reached a semicordial relationship with Echeandía. Pico and the other diputados issued a circular to the ayuntamientos, asking them to preserve the peace, to recognize the assembly's authority, and to refuse the temptation of joining the northern junta.[78] The diputación also resolved to avoid any further public disruption. Pico had accomplished his goal of deposing Victoria and, in doing so, made his mark on California politics. However, he never challenged Echeandía or Zamorano for the governorship. Unfortunately, the political feud sparked an open animosity between northern and southern California that had existed below the surface since the early 1820s.

With two Mexican officials in control of their own forces and in open rebellion with each other, the Californios knew that it was only a matter of time before the power struggle would catch the attention of the federal government. Moreover, California's representative in the Mexican Congress, Carlos Carrillo, was somewhat conservative, opposed to secularization, and a mild supporter of Victoria.[79] By early May, a sort of truce was made giving Zamorano military control in the north and Echeandía military control in the south. During this same time, Mexico City sent Brigadier General José Figueroa to California with the dual command of jefe político and comandante general. He wouldn't arrive until the new year, however, and California remained a vast territory without a single true leader. Although Pico took the oath as governor, Victoria had relinquished command to Echeandía. Internal conflict remained in California until the arrival of Governor Figueroa on January 14, 1833.

California's political upheavals from 1830 to 1832 mirrored the national crisis. It is impossible to view California's trauma as isolated from national politics. As part of the nation, California experienced the same growing pains that allowed men like Pico to assert themselves. Despite the question of leadership in California, Pío Pico had won a complete victory in terms of establishing himself as a political force. More than any other politician of his generation, the thirty-two-year-old Pico had accomplished what other Californios of his class were pushing for: the establishment of California as an independent force within the Mexican republic. Although a battle for genuine recognition lay ahead, the Californios had gained much confidence. They now had a clear vision of how they would wield absolute power over California. They could now determine how their relationship with Mexico City would proceed.

After the revolt against Victoria, Pico became a vital force in politics, but he had yet to establish the Picos as one of

California's prominent families. He began by cultivating his ranching business in Jamul. The young politician understood that power came with land ownership and by raising livestock. Few Californios had the connections and resources to become wealthy on their own terms, but, using a combination of family patronage and self-determination, Pico was able to climb the ladder of success. Ultimately, for Californios in Pico's position, the acquisition of complete power over California's political and economic interests could only be accomplished by attacking the Church. In their quest to transform society and to enrich themselves at the same time, the Californios found the secularization of the missions to be a critical issue. Pico emerged as an important leader in this movement.

CHAPTER 3

Secularization and Rebellion

Pico at San Luis Rey, 1835–1840

By the summer of 1833 Pío Pico had experienced first-hand the effects of national politics on California. The central government's policies influenced every major development in California. Local politicians were deeply involved in the national debates of the time. Of the many issues that divided the nation, the debate over secularization had direct consequences for California.[1] The missions held the region's most valuable real estate, arousing the jealousy of many. As tensions rose, a bitter debate between politicians and missionaries erupted in the 1830s. Although the California diputación had argued for secularization on the basis of ending "Indian bondage," the priests understood greed as the real motive. The mission Indians, however, would use the dispute to resist exploitation and manipulation from both sides of the debate. Despite their continuous resistance against the Spaniards and Mexicans, secularization would present a new set of laws that would allow them a small degree of political autonomy. The foremost goal of secularization was to distribute mission land to Indian neophytes and turn the buildings into parish churches that would serve pueblo citizens. This meant that Indians would be freed from the control of the missionaries, would become landowners, and with their newfound liberty would gain most of the rights of Mexican citizens. This idea of liberty ultimately gave California Indians the power to resist exploitation.[2] If secularization aimed to reorganize the lives of Mission Indians, it became a political battle among Mexicans. After independence in 1821, liberal politicians pushed for it. The secularization question challenged many entrenched conservative beliefs, such as the right of ecclesiastical land management, which would result in the loss of privileges for Mexico's predominantly Spanish-born missionaries.[3] In California, the situation was no different.

As secularization gained support, it also advanced liberalism's progressive ideas and simultaneously empowered local politicos. It was one of many issues liberals used as an attack against Spanish supremacy in Mexico. In 1824 and 1829 respectively, the government abolished the colonial systems of *castas*, castes, and African slavery.[4] In California similar decrees emancipated Indians from missionary control.[5] But for many of them, the California padres remained influential. Although some neophytes did take advantage of the decree of emancipation, few qualified because they lacked self-sufficiency.[6] A major effort to secularize California's missions finally came in 1830, when Governor José María de Echeandía issued his *Plan para convertir en pueblos las misiones de la alta California.*[7] Liberal politicians argued that missionaries held the indigenous population captive, failing to advance their assimilation into the larger culture. The Indians became the liberals' prime example of conservative and religious exploitation. The missionaries, of course, believed that Californio politicians wanted only to take the land for themselves. Church leaders especially singled out Pico as a man who hoped to profit from mission land. They saw him as "the arch-enemy of the missions, and, doubtless, the chief and most unscrupulous among the plotters for the possession of the mission lands."[8]

Nevertheless, Echeandía's plan, if adopted, would require the confiscation of mission land and its distribution to ex-neophytes for the creation of Indian pueblos. It said that ex-neophytes could effectively establish new pueblos in the form of communal property. The plan allowed one square league for pueblo needs, as well as the distribution of mission cattle and various other items. Echeandía's plan also outlined the management of surplus land and livestock, with the expectation of providing for a local schoolmaster, hospital, and other public institutions. Finally, it included the creation of positions to administer the remaining property.[9]

Echeandía's secularization decree, and two others issued from Mexico City, entrusted to government-appointed officials the control of each mission's land and its indigenous population.[10] These positions were highly sought after because of the enormous land base charged to the administrator. Men like Pío Pico scrambled to secure such an appointment.

Secularization issues were in line with the liberal notion of progress and the creation of a secular society. In his bid to become one of the most ardent opponents of the mission system, Pico fully supported secularization. Despite Echeandía's efforts, however, the plan did not materialize. As conservatives took control of the government in Mexico City, as we have seen, new appointments followed. The arrival of Governor Manuel Victoria in 1830 put an end to Echeandía's hopes. He was powerless to advance secularization in California. Not only would the Mexican Congress refuse to support the liberal plan, but Victoria controlled both the California government and its military.

Although with no authority to take legal action, Echeandía began to work with Pico's rebellion against Victoria. As tension between liberal California politicians and the conservative Governor Victoria erupted into violence, Echeandía hastily wrote several plans he hoped would again bring secularization closer to reality.[11] After the success of Pico's rebellion,

California's new governor, José Figueroa, was given orders to revoke Echeandía's secularization plans and to proceed on the matter with caution.[12]

A highly decorated veteran of the war for Mexican Independence, Brigadier General José Figueroa arrived in California as governor and *jefe militar,* or head of the military, in 1833. He immediately began to investigate the condition of the missions and neophytes. Figueroa, perhaps under the influence of the missionaries and the miserable condition of the neophytes, quickly decided to oppose full-scale secularization. In a dispatch to the federal government, he stated that secularization would bring about irreparable damage to the California economy.[13] Because the missions produced a great deal of trade, he reasoned, secularization could lead to financial collapse. As the missionaries did, Figueroa also thought of the neophytes as children incapable of functioning in Hispanic society. According to Figueroa, their incapacity to live as "civilized" Mexicans would lead to secularization's failure.

Figueroa's letter to Mexico City clearly outlined the belief among many Mexican officials that the Indians needed more exposure to western civilization. The Indians had been "only recently domesticated," he wrote, and must be "led by the hand towards civilization."[14] At Mission San Luis Rey, Figueroa spoke to the neophytes about the benefits of emancipation, including the granting of land, cattle, and other provisions. When asked who would like to take advantage of such an offer, Figueroa was surprised that only four families in one hundred accepted.[15] In light of such telling interaction, Figueroa issued a provisional law that gave partial emancipation to neophytes who had practiced Christianity for twelve years.[16] It is difficult to deduct to what extent the missionary fathers had influenced Figueroa's action. A possible clue is that his law also contained a provision that ordered recalcitrant Indians to be returned to the missions and back under the authority of priests.[17]

Before Figueroa could implement his plan, however, events in Mexico City once again caused drastic change in California. Since 1830 the conservative minister of foreign relations, Lucas Alamán, had advanced his plan to restore Mexico from chaos. He returned land expropriated from the Catholic Church. He attempted to fix the crumbling economy by strengthening international business ties. He heralded both California and Texas as the future of Mexico's economy and boldly issued a law banning further U.S. immigration to Texas.[18] However, the administration was not beyond the use of authoritarian measures to promote its vision. The government arrested individuals for promoting religious tolerance and attacked several people accused of siding with the liberals.[19]

By 1832 General Santa Anna began organizing a rebellion against President Bustamante's ministers, whom he accused of antifederalism. As the movement grew, liberals wanted the ministers punished for their role in the callous execution of Vicente Guerrero, who had led insurgents in the fight for independence and was overthrown as president. Alamán and the other ministers fled, and Santa Anna installed himself as Mexico's president. He chose as his vice president Valentín Gómez Farías, a prominent and radical liberal. When Santa Anna was called away to suppress a rebellion, he handed his responsibilities to Farías.[20]

Vice President Farías immediately began to issue liberal reforms that focused on weakening the power of the Church and the military. The state separated education from Church control, and for California, a secularization law followed in 1833.[21] The new law concerned the missions of upper and lower California alone and simply required that they be transformed into parishes.[22] The law also called for the creation of a vicar general in California to oversee the newly created parishes. The articles excluded discussion of land distribution and the manner in which administrators would be selected to oversee it. As the new decree circulated, it created anxiety in California, especially for Figueroa, because the new law immediately invalidated his plan to gradually secularize the missions. The padres wasted little time informing Figueroa about the dangers of secularization. Fray Francisco García, prelate of the missions, flatly asked Figueroa to resist secularization.[23] García argued that neophytes were childish, drunkards, and prone to aborting their pregnancies.[24] In other words, he implied that only the missionaries could guide them away from their uncivilized ways.[25]

In 1834 Governor Figueroa finally complied with the Mexican secularization law drawn up by Farías the previous year, although in a way that heavily favored the Californios. The political situation required Figueroa to create a regional secularization bill that satisfied all and took into account local political, economic, and demographic realities. Figueroa's *Reglamento provisional para la secularización de las Misiones* (Provisional regulation for the secularization of the missions) immediately secularized ten missions and made plans to secularize those remaining.[26] The reglamento issued from 100 to 400 *varas* of land to former neophytes and created communal plots for Indian pueblos.[27] The pueblos would have their own jurisdiction and government, made up of their own elected officials.[28]

With Figueroa's decree in place, naturally the padres lost administration of the temporalities to a government-appointed official charged with administering the transition. As in other secularization decrees, little was said concerning the duties of the administrator, except regarding property management. Figueroa's reglamento ordered that the administrator, or *comisionado,* once appointed, carry out the regulations of secularization. The comisionado took control of a mission from the padres, explained the reglamento to the neophytes, and "emancipated" them from Church authority. He also had to take inventory of the missions, pay mission debts with approval of the governor, and distribute property, including livestock and tools, to the Indians.[29] After the distribution of land, a far greater amount of surplus land remained, giving the administrator the potential to profit from his post.[30] Figueroa's idea to use surplus land for the benefit of the California economy seemed logical. Nevertheless, the failure to spell out regulations and Indian labor requirements allowed the administrator to take advantage of his position. This situation existed at Mission San Luis Rey, where Pío Pico was very satisfied to have been named the comisionado in 1835.

His appointment could not have come at a more opportune time. The year before, Pico had married María Ignacia Alvarado in the plaza church in Los Angeles. By this time Pico had become one of the most successful politicians in California, and many territorial elites attended the wedding, which became legendary as one of the grandest in early California history. In fact, Pío's compadre, Governor José Figueroa, served as the best man. The two had forged a strong friendship, which explains why Pico received the appointment as comisionado to California's largest mission. The elegant wedding reception, held in the house of Pico's brother-in-law José Antonio Carrillo, lasted for eight days. María Ignacia was the daughter of Francisco Javier Alvarado, a sergeant in Los Angeles. Alvarado's son, also named Francisco Javier, was alcalde of the Pueblo of Los Angeles. He had married Pío's sister, María Tomasa Pico, in 1829. This relationship extended Pío's clout by assuring him a healthy share of political appointments and access to land grants. Although Pico had uncles and cousins in northern California, his ties in the south helped him create an important nucleus of powerful landowners who sought to control regional politics. As comisionado of San Luis Rey, he positioned himself to become one of California's wealthiest citizens. Figueroa's untimely passing in 1835 did little to dislodge Pico from the powerful position he had carved for himself.

Situated just north of San Diego, Mission San Luis Rey at the time had enormous economic potential, which Pico clearly understood. The secularization policy required the former neophytes to work during the transition from subjects to free citizens. The mission's indigenous population, called the Luiseños because of their association to the mission, had very little trust in the new policies. In fact, very few Indian groups in southern California had faith in promises of "emancipation." From 1835 until 1840, Pío Pico and the other Californios in southern California faced increased Indian resistance to policies intended to manage them. By allowing the Luiseños self-representation, secularization actually encouraged them to organize against the California government.

The neophytes had had a difficult life under missionary control. Religious conversion, fatigue, disease, and general maltreatment contributed to their depopulation.[31] Under the care of missionaries, Indian converts could not practice the religion of their ancestors or travel freely through the country. Soldiers were assigned to protect the missions because of the constant threat of revolt. During the period of secularization, this arrangement began to deteriorate when Indians received "freedom" from mission control. Placed under the care of the government, however, they received land but in return were required to provide free labor for the newly secularized missions. This contradiction caused resistance to elevate.

Known as the "King of the Missions," San Luis Rey had vast acreage, including various Indian pueblos already within its domain. At the largest Indian villages the mission stored grain, grew crops, kept horses, and grazed cattle.[32] In the mid-1820s San Luis Rey had a total of 22,610 cattle, 27,412 sheep, 1,120 goats, 1,501 horses, and 235 mules.[33] Shortly after San Luis Rey was decommissioned, however, it faced financial collapse. By late 1834, the outgoing administrator, Pablo de la Portilla, could not entice the Luiseños to work.[34] Pressing the rights given to them under the decree of emancipation,

Drawing of Mission San Luis Rey, ca. 1855. Courtesy of the Bancroft Library, University of California, Berkeley.

on November 4, 1835, a large group of Luiseños rode into San Diego to compel the alcalde, José María Osuna, to intercede on their behalf. [35] They complained that Portilla held them against their will despite promises of freedom. Fearing a massive revolt, Osuna immediately addressed their demands.[36]

Despite Pico's dreams of prosperity, with secularization the Luiseños continued to resist political and religious controls.[37] Figueroa's decree became the impetus for their legitimate organizing against the actions of Mexican citizens, such as forced labor. It also allowed for the election in each new pueblo of an Indian alcalde, who became a political leader of his people and a conduit who interacted with Mexican officials.[38] Despite scant evidence, it is certain that Indians established new pueblos under the secularization order. At Mission San Luis Rey, Luiseños established Las Flores, an outpost of the former mission, as a pueblo. In May 1835, the governor wrote to the "Alcalde of the Pueblo of Las Flores" to proceed with the distribution of buildings to the inhabitants.[39] At Pala, a former rancho of the mission, Indians also created a pueblo with its own alcalde.[40] Although the ability to organize did not depend on Mexican law, secularization allowed the Luiseño population to assert itself politically.

Mission San Luis Rey was an ideal place for Pico to manage his business operations. He had deep political and economic ties to San Diego.[41] His Rancho Jamul prospered in the area and provided a comfortable life for his family.[42] As comisionado of the mission, he capitalized on his already burgeoning cattle business.

Secularization laws in California put into place a new bureaucracy. Figueroa's law continued the earlier practice of appointing an administrator for each mission.[43] Aside from managing the assets of the mission, Pico and other comisionados were required to gather Indians to provide labor on mission, now government, property. This complicated the task of administration because now Pico had to order the Indians back to work for an establishment they had been liberated from. How did he do it? One answer can be found in the creation at this time of an official entitled *encargado de justicia.* This officer administrated in the areas surrounding the missions of San Diego.[44] The act allowed him to work with military officials to punish individuals who committed petty crimes. The law was extremely unclear about what constituted a crime. Article eight, for example, stated that for offenses committed at the mission, criminals would receive imprisonment in chains for a period of sixty hours to eight days, with the possibility of an eight-day period of forced labor.[45] Aside from drunkenness, "public scandal" was also considered a crime. The vagueness of the regulations could have easily allowed an official to jail an Indian for refusing to work for the administrator. This law gave Pico the authority he needed for success at San Luis Rey. In an unbelievable twist of fate for the Luiseños, in 1836 the government also appointed Pico encargado de justicia.[46]

The laws establishing the encargado de justicia completely undermined the Indian alcalde's ability to function as an authority. This was potentially detrimental to Indians who wanted to establish independent Indian pueblos. The encargado could override their authority without sufficient justification. Pico himself recounted an episode when he had a Luiseño alcalde shackled and given fifty lashes for attacking a Mexican mayordomo; apparently Governor Figueroa was at the establishment at the time and did not object to the whipping.[47] This law is one of many instances that reveal the contradictory nature of Indian emancipation during the era of secularization in California.

Soon after he had established himself at the mission, Pico held great optimism about California's future. He attributed this to his belief that he had successfully reconciled Indian complaints. In a letter to his friend Mariano Guadalupe Vallejo, Pico spoke of "rumors" that the Indian population had begun to treacherously kill their cattle without regard for the future.[48] This behavior led him to conclude that the Luiseños had accepted their new life and duties at San Luis Rey. He also suggested that he had resolved the concerns of the missionaries, who had happily begun to produce a surplus of goods for sale. "Very soon," Pico wrote, "instead of being worthy of sorrow, we will be the envy of all of the inhabitants that form the confederation of the Republic of Mexico."[49] He worked with both Indians and missionaries to make the mission profitable. Pico believed he had finally brought order to chaos.

His letter to Vallejo reveals that Pico believed he was capable of propelling California into a new era of prosperity. It also reveals that he had a stake in Mexico's future. He was participating in the national dialogue of the time, and he marveled at the notion that an average citizen could make something of himself. Despite his differences with certain Mexican officials, Pico and many of his friends believed in and were loyal to the Mexican Republic. According to Pico, through the efforts of its leading citizens, California could possibly emerge as a dominant region in the Mexican economy.

It is difficult to determine, however, whether Pico performed his duties differently than other administrators. Although he worked toward building the future of California's economy and attempted to entice the Indian community to work, few documents show that he administered other duties as stipu-lated in Figueroa's secularization decree.[50] Although we know about the formation of two Indian pueblos at San Luis Rey, the establishment of a school or other public buildings is uncertain. However, Pico was meticulous about determining the value of the mission. In 1835 Pico's inventory, conducted with the assistance of Fray Buenaventura Fortuni, listed San Luis Rey with debts of $9,300.87 and credits of $49,619.75.[51] The final value of the buildings was estimated at $48,000; the furniture and accessories at $24,193.75; the church at

$30,000; the sacred instruments at $11,485.50; and the ranchos at $40,437.50.[52] In total, Mission San Luis Rey's inventory was valued at $194,436. By comparison, the value of San Luis Rey dwarfed other missions. For example, Mission Santa Inez had assets of only $50,962.62.[53] Shortly after the estimation of the San Luis Rey's value, Pico set out to make a profit for the mission. By 1836 he managed to increase cattle production, using the hides for trade from San Luis Rey.[54]

Pico had the luxury of studying his predecessor's failures. Pablo de la Portilla had left San Luis Rey nearly in ruin and with an indigenous population constantly on the verge of rebellion. He believed discipline alone produced results, as the padres had proved during the mission's productive heyday. Years later, when he recorded his narrative, a boastful Pico recalled that he "imposed the condition on Jefe Politico Figueroa that [he] be allowed to govern the Indians the same as they had been governed before by the padres."[55] Like Pico, many saw the Indians as children incapable of governing themselves. The Indian population soon came to despise Pico. Luiseño neophyte Julio César, in one of the few testimonies taken of a native California Indian during this period, recalled that Pico made them hold their hats in hand when he passed by. César stated that of all the despotic administrators, none abused them more than Pico.[56]

The conflict that came to characterize Pico's administration was a result of his notion of progress. His primary aim was to operate an enterprise rather than to ensure the transition of former neophytes into Mexican society. Various complaints surfaced that he allowed his cattle to pasture in Temecula and Las Flores, Indian areas he would eventually attempt to acquire.[57] Furthermore, Pico himself recalled that he attempted to maintain order in a paternalistic manner. For example, he upheld the moral standards of the padres by keeping young, unwed women in the convent, while young Indian men lived in the *departamento de varones*, that is, men's quarters.[58] The

Luiseños protested that the missionaries showed more restraint than Pico did, and that he demanded work without compromise.[59]

Even before he was selected as comisionado Pico recognized the mission's huge potential as an economic source. Its land contained thirteen large, populated Indian ranches, including San Mateo, Las Flores, Santa Margarita, San Juan, Pala, Temecula, San Jacinto, San Marcos, Pamuza, Pauma, Potrero, Agua Hedionda, and Buena Vista.[60] These ranches produced a wide variety of agricultural and other goods. Even so, forcing the Indians to work, denying their promised liberties, treating them harshly, and encroaching on Temecula, where he grazed his own cattle, led to Indian protests and eventually their rebellion.

The Luiseños' organized protests against Mexican officials like Pico and Pablo de la Portilla demonstrate that they at first sought change from within the legal system. Similarly, throughout Latin America, Indians also utilized legal means to redress their concerns and to seek justice. In California, however, such action proved to be an anomaly. The practice of legal action taken against soldiers and citizens for crimes against California Indians existed, but it was usually ecclesiastics who made these charges. By the 1830s, however, many native communities began appealing to Mexican authorities for redress of their grievances.

After secularization, with increasing frequency the Luiseños filed legal complaints over their treatment. But, as encargado de justicia, Pío Pico's ability to punish them with seemingly little regard for justice hindered organized petitions among the Luiseños and other Indians of the San Diego area.

Within six months of his arrival as comisionado, complaints against Pico began to mount. Aside from grazing his cattle in Temecula and his harsh treatment of the Indians, they also accused him of squandering mission property.[61] Despite Pico's authority, the Luiseños did not give in to his demands. In fact, they attempted to foil his administration and drive him from the area. In 1836 they formed a coalition and selected Pablo Apis from Temecula pueblo to represent them. Apis was educated and possessed the leadership qualities the Luiseños needed. They did not count out the use of force against Pico if negotiations did not work, and knowing Pico's angry temperament, they probably *did* count on violence. In June they petitioned the alcalde of San Diego, citing Pico for wrongful treatment and misappropriation of mission property.[62] When Pico learned of the protest, he reported it to the San Diego Presidio and asked for military assistance. Comandante Nicolás Gutiérrez left the presidio with four soldiers to inquire about the confrontation. Gutiérrez soon located Apis and told him that he had permission to travel to San Diego to address his complaints to the new alcalde, Santiago Argüello.[63] When Pico learned of Apis's intentions, he ordered the Luiseño arrested and accused him of being the ringleader of the protest. While Apis and the Luiseños had simply utilized their legal rights to protest against abuse, as encargado de justicia, Pico could arrest Apis for many broadly defined reasons. In the end, it was Pico's word against Apis's.

It is difficult to understand the true nature of the incident since Pico's version differs slightly from that found in the official military documents. The official report states that Sergeant Pablo Rodriguez incarcerated Apis upon Pico's orders.[64] According to Pico, nearly one thousand Luiseños, many armed, had gathered in front of his quarters, demanding their leader's release.[65] The Luiseños knew their actions would provoke a military response from the territorial government. Nevertheless, the showdown lasted until the early morning hours, resulting in the unconditional release of Apis. Pico eventually gave into Luiseño demands because he feared for his life.[66]

Pico's response to the Apis situation was only a temporary solution. Just days before the incident with Apis at San Luis Rey, Pico had secured the aid of San Juan Capistrano's military guard.[67] Although the guard had not returned in time to prevent the Apis affair, Pico decided to prevent any further altercations. With the help of San Diego troops, Pico had Apis arrested. To completely eliminate him as a threat, Apis was forcefully enlisted in the military company at Monterey.[68] Pico took many precautions to prevent further Indian uprisings, particularly by having the military arrest more Indians to help secure Pico's control over San Luis Rey.[69]

The general discontent among the California Indian population toward Pico persisted. Nicolás Gutiérrez reported in June 1836 that Indian hostilities had occurred in San Luis Rey, San Diego, and San Juan Capistrano.[70] The Luiseños continued to protest Pico's administration without regard for retaliation. Less than a month after Apis's arrest, they organized again and petitioned the government to remove Pico as administrator.[71] Pico was still an influential person, however, and Californio officials did not think his method of maintaining the Indian workload was unorthodox. Most importantly, Governor Mariano Chico refused to have Pico removed despite Indian complaints.[72]

Constant arrests could not solve the problem, however. In order to succeed, Pico had to make amends. Hoping to turn the situation in his favor, he tried to mediate various complaints. When Indians at the pueblo of Las Flores complained about unfair treatment from their alcaldes, Pico went in person and appointed a new alcalde and *regidor*.[73] In November 1836, he took steps on behalf of the people of Agua Caliente to prevent Pablo de la Portilla from acquiring Luiseño property rights.[74] However, the fact that Pico had acquired some Luiseño property rights for himself might suggest that he simply tried to prevent Portilla from acquiring what he himself wanted.

In his various positions as administrator of San Luis Rey, encargado de justicia, and regidor of the San Diego ayuntamiento, Pico faced many local issues from 1835 to 1840. While concentrating on his administrative duties, his regional political posts, and his cattle operations, he found himself being pulled into territorial issues. A major setback in his administrative climb came in 1837 when he joined a southern California rebellion against the new governor, Juan Bautista Alvarado, from Monterey.

The previous year, Alvarado, a young northern politician, had led a revolt against the constitutional governor of California then, Nicolás Gutiérrez. The revolt was partially based on policies of the conservative government in Mexico, which annulled the 1824 Mexican Constitution in order to create a more powerful centralist government. The 1836 Constitution, or *siete leyes*, the seven laws, as it was also called, severely diminished the power of the states and territories, leaving California helpless to determine its own political future. Alvarado became interim governor after his successful revolt against Gutiérrez and declared California independent from Mexico until the government restored the federalist system of the1824 Constitution.[75] He also elevated the diputación to a state legislature, now called a *junta*, or assembly. Because norteño politicians led the revolt, southern politicians like Pío Pico and Carlos Carrillo worried that the north would dominate California. Eventually, many sureños would resist Alvarado's claim to the governorship, causing a two-year regional conflict. Pico and his southern colleagues supported their own candidate, Carlos Carrillo, and remained loyal to the federal government.[76] The two leaders eventually met on the battlefield to determine the outcome. By March 1838, Alvarado's army had defeated the sureños. Carlos Carrillo surrendered and signed the Treaty of Las Flores on April 23, 1838. The treaty required the dejected Carrillo to surrender to the authority of Alvarado, his cousin. In the aftermath, Pico and others were arrested and held as Alvarado's prisoners. Through mediation, the federal government eventually recognized Alvarado as governor, ending the conflict for all parties involved. During his brief incarceration, Pico was informed that his Rancho Jamul had been attacked and burned to the ground.[77]

It was during this period that numerous Indian attacks in southern California were reported to the military.[78] With Pico confined, his rancho was a perfect target for a surprise attack. Jamul was located about twenty-two miles east of San Diego, within Kumeyaay Indian territory. Few Mexicans lived this far from the coastal region, and the interior Indians had never been subdued; their attacks on Mexican settlements were common. An Indian servant warned Pico's mother, Doña Eustaquia, that an attack was coming. The fact that the servant knew about it suggests that it may have been a local Kumeyaay reprisal. Nevertheless, the warning was critical because it saved lives. Doña Eustaquia gathered her daughters and urged the mayordomo, Juan Leiva, to flee with her.[79] Leiva felt the threat was insignificant and remained at the rancho. In the attack, Leiva and his employees were killed, and his daughters were kidnapped and never heard from again. The news of the Indian attack at Rancho Jamul quickly circulated throughout the California pueblos.

Pico's incarceration during the Alvarado affair and his loss at Jamul marked the first major blows to his still-promising career. Despite the raid's fatal outcome, Californios should not have been so surprised about it. In southern California, violent reaction to Mexican rule was, as we have seen in the case of San Luis Rey, becoming uncontrollable. In Pico's absence, the Luiseños had continued their defiance and had begun to leave the missions in large groups. Upon Pico's return, he attempted to regain control. It was a stroke of luck, or perhaps because of his continued influence, that in 1839 his older brother José Antonio Pico was promoted to coman-dante general of the troops at San Luis Rey. Pico and his family spent that year trying to put their once burgeoning cattle empire back in order. Andrés left the military to take over at the devastated Jamul.[80] Pío was attempting to protect and rebuild his interests. With Andrés taking care of the family's financial matters, José Antonio commanding the military and looking out for Indian uprisings, and Pío administering and controlling the vast lands of San Luis Rey, everything again seemed to be in place.

Nevertheless, various Indian attacks in the southern region put José Antonio on the defensive. Andrés Pico wrote to the alcalde of San Diego, José Antonio Estudillo, that Indians had threatened Jamul once more and were still a serious threat to the pueblo of San Diego.[81] In July 1839, José Antonio Pico wrote to General Vallejo, begging him to use his influence with Governor Alvarado to apprehend and punish the various bandits who put San Diego in danger. Pico explained that the *malhechores*, evildoers, had set ranchos ablaze and had killed *gente de razón*.[82] According to José Antonio, many in southern California, including residents of Los Angeles, were terrified of Indian rebellion. José Antonio was in need of the military's assistance and desperately appealed to Vallejo and the governor for help. Supplies were low at many of the large ranchos, including Jamul, and the missions had few extra provisions. Furthermore, the lack of money and resources made it extremely difficult to find new recruits, placing the military in a dire situation. José Antonio Pico told General Vallejo that the soldiers had no food, uniforms, or ammunition.[83] He feared that without prompt assistance Indians and any other enemies of the nation might devastate the pueblos of southern California. Citizens did not sit idle and wait for the military to come and protect them. In a June 1839 petition, the leading citizens of San Diego and Los Angeles asked for substantial military assistance from the supreme government in Mexico City.[84]

The petition to Mexico City is important because it opens a number of possibilities for viewing California's financial situation at the time. Why was the economy failing if secularization was meant to bring prosperity? Indian protest was on the rise, the number of military troops had dwindled, and a state of panic existed among Californios and Mexicans alike. In historical records for this period, the only clues to this economic decline are the corrupt administration of mission land, the constant political turmoil within California, and the increasing relevance of Indian resistance.

While at San Luis Rey, Pico encountered financial problems of his own, causing him to take drastic actions. The Luiseños continued to refuse to work, and their ongoing objections to Pico's administration compounded his problems. By mid-1839, it was urgent that Pico stabilize operations at San Luis Rey. To raise money, he first had to sell his property in the pueblo of San Diego. In June he moved his mother and sister Jacinta, who was ill, to San Luis Rey. He wrote to his brother José Antonio that he was going to sell the family home in San Diego and asked José to use his influence with the governor and General Vallejo to sell the building, conveniently located near the presidio, to the military.[85] Pico's letter also noted his petition to Alvarado asking for ownership of the lands of Temecula. In response, Governor Alvarado gave him temporary custody of Temecula. To the Luiseños this was just one more act of betrayal, especially because the Californios had issued statements concerning the new liberties of Indians. Shortly after he moved his mother to San Luis Rey, Pico wrote to William Hartnell, inspector general of the mission, an Englishman turned Mexican citizen. Hartnell's duty was to take inventory of the missions, listen to the complaints of the Indians, and deal with unmanageable administrators, a sure sign of the failure of the current system. Pico asked Hartnell for help with the return of fugitive Indians. The mission was falling into ruin, and under threat of resignation, Pico asked Hartnell to round them up.[86] However, in an interview with the Luiseños, Hartnell learned about their objections to Pico as administrator. Numerous complaints came in against Pico, including that he exploited the wealth of the mission, leaving the Luiseños without such basic items as clothing.[87] After Hartnell reviewed the situation and visited the mission, he made the recommendation to Governor Alvarado that Pico be discharged. That done, Alvarado also issued a new order for the management of California's missions, which called for qualified mayordomos to replace the administrators—and at less cost. The friars were also given a greater role in mission management.[88]

Though he was not entirely upstanding, Pico was no different from many administrators. In his inspection of 1839–40, Hartnell recorded many instances of inappropriate activities by various mission administrators. For instance, Hartnell wrote in his notebook that the neophytes at San Juan Capistrano requested the removal of comisionado Santiago Argüello for various abuses. When Hartnell refused to remove him, the Indians became angry and warned that they would only work under the care of the padre. Similarly, the neophytes at San Gabriel accused comisionado Juan Bandini of wrongdoing, including stealing the mission's finest horses. They demanded his removal, and Hartnell complied. At Santa Barbara, too, Hartnell reprimanded comisionado Manuel Cota for attempting to alter the mission inventory of cattle in his favor. Hartnell soon received word from Padre Narciso that Cota "had become possessed of the Devil." Cota, in a fit of rage, had dragged an Indian along the ground by the hair. Ultimately Hartnell suspended Cota from his duties for refusing to obey orders.[89]

Even after Pico left the mission, he continued his attempt to secure ownership of Temecula. He is said to have passed out provisions to the Luiseños there, just as he informed them that the government had given him provisional custody of the land. The inhabitants of the pueblo had fought Pico for years over this issue and were not about to give up then. Pico had cattle grazing in many parts of the mission, which was customary among the administrators, and in the process gained the disdain of the residents. At Temecula, however, the Indians armed themselves and warned of a massive uprising if Pico did not remove his cattle.[90] With the arrival of the new mayordomo, José Antonio Estudillo, alcalde of San Diego and Pico's godson, the Luiseños eventually got their wish. Incidentally, and unfortunately for the Luiseño residents of Temecula, Estudillo's goal was to secure Temecula for himself.

Pico finally left the great mission in 1840 but fought the entire time to prevent his dismissal. Hartnell, in fact, threatened to force him out of his post and recorded that in August 1840, Pico satisfied his debt to the mission of $170.00.[91] Yet for the Luiseños, the debt could never be repaid. Although many historians say he was the worst exploiter of the missions, he seems to have done no worse or better than the other administrators.

The proponents of secularization believed that liberty, private ownership of land, and the "gift" of entering Mexican society would transform the Indian population. Yet, in many instances, the Indians simply wanted to be left to themselves. Secularization from the "liberal" standpoint was an absolute failure. Few Indians acquired land, and proclamations of "emancipation" left much to be desired. Pico was typical of the administrators who on one hand believed in Indian emancipation from the friars, but who still wanted to profit by using free Indian land and labor. In the end, however, the recalcitrant Luiseños managed to help depose Pico as they had the previous administrator. And as the records show, Luiseño resistance hurt the San Diego economy. Pablo Apis, along with his Luiseño followers, had the courage and means to resist their exploitation. Similarly, the strong Indian resistance at Temecula led Pico to reconsider the wisdom of acquiring it. Nonetheless, he petitioned once more for Temecula in late 1840 but agreed to relinquish his claim as a condition of receiving the 131,400-acre Rancho Santa Margarita, an enormous grant.[92] Through everything, Pico continued to excel as one of California's most influential politicians. Not long after his removal from San Luis Rey, he became the first voting member of the California assembly, and in 1845, Pico granted Pablito Apis, the son of his old Luiseño foe Pablo, a claim of 2,233 acres in Temecula.[93]

The chaotic atmosphere in California mirrored events throughout Mexico that gave way to the rise of *caudillismo,* rule by military-political dictatorship, in which regional strongmen took control of government by force, often in order to protect state rights against centralist attacks.[94] Although Juan Bautista Alvarado and Pío Pico were not typical caudillos, the political atmosphere in Mexico helps to explain their rise.

CHAPTER 4

The Pivotal Years, 1840–1846

Although California became increasingly aware of its sus-
ceptibility to being seized by any of several powerful
nations of the outside world, it nevertheless saw the escala-
tion of internal conflicts. Californios were embroiled in a
bitter dispute over the location of the customs house and the
California capital, both of which were in Monterey. Sureño
politicians feared domination from the north, which would
mean loss of power to regulate trade, to access valuable land,
and to win important territory-wide assembly seats. Although
Pico took a brief hiatus from politics, he could not ignore
the agitations from northern leaders. He was understandably
upset after Governor Alvarado removed him from his lucrative post at San Luis Rey. He continued to oppose Alvarado
at least until 1841, when Alvarado granted him the vast Rancho
Santa Margarita.[1]

The terms of the grant stated that both Andrés and Pío
Pico would relinquish their temporary claim on Temecula
for Santa Margarita.[2] Pico was satisfied and seems not to have
disturbed the governor further. However, within the next couple
of years, he became the most spirited southern leader in opposition to norteño power. After leaving his post at San Luis Rey,

Pico remained influential in the assembly and concentrated on developing his business activities. With Alvarado's triumph in the south and a stint as temporary governor after his successful rebellion, the time came for Mexico to choose an official governor of California. Alvarado, José Castro, and Pío Pico, all members of the assembly, were put on a list from which Mexico's federal government would choose a governor.

Alvarado secured the governorship without much of a fight, but Pico continued to argue that Los Angeles, not Monterey, should be the capital of California. Pico himself admitted, however, that "from the time of my separation from the ex-mission of San Luis Rey until the end of Alvarado's administration, I did not involve myself in public affairs."[3] Instead, he was busy consolidating his ranching interests and settling issues that had arisen among the Indians living on his newly acquired land.

Pico had also purchased a house in the main plaza of Los Angeles after his expulsion from San Luis Rey. Although small, Los Angeles was considered a city during the 1840s, a place where elite southern rancheros conducted business. Los Angeles appealed to Pico. It was a city where other powerful rancheros resided and was the seat of the sureño political establishment. It eventually claimed Pico as one of its sons. It was San Diego, however, where Pico invested his wealth. His two large ranches, Jamul and Santa Margarita, were in full production, although Pico had little need to be there. His mayordomos managed the operations of the ranches and from those locations represented his interests.[4] The plaza of Los Angeles became a fashionable residential area for many politically and socially elite sureños. José Antonio Carrillo, Ignacio del Valle, Vicente Lugo, and Agustín Olvera, to name a few, were among the powerful rancheros and politicians who owned homes on the plaza and controlled the politics, trade, and commerce of Los Angeles.[5] As California slowly began to prosper, many families were able to acquire luxury items from abroad. The

Angeleños filled their leisure time with cockfights, bullfights, gambling, horse races, plays, parades, and religious processions.[6] As the most populous town in California, Los Angeles gradually became a city that commanded respect. Pico spent a brief period as tithe collector of Los Angeles and became acquainted with its residents.[7] And as a ranchero, he was part of the city's lifeblood. Few professions, aside from the clergy, existed in Los Angeles that did not revolve around ranching. Saddlers, ranch hands, tavern keepers, blacksmiths, vaqueros, household servants, and farm workers lived side by side, making Los Angeles a lively and industrious place to live.[8] With his enormous wealth and influence, Pico became one of its most respected residents.

Pico remained busy with his new acquisitions. His Rancho Santa Margarita totaled 133,440 acres after he purchased Las Flores in 1844.[9] Two years earlier he had effectively stopped expansion of the Indian pueblo at Las Flores. In his continued capacity as encargado de justicia for the municipality, Pico decreed the land too arid and lacking resources for further settlement.[10] This opened vast areas around Las Flores for the development of his ranching operations, and two years later he purchased the land. Rancho Santa Margarita y Las Flores had seven rivers and creeks, seven lakes, thirty-five miles of coast, two mountain ranges, and vast grazing lands.[11] Pico's brother Andrés, corecipient of the grant, was busy with his own commercial interests. The two brothers oversaw construction of a corral and an adobe structure where they would conduct business and entertain guests. Pico's herds had grown considerably as a result of using land belonging to Mission San Luis Rey. From Jamul to Santa Margarita, Pico's mayordomos moved products. In the process, the Pico brothers grew wealthy.

This was a pivotal time for the Picos and for California alike. Had it not been for California's never-ending political crisis, Pico's opportunity to exert his political authority across California might never have arrived. In January 1842, President

Santa Anna replaced Alvarado and appointed Brigadier General Manuel Micheltorena as governor, *comandante militar*, and inspector of California. Santa Anna was still troubled over his defeat at the hands of U.S. rebels in Texas during the mid-1830s. To confront a possible attack on California, he sent Micheltorena north as political and military chief. Micheltorena had sufficient experience to face the United States should hostilities continue. He was a veteran of the war in Texas and had distinguished himself as a commander. The general took with him an army of more than three hundred men, many of whom were criminals, to defend Mexico from another humiliating loss.[12] The criminal soldiers, or *cholos*, antagonized the citizens of San Diego, and then Los Angeles, almost as soon as they arrived. Even so, many sureños received Micheltorena with open arms simply because he came as Alvarado's replacement.

Micheltorena's appointment as a defensive strategy made sense to some Californios. Many believed that war with the United States was inevitable. These fears nearly came to pass in October 1842. As Micheltorena and his army were en route to Monterey, they received the news that Commodore Thomas ap Catesby Jones, in charge of the U.S. Pacific squadron, had captured Monterey. Commodore Jones believed that Mexico had declared war on the United States, and that France or England would take control of California if he did not act.[13] After negotiation and the realization that the two countries were not in a state of war, control of Monterey was restored to Mexico. But this disaster confirmed that California was too poorly equipped to defend itself, even against a mere two warships. The next day, although Jones had admitted his mistake and invited Alvarado to return to the capital, Alvarado refused and asked that all matters be taken up with the newly appointed Governor Micheltorena.[14]

Micheltorena's arrival actually opened a door for Pico to reassert himself politically. Micheltorena was seen as an arrogant officer with little regard for public opinions. His soldiers had become a public nuisance; intoxicated and violent, they disturbed the residents, and many demanded their removal. The new governor also angered some prominent norteños by deciding to take the oath of office in Los Angeles. Delayed for weeks by the Jones affair, Micheltorena decided that Los Angeles was a suitable place for the transfer of power. It was December before the ceremony was scheduled. Perturbed, Alvarado refused to make the journey, sending Jimeno Casarín in his place.[15] Once Alvarado's term ended, Pico found new hope and renewed energy to continue his political career. In addition to questions about the new governor and mounting concerns about the United States and sectional strife in California, Pico was still concerned about the unfinished business of secularization.

Governor Micheltorena's view of secularization did not drastically differ from that of Pico and other Californios. But the deplorable state of the missions and the lack of funds in the treasury caused the new governor to take drastic action. In late March 1843 Micheltorena restored church control over the neophytes. The missions had been so degraded and stripped of wealth that they were falling into a state of ruin. Hoping to save the system and help destitute former mission Indians, he returned the administration of vacant lands and buildings to the missionaries.[16] Like the proponents of secularization, Micheltorena hoped the revitalized missions would strengthen California's economy. To help support the missionaries, citizens would have to make "voluntary" charitable donations, or tithes, a policy which angered liberal Californios.[17]

Pico was at first suspicious of the governor because of the privilege he afforded certain foreigners. The arrival of illegal immigrants from the United States began to alarm Mexican officials. Foreigners were welcomed in California, although the residents understood that if immigration went unchecked, they might suffer the same fate as the Tejanos. Nevertheless, Micheltorena was generous in his grants of lands to foreigners,

angering many Californios. For a time Pico suspected Micheltorena of working with the Swiss-born John Sutter to secure
the independence of California from Mexico.[18] This suspicion
was the beginning of Pico's troubles with the general.

Juan Bautista Alvarado, displeased with Micheltorena
since surrendering the governorship to him, was suspected
of fomenting a revolution against the general, who had him
arrested in January 1844. Alvarado had protested that the
streets were not safe with Micheltorena's convict soldiers roam-
ing around the capital.[19] Others also complained that the
soldiers committed robberies, beatings, and rapes, and that
their actions were costing the government much-needed funds.[20]
But whatever his perceived faults, Micheltorena cannot be
accused of denying elite rancheros the security of their
economic status. In fact, only a month after Micheltorena
arrested Alvarado, he granted the former governor the 44,386-
acre Rancho Las Mariposas.[21]

Complaints against Micheltorena began to mount around
California. A rebellion erupted on November 14, 1844, when
Pío's cousin Jesús Pico, Manuel Castro, and Antonio Chávez
drove off all the government horses in Monterey, seized
ammunition stored at San Juan Bautista, and began to promote movement against the governor. Alvarado and Colonel
José Castro immediately joined the rebellion, which grew
steadily. Castro was at the head of a 220-man rebel army when
he met and overpowered Micheltorena's smaller army in late
November 1844 near the pueblo of San José. Alvarado and
Castro wrote the Treaty of Santa Teresa, which demanded,
among other things, that the cholo soldiers be sent back to
Mexico. Outnumbered, Micheltorena promised to send the
troops back to Mexico and attempted to dissipate hostilities.
It soon became clear, however, that Micheltorena *had* plotted with John Sutter, as Pico had suspected, and together
the two soon raised a larger army of Mexicans, Indians, and
foreigners to squash the rebels.

Hoping they could match Micheltorena's forces, José Castro and Juan Bautista Alvarado marched to Los Angeles with an army, urging the south to join it. Upon his arrival, Castro had a skirmish with the troops of Andrés Pico, whom he suspected of siding with Micheltorena. The sureño soldier José María Barrera was killed sometime after the battle, which Pico considered "murder in cold blood."[22] At the time, Pío Pico was at San Juan Capistrano complying with Micheltorena's orders to sell mission property to raise money for the defense of the country. Castro told him about the rebellion in Monterey and described the serious state of governmental affairs. As an important southern partisan and the senior voting member of the assembly, Castro understood that Pico's cooperation was indispensable. Legally, the assembly was the only political body that might have the power to justify rebellion against a standing governor. Castro explained to Pico the circumstances leading to the rebellion, blaming it on the depredations of the cholo troops, and promised that if he joined the rebellion, the north would recognize him as governor. Legally, Pico would have been named governor without norteño approval. Nevertheless, he agreed to listen to the views of other important leaders. He then called for a special meeting of the assembly. All the members, including Francisco de la Guerra, Carlos Antonio Carrillo, Francisco Figueroa, Narciso Botello, Agustín Olvera, and Pico, were present.[23]

The assembly decided to send a three-man commission— Vicente Sánchez, the alcalde of Los Angeles; Antonio María Lugo, a personal friend of Micheltorena; and José Antonio de la Guerra, commander of the Santa Barbara Presidio, to negotiate with the general, who was then approaching Santa Barbara with four hundred men. The commission, however, only increased Micheltorena's anger and determination to squash the rebels. Pico received information about Micheltorena's approaching army in early February. In his letter to Pico, Guerra wrote that Micheltorena wished to maintain public tranquility and would end his march and pardon the leaders if the rebels disarmed themselves and respected his authority.[24] Pico wrote back to Guerra telling him to inform Micheltorena that he had one hour to give his answer to the commission and that his authority would be respected only if his troops were sent back to Mexico.[25] The assembly was also concerned that Micheltorena had within his forces armed foreigners.

For Micheltorena, the hour came and passed. Pico immediately reconvened the assembly, which decided not to recognize Micheltorena's authority because it was "destructive to the country," as Pico later wrote.[26] When Micheltorena refused to recognize the legitimacy of the assembly and accept its offer of truce, Pico believed the governor's days were numbered. As the senior member, he took the oath of office that same day and was recognized as interim governor.

Although in a position of power, Pico still had to defeat Micheltorena and his army. He issued a public decree calling all foreign and native citizens to arms in Los Angeles, where he gave a speech detailing why Micheltorena's powers had been revoked. He also asked for citizen "cooperation in defense of their liberty and interests."[27] Pico, in order to establish political control, warned that failure to respond to the defense of the country would be seen as a criminal act.[28]

On February 19, 1845, Micheltorena and his army arrived at Encino, in the San Fernando Valley. Alvarado and Castro joined forces in Los Angeles, and Pico led a separate detachment of soldiers that arrived there the next day.[29] The battle that followed was typical of those fought on California soil during these years. Micheltorena and the rebels exchanged fire for one day, without a single casualty. Pico dismissed Micheltorena's request to suspend fire and negotiate, giving orders not to stop the attack until the general surrendered. That night Micheltorena attempted to flank the rebels but the plan failed. The Californio forces followed his movements. As more reinforcements arrived, Micheltorena's chances grew dim. The

Californio forces surrounded him, and some of his men began to defect. The next day, without supplies, food, or a chance to escape, Micheltorena sent word that he wished to hand over the reins of government to Pico, who later met with Micheltorena to discuss terms of his surrender. The dejected Micheltorena had no choice but to leave the country with his soldiers. Years later Pico recalled that Micheltorena had told him not to trust José Castro and that he should, rather, seek out Vallejo as the new comandante general.[30] Pico had no quarrel with Micheltorena's position. After all, Pico's animosity toward General Castro went back to the days of his opposition to Governor Alvarado, when he, Pico, was arrested by Castro—a personal insult. Despite Pico's objections, Castro took the leadership of California's military.

As for Pico, although opposed among some in the north, most Californians recognized him as the legitimate governor of California. However, the tension between the north and south created political instability. The two regions distrusted each other. Although most of the prominent families were connected through marriage or compadrazgo, many of the most powerful officials created a rivalry, whether it was real or imagined. Pico's grudge against Castro also included his belief that military officials should serve the citizenry, not have power over it. Many years later, even after Castro had been brutally killed in a fight in Baja California, Pico had no kind words to say about his foe.[31] Although the two came together for the common good, their differences did not end with the defeat of Micheltorena. This was unfortunate for California because, as most suspected, war with the United States was approaching.

Unfortunately, too, a growing number of norteño critics called for a movement against Pico. The fear and jealousy they felt toward Pico increased when he strengthened his hold over California politics, as Alvarado had done from the north. In October 1845 an election brought Juan Bandini, Santiago

Argüello, and the norteño José Abrego into the assembly. They joined sureños Botello, Figueroa, Carlos Carrillo, and Ignacio del Valle. Other members, Ignacio Palomares, Santiago E. Argüello, Abel Stearns, Agustín Olvera, Pico's brother-in-law Joaquín Ortega, and his norteño cousin Antonio María Pico, were substitutes, and all had family or business connections to the governor. This left norteños with only one representative in an assembly that now met regularly in Los Angeles.

However, the assembly was not enough; Pico also wanted his influence to extend to the Monterey treasury, reigniting a decades-old regional dispute. Between 1840 and 1846 the customs house experienced increased activity. Importation of foreign goods and exports from the cattle trade and other goods increased so that in 1845 the total revenues were approximately $140,000. Pico was eager to take advantage of increased markets, so he overturned Micheltorena's 1844 law prohibiting the importation of nationalized foreign goods.[32] Juan Bautista Alvarado had become the administrator of the customs house through an official appointment. In June 1845, however, he handed in his resignation when General Castro appointed him to command an expedition against Indians.[33] Thereafter, Pablo de la Guerra, a man who was equally respected by both northern and southern partisans, assumed control of customs.

Yet it was the treasury, the body that controlled funds collected at the customs house, which Pico was most interested in. After successfully naming Los Angeles the new capital of California, Pico attempted in early 1845 to move the treasury to Los Angeles as well.[34] José Abrego, the norteño assemblyman, argued that Pico lacked the authority to do so. Abrego was treasurer during 1845 and an enormously influential politician, elected to the assembly in late 1845. His protest to federal authorities, in fact, prompted officials to reject Pico's relocation plans. But because the position paid very little, in August Abrego resigned. Relieved, Pico appointed sureño

Ignacio del Valle to head the treasury. This move aroused a
fiery protest by Castro, who refused to accept Abrego's resignation and denounced the appointment of del Valle.[35] Castro
knew Governor Pico would not abandon his request to remove
the treasury to Los Angeles and leave the north without either
political or economic control. In fact, Pico was worried that
the norteños were attempting to hold funds rightfully belonging
to the government.

In a letter to Juan Bandini, Pico expressed his concern
that the norteños would defraud the government of its rightful
share of customs duties.[36] Writing about the customs house
revenue, Pico said that the residents of Los Angeles "would
take one [peso] and that [Monterey] would take ten as a
reprisal."[37] He believed that with Ignacio del Valle as treasurer,
the government would at last have just administration of the
duties. He was not against shutting down the port of Monterey if the norteños attempted to block del Valle's appointment.
In fact, Pico appointed del Valle with the very intention of
moving the treasury and customs house to Los Angeles, a
plan that Abrego and other norteños bitterly protested.[38]

Friction intensified when Pico attempted to enforce a
new territorial law that would give two-thirds of all revenues
to the government, leaving only one third for the military.
Castro again objected, stating that because of the dangerous
military situation, the law could not apply to California. When
Pico ordered the customs administrator to issue the required
duties to the prefect, his cousin Manuel Castro y Pico, General
Castro effectively stopped the transaction.[39] The battle over the
treasury marked the boiling point in the relationship between
the governor and the general. Castro's contempt marked a
rise in norteño criticism of Pico.

It seemed a blessing to Pico when in December 1845
Alvarado was elected to the Mexican Congress; Pico urged
his rival to leave soon. But Alvarado was unable to accept his
appointment because of the lack of governmental funds for

the trip.[40] Alvarado was the most prominent norteño politician, who many believed was behind Castro's schemes, and Pico wanted nothing more than to rid the country of him. The incident reveals the desperate financial paralysis of California's government in the months preceding the war with the United States.

Along with regional animosities, the other crisis Pico inherited was the unavoidable war with the United States. In 1844 James K. Polk won the election for president of the United States on an expansionist platform. Even before the Democratic convention, Polk wrote, "I have no hesitation in declaring that I am in favor of the immediate re-annexation of Texas."[41] This stand was in stark contrast to his opponent Henry Clay, who understood that Texas annexation meant war with Mexico. Polk was aware of the risks as well but viewed them as a necessary step in achieving his ultimate goal of acquiring more territory. Thus, when he won, Mexico knew the new president would have little regard for its sovereignty.

Despite the tremendous obstacles Pico faced as governor, he enthusiastically appointed qualified individuals to official posts. Perhaps as a way to calm regional antagonism, he also repaired the rift he and Alvarado had felt for years. He appointed the former governor administer of customs at Monterey. This move may also have been meant to repay Alvarado for granting him Rancho Santa Margarita. In 1844 Castro also encouraged Alvarado to take the governorship for himself because legally he had not finished his term when Micheltorena arrived.[42] Alvarado, however, kept his promise to respect Pico's authority, perhaps out of good will.

Pico also appointed officials to serve the northern and southern prefectures; San Diego, Santa Barbara, and Yerba Buena (San Francisco) served as subprefectures. In the northern prefecture of Monterey, he appointed his nephew Manuel Castro y Pico, who had aided him during the revolt against Micheltorena. Although this can be regarded as nepotism, Castro y

Pico was highly qualified for the position. In 1839 he was secretary and collector at Monterey and then secretary of the prefecture from 1842–43.[43] Furthermore, Castro y Pico was a cousin to José Castro, Pío's rival. Other appointments included his brother-in-law José Antonio Carrillo as minister of the supreme tribunal of justice and his compadre Juan Bandini as secretary of government. Pico's leniency with regard to his administration's political opposition caused Bandini to resign after a brief period.[44] Nevertheless, it was exactly this approach and Pico's ability to ameliorate certain conflicts that made him a success. He proved to be a talented negotiator, and had it not been for the animosity between him and Castro, the governor might have united California under a common cause. His reliance on family networks and creating new and lasting bonds facilitated his ability to maneuver between dangerous political divides. Pico had matured as a sharp negotiator, a trait that would take him a long way in the years to come. The consolidation of his power base was no different than that of other regional leaders in Mexico. He was typical of liberal leaders who promoted state rights and passionately argued for individual liberties, but who also empowered themselves at the expense of the opposition.

The opposition of José Castro was another issue entirely. Castro created problems for Pico among the sureños when he began to appoint unqualified men to important military posts, and in the process gained their support. Pico stated that he "asked [Castro] for what reason he gave posts to those ignorant men instead of advising them to dedicate themselves to working and supporting their families."[45] By 1845, Castro was plotting against Pico and managed to win the support of his brother-in-law José Antonio Carrillo.

As early as that May, there was suspicion that Carrillo was planning to overthrow Pico. John C. Jones, a U.S. citizen traveling through California, described the situation to U.S. Consul

Thomas Larkin in Monterey. "I have just returned from the pueblo; they are all at loggerheads there," he wrote. "Pío Pico is most unpopular, and José Antonio Carrillo, in my opinion, is endeavoring to supplant him. The present government of California cannot exist six months; it will explode by spontaneous combustion."[46] Jones's prediction had some merit. Pico had temporarily suspended Carrillo, then head of the southern military forces, probably because of his maltreatment of prisoners. When Andrés Pico replaced him, Carrillo harbored enough resentment to plot a rebellion. Carrillo, Sérbulo Varela, and Hilario Varela conspired to seize Pico and depose him as governor. Although Carrillo had by this time regained his position as comandante, he still resented Pico. He had been won over by anti-Pico partisanship from the north. He and several supporters then planned to attack Pico at his home in Los Angeles on the night of May 28, 1845.[47]

If Pico had enemies, he also had loyal allies. A soldier from the army who was supposed to oust Pico instead intercepted and gave the governor Carrillo's private correspondence concerning the plans, which foiled the plot against him. Pico also learned that Carrillo was acting in accordance with his northern enemy José Castro.[48] Pico used his informant as a spy to track Carrillo's movements. He waited for information and then called for help from his friend Luis Vignes, who gathered a group of French riflemen.[49] Pico also enlisted the help of his brother Andrés, who eventually overtook the rebel army and arrested the leaders. Carrillo, the Varelas brothers, and Felipe Lugo were found to be accomplices. Carrillo was put in irons and sent to jail. The brothers briefly escaped but were soon recaptured, apprehended, and likewise put in jail. In the investigation these three were charged with conspiracy to overthrow the government; Lugo was set free when it was determined that the others had misled him. As their ultimate punishment, Carrillo and Hilario Varela were banished from California by Pico.[50]

Pico recalled that he notified Carillo of his punishment and offered to help his defeated brother-in-law "in any way [he] could."[51] Yet Pico was stern enough to impose the punishment despite the deep family connections between him and Carrillo, who refused to accept help. Pico stated that he "reminded him of another occasion when [Carrillo] was being banished to Mexico at the time of Señor Victoria and had helped him with money and whatever else [he] could."[52] Carrillo and Varela were shipped to Mazatlán, the former making it back to California in early 1846 to join forces with Castro in Monterey.

Despite the dissension that existed in the government, its overall stability was less critical under Pico than in previous administrations. Pico had from the beginning appointed norteños like Alvarado to important posts in order to avoid revolts. As a gift for his services, Pico also sent Alvarado six yards of fine wool cloth.[53] However, he would not let norteños take control of power and energetically protected his position. As prefect of Monterey, his nephew Manuel Castro y Pico kept an eye on movements in that vicinity. Although some powerful men were eager to seize Pico's authority, none succeeded. Some potential rivals, such as Vallejo and Alvarado, were reluctant to govern the territory themselves because of the threat of a U.S. invasion. José Antonio de la Guerra y Noriega, who was supposedly mixed up with the Carrillo overthrow scheme, sent his resignation as comandante of the Santa Barbara Company in February 1845.[54] Thus Guerra, without an army at his disposal, was also eliminated as a possible threat.

As the last few months of 1845 approached, it was evident that both internal and external factors threatened to disrupt public tranquility. It was clear that some norteño elites were unifying in opposition to Pico's rule. The timing was unfortunate because Californio unity just then was critical. In late August Pico sent a circular to the citizens of California, relating news from the federal government of an impending war with the United States.[55] Pico asked that all citizens prepare for the protection of the *patria*, the homeland, in the case of invasion, but also warned that in the meantime, no foreigner of any nation should be harmed. Soon all Californios were aware of the possible conflict. Pico braced for war and was alarmed by California's lack of preparedness.

When the United States annexed Texas in 1845, virtually everyone understood that it was only a matter of time before war would erupt between the two countries. Instead of adequately preparing, however, the Californios continued to plot against each other. In his testimony, Pico recalled this period of his life as one of doubt and frustration. But on September 13, 1845, the supreme government officially recognized Pico as governor.[56] But in candor, he admitted that the task of governing was beyond his control at the time. With continued antagonism from José Castro and the threat of invasion from the United States, Pico had little chance of unifying and strengthening California's situation, especially because aid promised from Mexico never arrived. He was unable to protect California from invasion. Defense would require money, supplies, and reinforcements from the federal government. With the odds stacked against California, few men in the territory, even ambitious politicians, would have taken Pico's place. Nevertheless, Pico struggled to help the territory prosper.

Pico focused as well as he could on governing California. But with sectional strife crippling the government and taking much of his time, he was hardly in the position to manage effectively. In May 1845, however, he managed to get a law passed that made it illegal for anyone to cut timber on private property, something many landowning assemblymen could agree on.[57] Pico also spent much of his time promoting secularization and public education, organizing his cabinet, distributing land, managing commerce, and communicating with Mexico City.

To address the public's fears of continuing Indian raids, he issued a government contract to foreigners John Gantt and

John Marsh to capture all raiders. The contract stipulated that the team would apprehend rebellious Indians—or kill them if they resisted. Marsh and Gantt were allowed to take half the Indian cattle they recovered. Although certain tribes were granted amnesty, others—probably those who lived outside Mexican society—were not.[58] Little seems to have come from this contract, apparently because Marsh and Gantt could not gather enough men. Pico also attempted to form a party to capture southern horse thieves. Despite the occasional attack, however, Indian revolt seems to have been less of a problem than in previous years. This was a relief for Californio officials, who at the time were more concerned with international issues.

With little help from Mexico, Pico had to find another way to raise money. The preparation for war with the United States created the immediate need for revenue. Because of Mexico's inability to send assistance, the missions, with their readily disposable assets of great value, became Pico's obvious focus. But selling off their contents was not a simple matter. The previous year, 1845, Mexico had broken diplomatic relations with the United States because of its illegal annexation of Texas. The president of Mexico, José Joaquín Herrera, had written to Pico in November 1845, suggesting that to advance secularization, Pico suspend the sale of the missions. The Ministry of Justice and Public Instruction wrote that the government of California "must report on those particulars, suspending at once every proceeding connected with the alienation of the property in question pending the resolution of the supreme government."[59] The letter, however, arrived in April of the following year. By that time the Herrera government had been overthrown, and the California assembly had advanced its mission policies beyond the point of return. Although the matter was brought before the body, it seems to have been dismissed.

Pico and most of his colleagues saw the destruction of the missions as inevitable and proceeded to sell them off for desperately needed funds. The missions may have survived ruin had Pico not interfered. On the other hand, the friars were by now discouraged and nearly ruined because of the effects of secularization.[60] Pico rushed the advancement of his secularization policy not only for the sale of mission treasures, but also because Californios at the highest levels wanted to ensure for themselves the lion's share of mission land in case the United States declared war.

We will never know if Pico's plan to sell the missions would have improved the economy because of the chaos cast upon California and Pico's administration during the U.S.-Mexican War. When Pico took office in 1845, the treasury was already in need of funds. Although 1844 had been a prosperous year for the customs house, Pico was obliged to pay $11,000 to transport Micheltorena and his men out of the country. Besides the impending war with the United States, the desire for personal wealth also played a role in the final secularization decree.

From governors Echeandía, Figueroa, Alvarado, and Micheltorena, the idea was always to gradually secularize the missions so the economy could adapt to the change. Pico, along with many in California, believed that the mission system was a failure, that the missionaries had had their chance at converting the Indians into settlers and had failed miserably. Liberal Mexicans of his generation liked to think that they understood the degradation the Indians suffered under mission authority. Secularization policies, at least on paper, considered the interests of the Indian population, although little that helped them was ever accomplished. Pico was not one to see land that could be grazed go "to waste." After all, ranching had become the main business of California and was an industry that he had great stakes in.

Pico's plan for secularization went a step beyond previous policies. His first act was to send Carlos Carrillo and Ignacio del Valle to discuss his plans with the missionary superiors.

Pico wanted to sell many of the missions to private individuals, using the proceeds to help the government. Others he would lease, using those proceeds for the exclusive benefit of the Indians.[61] Pico presented his plan to Fray Narciso Durán, president of the missions. The assembly would later pass it. Although Pico asked for Durán's assistance, the friar was hostile to the idea from the start. His futile argument was that the government's real motive was to assist the ranchero elite in acquiring the property at less than its real value. He believed that once the Indians were segregated into Indian pueblos without the care of the missionaries, they would return to their old ways and, in addition, be at the mercy of unscrupulous landowners.[62]

Fray Durán wrote a lengthy reply to Pico concerning secularization. "I cannot but express my amazement that the government of Your Excellency, which is no more than temporary, presumes to undertake such a serious innovation in the missions as is the destruction of their system under the title of enjoyment and liberty of the Indians," he wrote, "who for their foolish and unsteady judgment are no more than so many school boys, and who are led only by the present without providing for the future."[63] This letter reveals the paternalistic attitude of the friars concerning the Indian population. According to Durán, if the Indians were given complete liberty to do as they pleased, they would not survive, especially without the padres to guide them. This was the type of control over Indians liberal politicians in mid-nineteenth-century Mexico detested, even if many were more interested in the land than in Indian lives.

Durán did present some logical points concerning secularization, however. He understood that if the missions were made into pueblos, a vast amount of surplus land would fall into the hands of private individuals and away from the Indians. Both the government and the missionaries accused each other of exploiting the Indians. Durán asked Pico, "If Your Excellency, for lack of laborers, were not able to attend to all your possessions, would it seem right to you that the government came and directly by itself sold what Your Excellency cannot render productive? Surely not. Well, why then is it intended to do the same thing to a few unfortunate Indians?"[64] Durán suspected correctly that politicians would leave the Indians without a home, forcing them to work for reduced wages on lands once claimed as their own.

Despite the objection of the friars, and with the consent of the assembly, Governor Pico issued a bando on April 21, 1845, that called for a moratorium on land grants near the missions.[65] The purpose, as previous governors had also called for, was to eventually create Indian pueblos on mission land. Pico also demanded that Durán order the missionary fathers to refrain from selling any movable property from the missions in their charge. He wanted an account of all debts and assets from the administrators so that the matter could be reviewed before the sale of the property. Pico sent another letter to Durán asking that he see to it that the friars take inventory of all mission assets and debts incurred. Naturally, the friars were upset. Although all complied, many did so under protest.[66]

One of those who spoke out was Fray José Real of Santa Clara Mission. In his scathing criticism of Pico, he pointed out that the governor had forgotten the sacrifice the padres had made for the nation. "I assure you it caused me a great surprise to see how quickly and willingly the governor accuses of crime the poor missionaries who have sacrificed their tranquility and their health in the discharge of the ministry," he wrote.[67] Through the correspondence we can see how the friars came to regard Pico as the "enemy" of the mission system in California. They were not only angered by the accusations, they were also resentful because the missions had strengthened California's economy. The mission debts that existed were in most cases inherited from civil administrators like Pico. Nevertheless, Pico wanted the little they owed to be paid back to the government immediately, an action that earned him their further scorn.

At this point, after many words between the friars and the government, Pico simply desired the consent of Fray Durán. He understood that the protests of the friars meant little, but with the consent of Durán, president of the mission system, he could go ahead with his plan without interference from the federal government. Furthermore, Durán's consent meant that the general Californio population, which was still made up of devout Catholics, would not see the governor as an enemy of the faith. For the task, Pico sent his compadre and governmental secretary, Juan Bandini. The object, of course, was to convince the old padre that the government's plans gave strict consideration to the welfare of the Indians. Bandini made the trip to Santa Barbara and seems to have convinced Durán of the government's good intentions. Durán wrote back to Pico, praising him for seeking the advice of the friars. It is also evident that Fray Durán believed that the government's intentions were not completely destructive, "inasmuch as, from the conference with Bandini, I have learned that the territorial government had in mind better plans for arresting the total destruction of the missions."[68]

Thus, on May 28, 1845, the assembly passed the last laws of secularization, modeling them after many of the suggestions Fray Durán had given.[69] The first article of the decree described Mexican-Indian relations in California, at least as far as the ecclesiastical and governmental branches were concerned. It required the Indians of missions San Rafael, Dolores, Soledad, San Miguel, and Purísima to gather and occupy mission lands within a month; otherwise the government would transfer the property into the public domain. This vague article could have meant many different things but seemed to play into the hands of the government. The government would, of course, sell the excess land for profit. As private individuals began to lease the mission property, the Indians remaining around the land, according to the plan, would be able to work for the renters, cultivate any land distributed to them, or seek employment with other parties. The plan, as spelled out in the second article, allowed the padres to retain the church, courthouse, and quarters of the curate for religious services.[70] Although the assembly would pass this decree, it would do so keeping in mind the influence of Fray Durán. The fifth article allowed for rents to be divided among the government, with funds going toward public education, the Indians, and the maintenance of the padres.

Despite the apparent concessions to the prelate, Californios understood that the era of the missions had ended. Pico wasted no time in notifying Fray Durán of the assembly's order. He informed the prelate that his brother Andrés Pico and Juan Manso had been appointed to undertake the inventory of the missions as stipulated by the decree of May 28. "I hope, then," he wrote, "that Your Reverence may be pleased to send your orders to me through the messenger, whom I am dispatching today, so that the comisionados may operate soon and without obstacles."[71]

Durán wrote back with approval of the plan but had a few remaining concerns. He told Pico he was pleased with some of the directions of his plans for secularization, but that he was skeptical about the "absolute liberty of the Indians."[72] Durán understood the need the new caretakers had for laborers. But he warned, with a cynical tone, that the Indians did "not want liberty in order to work, but that they may be idle."[73]

Durán soon realized, however, that he had been duped. Pico had written a very different letter to Fray Esténaga at San Gabriel, requesting that he surrender mission property, apparently so Pico could sell it immediately.[74] To this request Fray Esténaga refused to comply, arguing that he had not received the commands from Prelate Durán. Durán, equally shocked, wrote to Pico in disbelief, arguing that there first had to be some regulation concerning the distribution of property. Fray Durán wrote, "I at last see that I have committed an error by yielding and concurring through love of harmony and submission to the government, and that I can take no further active share in this matter, as I have done so far."[75] Fray Durán pointed out that the move was without regulations of any kind to determine the true value of the land, to set up an auction, or to distribute the land properly.

Pico had written to Fray Esténaga out of desperation. The governor addressed the assembly in late August 1845, with concerns that creditors were demanding their money from the missions. The friars seem to have decided that the concerns were merely a pretext on which Pico and the assembly could promote the sale of the missions. In fact, it is true that the matter of mission debt had never gained such urgency. In previous years creditors were content to wait because they knew the friars would eventually pay.[76] But Pico believed that the government was responsible for settling the debt and caring for the Indians who had been abandoned without resources. He felt that the sale of the missions would help promote their welfare by creating a ranching and agricultural economy that would provide employment for them. After much deliberation, Pico submitted his plan for the sale and leasing of the missions.[77]

The plan, or reglamento, which took into account some of Durán's concerns, provided for the public auction of the abandoned missions of San Rafael, Dolores, Soledad, San Miguel, and Purísima. With the exception of the curate's house, the church, and a space for a school and a courthouse, the buildings at the mission pueblos of San Luis Obispo, Carmelo, San Juan Bautista, and San Juan Capistrano were also to be sold to the highest bidder. The priests felt that the Indians had abandoned these places because of their belief that the new landlords would force them to work. The sales were to take place in December and January 1845–46 and the proceeds to be split between the government and the friars. From this money, the government would erase the mission debts. The rental of the remaining missions was to take place in December, and the revenues were to be split among the government, the friars, and the Indians, with the latter receiving a share of the profit and individual parcels of land. Pico made it clear that traditionally occupied Indian land was off limits to renters.

As decreed, on December 4, 1845, those who had money to invest in property gathered at Los Angeles and began to bid at a public auction. San Juan Capistrano was sold to John Forster, one of Pico's brothers-in-law, and James McKinley for only $710. San Fernando was leased to Juan Manso and Andrés Pico for $1,120.[78] This elegant mission would become the home of Andrés Pico after the U.S. invasion. Other individuals were able to purchase or lease the missions during December and January. Pico allowed Durán and other friars to manage the distribution of property to the Indians.[79]

Yet in 1846 Pico was forced to take further steps against the missions. An armed band of Americans had taken Mariano Guadalupe Vallejo prisoner, and war with the United States was looming. With little or no help from Mexico, Pico believed he had no choice but to sell the remaining missions to raise funds for defense.[80] However, it can be safely argued that the governor made little or no gain by selling the missions. In fact, the pending war made the transfer of property to private citizens critical. The act itself was not his alone, nor can it be said that Pico deliberately attempted to sell off the missions without recourse. On April 4, 1846, the assembly ruled in favor of selling the remaining missions. Pico's decision to abide by the ruling of the assembly was made when the defense of the country was in jeopardy. Internal and external factors led the sureño-dominated assembly to react; few were willing to lease the debt-ridden establishments. It is true that the debts were largely incurred by the Californio elite in general, and that some actions were not altogether honest.

No evidence exists to support the popular notion that Pico somehow made away with thousands of dollars from mission sales. It seems impossible that Pico would have been able to carry out this scheme without the knowledge of government officials. Pico himself claimed, "I put the missions up for sale, succeeding in getting rid of some of them for such an insignificant amount that it makes one ashamed to mention it. But I was determined to end the mission system at all costs, so that the properties could be bought by private individuals, as it was set forth in the law of colonization."[81]

Between May and June 1846, the government sold the remaining missions at auction. The assembly may have acted to prepare for the war, but it collected little revenue.[82] The claim that Pico hastily sold the missions in order to put as much property into the hands of the Californios before the arrival of U.S. citizens seems plausible. Pico had finally managed to sell the missions and put an end to the system. The contracts all had stipulations regarding the care of the missionaries. But with the coming war, focus on the missions quickly faded.

CHAPTER 5

Governor Pico and War with the United States

The Californios were not blind to the designs the United
States had on their beloved homeland. After the unsuccess-
ful attempt to purchase California from Mexico, the United
States decided to take a more aggressive approach.[1] Many
Yankees saw California as the jewel of the West. It had fertile
and abundant lands, natural beauty with bountiful resources,
and of course, the San Francisco Bay. As an untapped resource,
the bay would open a lucrative trade route to Asia. It would
also provide for protection against foreign powers. Simply put,
the United States would be better off with California than without it. Possessing San Francisco would enable the United States
to fully realize its unique geographic position in the world.
Underlying these issues was also the assumption that the United
States should possess California by divine right. Many adventurers carried the idea of manifest destiny into the West, making
their way to California in the 1840s. As official or unofficial
agents of the U.S. government, many of these men came with
an appetite for conquest.

The first signs of U.S. intrigue came on January 29, 1846,
when John C. Frémont arrived in Monterey by way of Sutter's
Fort, near modern-day Sacramento.[2] Frémont, the son-in-law
of Senator Thomas Hart Benton, "the high priest of Manifest

Destiny," attempted to disguise his arrival as a friendly expedition.[3] While in Monterey he stayed with U.S. Consul Thomas O. Larkin, who at the time had received orders to discuss with Californio leaders the possibility of a friendly annexation. Prefect Manuel Castro y Pico wrote to Larkin asking why armed U.S. troops had entered California. Frémont later explained that the United States had funded him to conduct a scientific mission in order to investigate a practical route to the Pacific. The prefect informed Pico of Frémont's answer, but no objection seems to have been made to his presence. Pico did, however, order men to observe Frémont's movements.

Pico had good intuition. Captain Frémont quickly broke his promise to retreat from California and instead began to explore freely. Ultimately, after he refused orders to leave, General Castro marched against the captain's camp at Gavilan Peak, where Frémont had raised the flag of the United States in defiance.[4] Soon after, parties from Oregon also began arriving, increasing the chance of an armed movement against California. In some cases the intruders were perceived as a threat to Californio landowners. Others saw them as an opportunity. Whichever position they took, in early March 1846, the California assembly began to meet continuously.

The assembly addressed the disorder of education, the administration of justice, and the state of the military. They talked a great deal about reorganization of the military because of the threat of foreign invasion. Officials in Mexico City also understood the dangers facing California. The supreme government ordered Pico to prevent the immigration of foreign families and the arrival of nearly two hundred U.S. citizens from Oregon.[5] Pico seems to have complied. He called upon General Castro to work in harmony with the political branch of the department so that military reorganization could begin. Pico sent Pablo de la Guerra north to Monterey as a representative. Guerra attempted to negotiate a harmonious relationship between Pico and Castro toward the improvement of California. General Castro, however, did not respond to Guerra.[6] Instead he sent Pico a separate communication regarding the Frémont incident and warned that if necessary, he would take military actions in defense of California without Pico's consent. He also announced the return of José Antonio Carrillo from exile and asked the governor not to arrest him, as the government required Carrillo's services. This correspondence, read before the assembly, provoked an outcry among the sureños, especially Pico and Juan Bandini, who denounced Castro's actions as unlawful. At the same time, Pico publicly announced his federal appointment as governor, perhaps because he hoped it would bolster his sense of legitimacy.[7] He took the oath in public on April 18, 1846. Some citizens protested the act of the supreme government, and for a time, some important norteños considered withdrawing their approval of Pico as legitimate governor.[8] Pico and his associates, not surprisingly, believed Castro and Alvarado had provoked the movement against his authority.

In late March, Castro convened a military junta in order to discern what actions to take toward the protection of California. The junta also hoped to weaken Pico's control over California politics. It produced a bando giving Castro the right to act in the defense of the country with or without Pico's approval.[9] In later deliberations the norteño junta declared that it did not recognize some of the proclamations of the current Herrera regime in Mexico City, one being the official appointment of Pico as governor.[10] In the same light, the junta recognized General Mariano Paredes y Arrillaga as president of Mexico, which went against the common goal of protecting California. If the norteños' only reason to support Paredes was to challenge Herrera's appointment of Pico, they made a grave mistake.[11] Many of these norteño officers, including Castro and Alvarado, had previously given their word to recognize Pico as legitimate governor. Paredes left central Mexico with a large army, purportedly to protect northern

Mexico from encroaching Americans. Instead, he used his force to overthrow Herrera's moderate liberal government.[12] The junta's support of Paredes, furthermore, led to political chaos and shattered any unity Mexico had to effectively defend itself against the United States.

News of the norteño junta and its decrees of April 11 startled the south. Pico denounced the movement as a plot to ignore the authority of the assembly, the governor, and the entire south.[13] He wrote to Mariano Guadalupe Vallejo asking why he would participate in an illegal junta. Pico warned Vallejo that the junta sought to impel the northern pueblos to act without the authority of the legitimate government.[14] Vallejo, always attempting to maintain a moderate position, replied to the governor in the friendliest terms, and assured him that his involvement with the movements in the north was a precautionary response to the threat of war.[15] He warned Pico that the governor's southern partisanship hurt his ability to govern California. Despite Vallejo's criticism, Pico and the assembly believed that the north had indirectly waged civil war on the south. Because the north refused to abide by the orders of former president Herrera, who had appointed Pico governor, the sureño assembly in turn felt threatened and so authorized Pico to leave the capital to restore order. Pico would do so, and he also intended to depose General Castro.

Before taking such a drastic action, however, Pico attempted reconciliation. He issued orders to all pueblos to elect representatives to a *consejo general,* a general council, that would convene at Santa Barbara on June 15, 1846. Pico hoped to resolve regional differences and to discuss the best method of protecting California from outside attack. The norteños bitterly protested the meeting because southern representatives held more seats. Pico and his colleagues in fact wanted to give the south a prominent role in the defense of the country. Although the Santa Barbara meeting never took place, a meeting of northern military officials may have, where many leading figures proposed independence as either a separate nation or as a protectorate of England, France, or the United States. Some are said to have favored a French protectorate, while a small minority, including Vallejo, advocated U.S. annexation.[16]

Having failed in their attempt to meet in a neutral setting, the sureños regarded Castro's junta militar and his refusal to abide by President Herrera's decrees as a declaration of civil war.[17] The assembly decided to raise an army in order to provide protection from a U.S. invasion, seeking first to attack Castro, however. It seems likely that Castro also had plans against Pico, yet the situation in the north, with regard to a U.S. invasion, demanded his immediate attention.[18] Between March and June 1846, Castro pursued Frémont, who had ignored orders to leave California.[19] Perhaps Castro desired to remove Pico by force, but Frémont's movements prevented him from doing so.

In a letter to his compadre Juan Bandini, Pico announced that the assembly had suspended Castro until the restoration of public tranquility.[20] Pico, with his army of men from southern California, prepared to march on the northern pueblos and ordered Bandini to turn over all arms to the subprefect of San Diego for distribution to the soldiers. He also asked him to use all of his influence in San Diego to gain favorable public opinion. Bandini hardly had to be persuaded. Like Pico, Bandini unquestionably held southern partisanship and animosity toward Castro.[21]

After raising some money from prominent sureños, Sonorans, and New Mexicans, Pico left Los Angeles on June 16.[22] Within three days his army of seventy men arrived at San Buenaventura. Although aware of Pico's movements, Castro himself did not march to the south, as leaders in Los Angeles had feared. He did, however, prepare his forces to meet an invasion from either native or foreign enemies.[23]

In an official letter to Pico just days before his march, Castro criticized the governor's recently proposed consejo in

Santa Barbara. Castro characterized Pico as a "serpent" whose actions were like "a vibrant and destructive flame."[24] This referred to the fact that Pico had suspended Castro's command during such a critical time. Castro questioned sureño loyalty to Mexico. He called the consejo illegal and asked what authority the assembly and the governor had to initiate such a meeting. He then warned Pico, "In the name of the armed forces under my command, I protest against all of the subsequent acts that emanate from the clandestine junta."[25] In the eyes of Pico and the assembly, this act of hostility proved that Castro planned an armed attack—essentially against the government of California.

Unaware of the hostile events occurring in Sonoma, Pico wrote to Juan Bandini from San Buenaventura. With great confidence, Pico told Bandini of the men's enthusiasm toward the campaign and of his pleasure that another thirty men would soon join them. Pico reiterated his belief that Castro must be punished for his actions against the government and added that he had written to Castro, warning him of the campaign. Soon after he resumed the march from San Buenaventura, Pico received news from Sonoma that put him in the most difficult political position of his career.

While approaching San Luis Obispo on June 19, Pico learned that armed adventurers from the United States had taken General Vallejo, Vallejo's brother, and Victor Prudon prisoner in Sonoma. Captain Frémont had initiated the Bear Flag Revolt, as it came to be known. Pico wondered if the news was a hoax Castro had invented to catch him off guard. Soon, however, Manuel Castro y Pico and Juan Bautista Alvarado approached his camp. Castro y Pico, a close relative of both the governor and the comandante general, convinced Pico of the seriousness of the situation. Pico had disastrously miscalculated Frémont's expedition. Confusion over California's sectional clash allowed the Bear Flag Revolt to go undetected. Clearly, the United States intended to wrestle California from

Mexican control. Pico's partisanship had emerged at California's most vulnerable moment.

Pico reluctantly put aside his anger toward Castro and determined to prepare for the defense of the country. He wrote U.S. Consul Thomas O. Larkin a fiery protest and condemnation of the revolt and accused the consul of refusing to take "steps to cause the invaders to withdraw from their vile purposes."[26] Larkin had, in fact, done little to avoid war between the two nations. Governor Pico directly blamed the United States for the hostilities and warned that "such a sinister attitude as was observed on this occasion deeply compromises the honor of the United States and should it have upon it such a stain there is no doubt that it will be ineradicable in the eternal memory of all nations and will cause their scorn."[27]

Pico had a difficult task ahead of him. In an attempt to increase citizen morale, he issued a number of passionate bandos and gave animated speeches. He also issued a proclamation to the people of California in hopes of raising their patriotism and calling men to arms. He wrote, "I have the glory of raising my voice to you, in the firm persuasion that you are Mexicans, that there burns in your veins the blood of those venerable martyrs of the country, and that you will not fail to shed it in defense of her liberty and independence."[28] Some prominent sureños criticized Pico for calling the U.S. rebels bandits, which many misinterpreted as a declaration against all Americans. But Pico argued that the "North American nation can never be our friend. She has laws, religion, language, and customs totally opposed to ours."[29] Although many criticized the proclamation for putting California at risk of war, Pico defended himself, calling the Bear Flag Revolt an act of aggression against the nation. According to Pico, he never intended to offend norte americanos living among the Californios.[30]

As the war approached, the leaders of California discussed the possibility of seeking foreign assistance. Pico himself, once it appeared likely that California could not defend itself, had meetings with the Englishman Captain Patrick Blake to discuss the possibility of gaining British protection.[31] Blake commanded the twenty-six-gun English warship *Juno,* stationed off the coast of California. Pico went aboard on July 2, 1846, and discussed the terms for four hours. Pico told Blake of the dire situation in California, of the attack in Sonoma, and of the inevitability of war with the United States. He asked for British assistance "for the Mexican Departmental Government," but did not ask for protectorate status.[32]

In fact, Captain Blake had arrived in California with instructions from London to secure California's independence. Blake, however, needed the consent of California's top official—Governor Pico—which he never received. Thus Blake could not proceed with his plans. Pico also sent José María Covarrubias, who had replaced Juan Bandini as governmental secretary, to Mexico to secure reinforcements. Pico instructed Covarrubias to contact English officers only if he was unable to secure provisions in Mexico.[33] However, there is scant evidence of Pico seeking to establish ties with a foreign power.[34] The importance of this matter among Californios may have induced Pico to attempt this drastic step, but it was obvious to all that Mexico could not defend its northern frontier. Most Californio politicians realized their personal vulnerability. They had the duty to either forge new relations with the Americans or oppose them in defense of the country.

After the meeting with Blake, the governor marched north with his army and met Castro's army at Rancho Santa Margarita on July 12. Castro broke the news that days earlier, U.S. naval forces under John Sloat had captured Monterey. Given the serious circumstances they found themselves in, Castro and Pico publicly reconciled their differences in the presence of their men. Pico recalled: "Being all united, we embraced in token of reconciliation and all manifested great enthusiasm for the cause of our country, vowing to defend its independence and to die for it."[35]

Pico's earlier proclamation against U.S. immigrants had little to do with provoking the U.S. invasion of California as some of his critics feared. When Sloat declared California a possession of the United States, he also sent orders to Castro and Pico to surrender their authority. In order to make reparations against potential damages, Pico sent a circular to foreign residents, assuring them that because of their good faith they would not be harassed and would receive every right due to Mexican citizens.[36] He also issued a general proclamation to the citizens informing them of the attack at Monterey. He accused the United States of provoking the most "unjust aggression of late centuries," and having the arrogance to occupy and steal Mexican land "without disguising it with the slightest mark of shame."[37] Pico then ordered all male Mexican citizens between the ages of fifteen and sixty to report for duty to defend the country.

Pico's energy in mustering what few resources he could epitomizes the behavior of a loyal public official. Yet his actions during this period are clouded in skepticism. What real motives did he have in communicating with the British navy? Was he prepared to fight and die for his country, or did he simply look for a way to profit from the circumstances? The answer is difficult to ascertain but may be found in the lengths he took to repel the invaders. Pico wasted no time replying to Sloat. He lamented that the United States would commit such an aggression against a weaker, although civilized, nation. In the most cordial tone, Pico replied to Sloat's request—he could never surrender to his authority.[38] With his letter to Sloat, his proclamation to the foreign citizens, and his general call to arms, Pico had set California on an irreversible course toward war.

The swiftness of the U.S. attack prompted Pico to take immediate action. He set out for the south, where he and Castro began to organize a resistance to the U.S. forces who were quickly gaining control of the north. Pico also convened the assembly to discuss preparations for defense of the country. For months he had attempted to raise money for such a purpose. The sale of the missions is said to have been one such step. Perhaps in anticipation of a hostile takeover, numerous individuals petitioned Pico for land grants. The irregularity of so many petitions at once, coupled with the fact that they were made so close to the official U.S. occupation of California on July 7, would later arouse suspicion from the United States and again cast doubt on Pico's motives and behavior during the war.[39]

In June, leaders of the resistance gathered in Los Angeles, where the assembly met to discuss its options. In late July Pico heard that Frémont had landed at San Diego with a small force. On August 6 the forces of Robert F. Stockton landed at San Pedro and began to march inland toward Los Angeles. With information on the buildup of forces, Castro issued from his camp at La Mesa a proclamation stating his intent to leave California.[40] Dismayed at the illegal war waged by what he called "hordes of bandits," Castro announced that his forces were made up of only one hundred poorly armed soldiers. By leaving the country, he hoped to inform the federal government of the invasion and to seek help. He invited Governor Pico to flee with him.

Pico once again convened the assembly to discuss how to proceed without a military leader. Although Pico felt a defensive counterattack might not save California, he did argue for immediate military action in which he would take part. However, the assembly rejected his idea and decided that he too should leave California so that the United States could not capture the governor and force capitulation.[41] Eventually Pico did leave California to seek help from the interior of

Mexico. Years later Pico remembered that he had asked the assembly to authorize him to take command of the armed forces, "in view of [Castro] having failed us."[42] Although Pico later may have embellished his heroism, the decision of the assembly was a sound and necessary one. Pico's capture during hostilities could have compromised any chance the Californios had of self-defense. The assembly's difficult decision coincided with similar indecision for many leading Californios. Would they remain loyal to Mexico, or side with the United States?

U.S. representatives asked Abel Stearns, a naturalized Mexican, to bring Pico and Castro to Stockton's camp to persuade the two leaders to peacefully declare California independent and under the protection of the United States.[43] Stearns eventually became a confidential agent of Consul Larkin, although he maintained a neutral position. Juan Bandini, father-in-law to Stearns, allied himself with the United States and aided its officials in many ways. The California assembly faced many such obstacles as the United States was able to sway many prominent Californios toward their side. With northern California lost, the U.S. military besieged Los Angeles and San Diego, making it difficult for many landowners to defy the stronger invader. Despite the wavering of Californio loyalty, a handful of patriots took up arms and began a desperate fight to reclaim their homeland.

After the assembly meeting, Pico quickly left Los Angeles, taking with him the governmental archives. Before he departed, he left a pronouncement outlining the reason for his flight. In it, Pico clearly shows his desire to hold on to his position and defend the territory from invasion. He begged Californios to never "be taken in by flattery, cunning and false promises of the cringing enemy."[44] Pico wanted to make it clear to all that Californios were now impelled by force to live under the tyranny of the invader. He asked them to always be proud of their nation and promised that one day Californios would once again reunite as free citizens of Mexico. "That will be for me, beloved compatriots, the fulfillment of all my happiness and the only thing to which my heart aspires."[45]

From the capital Pico went to the ranch of Teodosio Yorba, and later to San Juan Capistrano, where he stayed at the home of his brother-in-law John Forster. Pico seems to have left there just in time. A number of influential sureños had sided with the invading forces. Juan Bandini and Santiago E. Argüello, now employed with the United States military, asked Forster if he knew Pico's location. They intended to persuade the governor not to leave the country and to begin negotiations with U.S. officers.[46] But Pico knew the assembly's decision did not authorize him to accept such an offer. Many individuals helped him escape capture even as Argüello led a contingency of U.S. soldiers to search for him. Argüello managed to capture fifty mules and twenty-five or thirty horses the governor had gathered for his trip. Finally, after packing provisions at his Rancho Santa Margarita, Pico rode into Baja California with Secretary José Matías Moreno.

Nearly a month after Pico departed from Los Angeles, the war in California took a violent turn. Pío's younger brother Andrés assumed command of the military forces and gained fame when he defeated Brigadier General Stephen W. Kearney's forces at San Pascual. Californios had also successfully retaken Los Angeles after U.S. occupation. But soon U.S. forces regrouped and acquired reinforcements. Meanwhile, Pico tried desperately to secure aid in Mexico.

In September 1846, while the war raged on, Pico and a contingent of soldiers arrived at Mission San Vicente in Baja California, where he found traces of the enemy.[47] In the nearby pueblo of San Vicente he saw the flag of the United States hoisted upon the door of the courthouse. He learned that Argüello and thirty Yankee soldiers under his command had come to force the inhabitants to declare allegiance to the United States.[48] An angry Pico had also just then received word from his sister that Argüello was pursuing him. Pico later

remembered that he had confronted the alcalde of San
Vicente, José Ignacio Arce, and asked if Baja California had
"put itself under the dominion of the United States."[49] The
alcalde claimed he could not subdue Argüello's forces. In a
fit of rage Pico "reprimanded him for having failed to defend
the sovereignty of the Mexican Republic" and asked the alcalde
if he recognized him as his governor.[50] According to Pico,
the alcalde began to weep and asked forgiveness for the grave
mistake he had made. Despite the contempt Pico felt for
Argüello's treasonous acts, he could not afford to wait to meet
him in battle. After finishing his business in San Vicente and
ripping the flag from the courthouse, he pressed on, making
his way to the pueblo of Mulegé on the eastern coast of Baja
California.[51] From Mulegé, Pico continued his previous commu-
nications with the Ministry of War and the Ministry of Foreign
Relations in Mexico City. From these documents, it seems clear
that Pico had few ulterior motives and intentions beyond that
of protecting California from the invader.

From Mulegé, Pico wrote to the Minister of Foreign Relations about his escape into Mexico. Pico had to secure immediate assistance. He had to make his escape look dramatic so as
to press the urgency of his cause. Pico explained that he fled
"over extremely rough roads, devoid of all human necessities."[52]
He portrayed the Californios with "intense anger against [their]
invaders," who would reconquer California "as soon as they
see themselves supported by the aid of troops sent to them
by the Supreme Government."[53] In an even more serious tone,
Pico implicated Juan Bandini, his compadre and assembly
member, and officials Pedro C. Carrillo and Santiago E. Argüello
as traitors to the Mexican nation, who acted under the command of the United States government.[54] Pico remained in
hiding at Mulegé until November, because the naval forces of
the United States were attempting to occupy the port. Pico
finally set sail across the Gulf of California toward Guaymas,
Sonora. Seeing U.S. vessels patrolling the area, and fearing

his capture, he ordered the captain to sail to safety. They landed at a place called Tetas de Cabra and from there went into Guaymas.

Arriving in Sonora on November 15, 1846, after a long journey, Pico continued to communicate with the federal government and urgently requested help from the government of Sonora. He wrote to the minister of foreign relations in Mexico City, informing him that Californio forces had reoccupied Los Angeles and San Diego.

Because of the war crisis in California, Pico urged the ministry to send forces and ammunition immediately. He noted that the victories of the Californios against the United States were "worthy of praise and of the immediate consideration of the Supreme Government."[55] Pico proclaimed that the United States saw the northern frontier of Mexico as a key element of their conquest, and that their power was increasing daily. He wrote that after the victory in California, a small number of government soldiers and ammunition would "be sufficient to reinforce the public spirit of those inhabitants who want no other country than Mexico; and with this aid the security of California, whose territory it is so important for Mexico to conserve, would be obtained beyond a doubt."[56]

Pico seemed to be optimistic in his belief that the Californios, with help from Mexico, could repel the forces of the United States. But even a small fleet of U.S. warships could have defeated Californio forces. Also, the United States determinedly sought to occupy the major Mexican ports on the Pacific, making a Mexican victory difficult to achieve. Pico continued to hope, however. The Californios had handily defeated U.S. forces at San Pascual and Los Angeles and had driven the enemies from the port of San Diego. With those victories, an atmosphere of patriotism and a true hatred for the enemy swept through California. Pico argued rightly that aid from the Mexican government might have rejuvenated the Californio forces. Furthermore, Lieutenant Colonel José

María Segura, a hero in the revolt of Los Angeles, had also made his way to Sonora to seek reinforcements.[57] Although many remained neutral, some Californios faced the challenge head on, and despite the treasonous acts of a few prominent citizens, loyal Mexican citizens enthusiastically sought reinforcements to purge the enemy from the land. Upon learning of Segura's arrival at the old presidio of Altar, Sonora, Pico sent the government another passionate letter, again pleading for support. He called the expulsion of the U.S. military from Los Angeles a "glorious victory" won only through the "patriotism and blind love for the Mexican Nation."[58] He championed the bravery of the Californios who exposed "their naked breasts against the destructive lead of the audacious and vile North Americans."[59]

Nevertheless, by late December the United States had regrouped and had begun its final conquest of California. Pico waited in vain for news from the federal government, which had, in fact, discussed the governor's requests. Pico and others had wondered why the government had forsaken them, but the general of the Mexican Republican Army, Antonio López de Santa Anna, made it clear in his letter to the secretary of foreign relations that relief to California was not a priority. The general congratulated the Californios for punishing the invading army of the United States. Thus Pico's continuous letters had in fact gained the attention of the most powerful military and political official in Mexico. In referring to Pico and his requests, however, Santa Anna could not send aid to "those distant States."[60] He insisted that all reinforcements and munitions were desperately needed in the interior of Mexico, where the war also raged.

Santa Anna's decision came only two weeks before Andrés Pico capitulated to U.S. forces. In January 1847 Andrés Pico signed the Treaty of Cahuenga, putting an end to the hostilities in California. Pico learned of the Treaty of Cahuenga in the middle of 1847, when his brother forwarded him the notification he had sent to the federal government. Pico received no reply from the Sonoran government, to which he pleaded for help, and thus no salary was paid to him from the government for his services from 1828 to 1847.

By any standards, Pico's term as governor ended in disaster. Yet the period during which he served and the events that unfolded while he was governor secured for him an important place in California history. Like other Californios, Pico understood the economic advantages of U.S. annexation. Juan Bandini and Mariano Vallejo, two other influential Californios, also recognized the many benefits to be gained by such an arrangement and supported it.[61] Such views, however, did not persuade Pico to abandon his attempts to ward off the enemy. His efforts revealed his deep love for California and his fatherland. His dream, as well as his duty, was to maintain California's connection to Mexico. But Pico had no choice but to accept reality. In mid-1848 he finally gathered the necessary resources and returned home to his Rancho Santa Margarita. He arrived soon after the signing of the Treaty of Guadalupe Hidalgo between the United States and Mexico, although news of it did not arrive in California until later that year. While some may say Pico "slipped back into the fold as a mere ranchero," this was far from the truth.[62] If California was severed from its roots, Pico still saw it as his homeland. As he had always done, he prepared to participate in its continued growth.

CHAPTER 6

Pico Reborn

In 1848 Pío Pico not only returned to a conquered territory, he was immediately seen as a controversial figure. Although the new United States political establishment, as we will see, made amends with wealthy Californios, some U.S. officials remained suspicious of Pico. His ambivalent stance on the U.S. presence in California worried many officials. He had never been friendly to the enemy's cause. Upon his return, although there were few obvious signs, Pico sensed he was entering a radically different California. As he rode through San Diego, San Luis Rey, and eventually into Los Angeles, he contemplated the magnitude of what had occurred only months before. The U.S. military now controlled California, and for the first time since his father's death, Pico was uncertain about his future.

The story that unfolds is not one-sided. The gringos did not come in and erase the Californios from memory. A new, unique relationship between drastically different cultures produced tension, animosity, and contempt, among other inter- actions. While many Californios fought back with brute force, others resisted politically and through the newly arrived system of justice. By contrast, Pico created alliances, participated in local politics, and successfully navigated drastic cultural differences.

Far from isolating himself as a rancher, Pico invested in real estate and remained influential in politics after California became a U.S. possession. Pico is seen here in 1852 with his wife, María Ignacia, seated next to him, and two of his nieces, María Anita Alvarado, left, and Trinidad Ortega, right. Courtesy of the Seaver Center for Western History Research, the Los Angeles County Museum of Natural History.

As the former governor, Pico naturally aroused the Americans' curiosity. His enormous presence and his extraordinary wealth brought him instant notoriety. Some saw him as a dangerous Mexican nationalist who had issued suspicious land grants just prior to the U.S. takeover. Still others took note of his uncertain racial mixture. To the racially conscious Yankees, Pico's African features made his wealth and influence problematic. When California became a state, less than two years after his return, blacks weren't allowed to own land or attend public schools. Racial tension was high, and some newcomers looked at prominent Mexicans as idle rancheros with questionable titles to their estates. As the 1850s unfolded, a period of unrelenting violence and prejudice against Mexicans created a dangerous business atmosphere for Pico; he had no other choice than to aggressively face his enemies.

Most influential Californios decided to make the best of the new situation. After the 1849 Gold Rush brought in thousands of fortune seekers, California became a state. Statehood, in turn, brought other dramatic reforms to California. Federal funding, electoral politics, and the U.S. judiciary created sweeping change in the established society. While Pico was confrontational, his brother Andrés took a less adversarial approach to the new government. Andrés's leadership of the Californio resistance had won him the respect of his enemies. He also won their esteem for signing the Treaty of Cahuenga in January 1847, which ended the war. Andrés rode the tide of his popularity to become a highly influential politician and military leader in postwar California.

Not all Californios were happy with the new political situation, however. Mexican residents of southern California in particular came to resent the prejudice they suffered at the hands of the Americanos.[1] Unlike the inundated region surrounding San Francisco, Californios still controlled much of southern California. In the gold mining region of the Sierra Nevada, on the ranches, and in the growing towns along the California coast, tension increased with each passing week. The cultural encounter between Anglos and Mexicans was on the verge of explosion, and no place in California was as tense as Los Angeles during the 1850s. California soon became a deeply divided state. Mexicans from different classes came together through common experience of racism and subordination.

Pico and others had once characterized U.S. citizens as the enemies of liberty. But the war brought about the need for reconciliation. New officials extended an open hand to Californios like Pío's cousin Antonio María, who signed the new California Constitution of 1849. Pablo de la Guerra, Andrés Pico, and Mariano Guadalupe Vallejo all maintained political influence during the early years of California statehood. Pío

himself was eager to forge new ties and resume the administration of his ranches. Unfortunately, the United States government considered him a potential threat and demanded he
answer certain pressing questions, particularly about land.
For those failed gold miners who made the arduous trip
across the continent, the only salvation was the prospect of
owning a piece of land. They quickly discovered that nearly
fourteen million acres of the state's most fertile land was tied
up in the hands of a small number of Mexican families.[2]
Some important families like the Picos had multiple grants,
a fact that caused additional resentment. Although the Treaty
of Guadalupe Hidalgo clearly protected Mexican property,
land grants from the Spanish and Mexican governments were
seen as a different issue. New settlers refused to be denied what
they felt was their right. Yankee immigrants received free grants
of land in Oregon and Washington; they expected the same
in California.[3] Hoards of squatters occupied the land, slaugh-
tering cattle for their own consumption, building houses,
and in many cases, resorting to armed conflict against the
landowners.[4]

To add insult to injury, Congress called for Mexican land
grant holders to prove the legitimacy of their titles. The Land
Act of 1851 set in motion a series of laws and trials that would
ultimately prove disastrous for Californios. The Land Act set
up a three-man board to determine the validity of claims, with
the ultimate goal of distinguishing between public and private
land. The law required that illegitimate or fraudulent grants
be returned to the public domain. Pico spent many weeks
from 1851 to 1856 testifying before San Francisco's Board of
Land Commissioners as a witness for grantees, and in the
process he learned a great deal about the U.S. legal system.
Yet California leaders accused him of antedating land grants,
making those he issued in the last months of his term as
governor suspect.

During his later governorship, Pico had issued approximately 146 grants from February 1845 to August 1846.[5] These grants totaled roughly 2.54 million acres of land, a far smaller amount than previous governors had issued. However, the California government criticized only Pico because of the timing of this many so closely preceding the U.S. occupation.[6] As governor, he had legitimate right to issue these "eleventh hour" grants, as they have been called.[7] Grant applications poured in during the final weeks before the U.S. invasion, and Pico had no obligation to turn them down.

The California government forced Pico to address the claim that he had antedated some grants to reflect their legality. The California Supreme Court deemed grants issued after July 7, 1846, when Commodore Sloat declared California under the protection of the United States, invalid.[8] Due to some apparent irregularities with the titles, most officials considered the grants suspect even before the state supreme court was created. In late July 1848, Colonel J. D. Stevenson wrote a confidential letter to the new American governor, Richard Mason, claiming that Pico had been involved in illegally granting property to prominent Mexican citizens. Stevenson also suggested that individuals who had received grants just before Pico fled California were eager to obtain certificates from the ex-governor upon his return.[9] Stevenson was one of several who believed that Pico had antedated the grants after Sloat's occupation of California. Stevenson's claims were based on his preliminary report of California land grants, and he based the allegation of fraud on rumors that Pico was not in Los Angeles at the time the grants were issued.[10] Naturally, this type of accusation justified the passage of the 1851 Land Act. Stevenson's main fear was that a Californio had taken the book of land grant records, which was missing from the territorial archives. Stevenson reasoned that as soon as these conspirators contacted Pico, they would persuade him to enter falsified dates into the records, helping to prove the legality of the grants to U.S. officials. Therefore, it was critical, according to Stevenson, to find Pico before he made contact with his old colleagues, and to establish the facts regarding the claims. It was never proved that Pico had antedated any claims, but even so, the accusation brought him scorn from many Anglo politicians as well as simple land seekers.

In its review of deeds, the land commission found that most that were suspect were tied to the distribution of mission lands. They rejected the majority of these. A review of the grants Pico issued, however, helps to clarify some misunderstood points. Although U.S. officials contested the land grants, most were eventually confirmed in appeal to the district court. Some of the disputed grants that Pico issued in the last few weeks before his departure were also eventually confirmed. This suggests that most individuals received legitimate and legal grants and that the accusation of fraud lacked proof. Some Californios were less fortunate, including Andrés Pico, who claimed tens of thousands of acres in multiple grants, most of which the court rejected. However, the court confirmed the 121,619-acre deed to former Mission San Fernando that Pío made to Eulogio de Celis.[11] Andrés Pico eventually purchased San Fernando and lived in its magnificent building for many years.

Although many Californios held legitimate titles to their land, the process of defending their legality often proved to be futile. Many factors, including appeals, combined to ruin Mexican landholders. It often required a decade or more of litigation to settle a claim. After lengthy trials and enormous legal fees, the claimants became so encumbered with debt that, ironically, their property was often used to pay it off. Or, the debts caused landowners to take out high-interest loans, using their property as security. During this period, too, land taxes were increased dramatically, which put a larger financial burden on the claimant. Finally, the rightful owners had to confront hoards of squatters who built homes, ranches, and farms while land titles were under investigation. In the end, most Californios had to sell their land in order to avoid absolute ruin.[12] Rather unbelievably, Pico maneuvered his way through the land commission years, paid his taxes, effectively dealt with squatters, and kept his land. This outcome is especially significant when we consider that Pico was scrutinized not only because of his large holdings, but also because his race and ethnicity somehow implied questionable rights.

Officials described Pico as kind but naïve and illiterate. Many other Californios were also thought to be illiterate. Although Pico was not well educated, he was clearly literate. The few remaining personal letters that Pico penned make this obvious. There is no doubt that his political decrees were written with the assistance of secretaries, a standard practice then. But Pico spoke with intelligence and authority, as is evident in his *Historical Narrative*. He may have been a victim of an attempt to portray the Californios as uneducated and contemptuous beings and therefore not deserving of the land they held. Many Americanos expressed sharp, mean-spirited criticism of Pico. For example, the successful San Francisco land-claim lawyer Isaac Hartmann detested the fact that a man like Pico had the means to protect himself. Hartmann described Pico as a "corrupt, non-English speaking, negroid, dwarfist."[13]

Although racism was a factor in American dealings with Californios, the Treaty of Guadalupe Hidalgo protected men like Pico. It gave them U.S. citizenship and, at least on paper, protected their rights. Because Pico had become a citizen, officials had few lawful means to disenfranchise him. They tried race, even suggesting that Pico was black. One official remarked that he was "about five feet seven inches high, corpulent, very dark, with strongly marked African features."[14] The first state legislature passed a statute prohibiting blacks, Indians, and individuals having at least one-eighth African ancestry from testifying against white citizens.[15] The admission of California, as either a slave or free state, became a major concern of the Constitutional Convention in Monterey in 1849. Although the majority of delegates saw no future for slavery in California, there were no attempts to protect the civil rights of blacks. They were not given suffrage and could not serve on a jury, homestead public land, or attend public school. With these restrictions, it is not surprising, perhaps, that a great effort was made to prohibit free black immigration to the state.[16]

It is unclear to what extent new Anglo arrivals viewed Pico's immense wealth as a contradiction of these anti-black laws. His brother Andrés, in fact, was an emerging politician who won a seat in the second session of the state assembly of 1851. It is possible that Andrés's European features allowed him to pass as white. Even so, there existed tremendous prejudice against Mexicans in California.

Ultimately, the tide of anti-black sentiment in California hardly touched the Picos. Pío refused to let racist policies disrupt his business enterprises, and he went on to testify in front of the Board of Land Commissioners with the goal of protecting the rights of Californio landowners. Nevertheless, Pico, who had been treated with such animosity upon his return, was careful not to expose himself as anti-Yankee. Pico's noted friendly nature was, in fact, a good business tactic. He could not afford Yankee enemies, politically or economically. He worked within the Anglo community, created new ties, and sought to expand his business networks. What he actually thought of the new residents is unclear. However, some Californios held tremendous animosity as soon as it was clear that the gringos had ambitions to divest them of their land. Juan Bautista Alvarado wished years later "that the foreigners that came to settle in Alta California after 1841 had been of the same quality as those who preceded them!"[17]

Despite the mutual dislike many Americans and Californios felt, Pico immediately began developing a business plan. He maintained connections with Californio landowners of all classes. In fact, in 1855, a group of Mexican landowners asked him to represent them because of flagrant land rights violations.[18] Pico successfully maintained a balance between his old and new contacts, which made him an extremely competitive businessman. With his growing financial influence, involvement in politics again was the next logical step. Before Pico could reassert his political clout, however, he had to deal with U.S. officials.

After the war, the armistice between the United States and Mexico allowed Mexican officials to continue governing until the ratification of the treaty.[19] Pico believed this law had temporarily restored his authority in California. Territorial officials immediately labeled Pico as a potential security threat and ordered his arrest. But because of his influence and his rights under the law, Pico was released from house arrest less than three weeks after his detention. Even so, many continued to view him with suspicion for some time after the event. A high-ranking U.S. officer remarked that if the Treaty of Guadalupe Hidalgo had not been ratified, Pico "would have been sent to Oregon or some other foreign country."[20] William T. Sherman, who accompanied Governor Mason on a tour of the goldfields, considered Pico dangerous, a potential spy, and deserving of punishment for entering California without a passport. Sherman warned that Pico "must be cautious how he acts towards our authorities, civil or military."[21] It seemed the highest-ranking officials in California were apprehensive of Pico. However, what Pico lacked in legitimate authority, his burgeoning wealth could supply. Unlike most Mexicanos, Pico could afford the legal council to shield him from ruinous political scrutiny. His growing influence also made him an important political ally.

Pío and Andrés became politically active in contrasting ways during the early U.S. period. Andrés, a rising military figure, was more successful in the new political arena than his brother. Most gringos saw Andrés as a respectable element of the Mexican population. Many considered him a skilled military leader and a responsible public official. Unlike Pío, Andrés was eager to reassure government officials that many prominent Californios were on their side. On numerous occasions he sided with law enforcement against Mexican resistance.[22] The trust he and others gained saved wealthy Californios from being compared with lower-class cholos. Some even began to mingle closely with the elite of Anglo society and, in fact, began to envision themselves as above commoners of all races.

On one social occasion, at an 1852 celebration of George Washington's birthday, powerful Californios and Anglos mingled with each other, to the chagrin of lower-class white settlers. An angry crowd of uninvited guests formed in front of the Los Angeles home of Abel Stearns, where the event was held.[23] Important Californios present at the celebration hoped for a commingling of wealth and influence that superseded ethnicity. Because of heightened racial tension in California, however, Los Angeles erupted in violence that lasted several days. To some extent, Andrés Pico's success proved that certain Mexicans maintained leadership roles in California. Andrés went on to claim a seat as a state senator and became the head of an enormous cattle empire and the owner of the redesigned Mission San Fernando, a lavish twenty-two-room building located on the 121,000-acre former mission grounds. During this early period of California statehood, Andrés seems to have had few problems with the mistreatment of Mexicans at the hands of gringos.

Aside from some meddling with the Los Angeles City Council, Pío appears to have been content with influencing politics away from the public sphere.[24] Although the circumstances were different, he continued his sectional strife with northern Californians. Along with lawyers Joseph Lancaster Brent, Benjamin Hayes, and Pico's brother-in-law José Antonio Carrillo, Pico was a member of a high-powered group that sought to separate the southern part of California from the north. Although nothing came of their efforts, the men were serious about their desire and even submitted a declaration to the local press.[25] By the time of this declaration, Pico was among the wealthiest men in California, having prospered from his enormous cattle empire. Even if men like Brent had little respect for Pico's brand of politics and his past allegiances, they could not dismiss the fact that he held considerable influence.

This period was a critical time for California politics. The previous year, 1854, the Know Nothings Party won numerous state elections, including the governorship. The Know Nothings were known in California for their anti-Mexican, anti-immigrant rhetoric. Although the Know Nothings held little power in Los Angeles, they were nonetheless a threat to the Mexican political establishment in California. On the other hand, Pico's main concern was the growing influence of the Democratic Party. Although the Democrats included many distinguished Californios among their elected officials, men like Andrés Pico and the mayor of Los Angeles, Antonio Coronel, Pío believed that the Republicans alone would protect Californio land interests and rights. The political tension soon escalated into outright hostility. *El Clamor Público* editor Francisco P. Ramírez wrote, "More than once we have had to refer to the grievances, the injustices, of which the Mexican citizens of California are victims."[26] Ramírez wrote about murder, various abuses in the gold mines, including the expulsion of Mexicans without recourse. "If a Mexicano has a complaint in the courts of this state, he is sure to lose it," he concluded.[27] The attacks on property rights and other flagrant violations of the Treaty of Guadalupe Hidalgo were so severe that a group of Californios called Junta Colonizadora de

Sonora began to discuss repatriation to Sonora, Mexico.[28] Pío Pico believed that the time was right to take a stand. Although Pico was perhaps more motivated by business interests than social justice, he understood the power of the Spanish-language press in Los Angeles. Californios continued to play an important role in the life of the city, but Los Angeles had changed. The growing Hispanic population now consisted of Mexicanos, Chilenos, and other Latin Americans. Many had new issues but wanted a government that protected their rights. Republican Party politics offered Pico the chance to protest what he believed were violations against Californio landowners and to begin expanding his influence in the business world. The Republican Party was new, founded in 1854, and represented a political rebirth. Among its positions, the party came out in opposition to the spread of slavery in the United States, particularly in the West. After Pico's initial turmoil upon reentering California in 1848, he had been looking for change, for something he could use to defend him against his enemies. The pro-citizen, pro-modernization, antislavery stance of the Republicans sat well with him.

Because of his influence and his ability to motivate people, Pico led the California Republican Convention in 1856, supporting the election of John C. Frémont for president of the United States. He issued statements in *El Clamor Público* on behalf of other Republican candidates.[29] The Republican Party understood Pico's importance. He was active as a regional *patrón*, that is, a power broker, and commanded vast influence over the working-class Mexican population. Still, it was a trying time for him. Despite his objections, his brother Andrés decided to join the Democratic Party. The pro-slavery position of most California Democrats had never sat well with Pío; he energetically defended the Republicans and the Union throughout the Civil War.[30] The Democratic Party was no friend to the Mexican population. It supported squatters, land reform policy, and had racist elements among its candidates.[31] Yet the Democrats offered generous political appointments to prominent Californios. Frémont, on the other hand, had opposed the Land Act of 1851 while serving as a senator; he also opposed the extension of slavery into California. Although Pico was no activist, Francisco P. Ramírez's sharp social criticisms began to influence him. Pico pledged $300 in 1855 for a defense fund for Californio landowners. Pico, Agustín Olvera, Abel Stearns, and other rancheros pledged "to aid and support each other by every legal means as free men."[32] The goal was to protect Mexican land claims against a prejudiced society and a biased court. When the land base of Mexican rancheros came under attack, Pico and other rancheros protested and did what they could to defend the interests and rights of Mexicans.[33] Even if he was not ready to denounce the Anglo community, Pico clearly recognized how unjust and prejudicial many were in their treatment of the new Americans of Mexican ancestry.

Los Angeles became the most violent city in California in the 1850s, and for a time it claimed the highest murder rate in the United States.[34] Lynch mobs were not uncommon, and many Mexicans fell victim to racial intolerance. This affected not only the poor. A mob nearly lynched the sons of wealthy Californio José María Lugo after they were accused of killing a white man.[35] Pío and Andrés were put in the awkward situation of having to act as intermediaries between the Anglo and Mexican communities. Their own nephew Salomón Pico reacted bitterly to Anglos during the Lugo case and later gathered a group of Californios to avenge the wrongs committed against his people, killing many whites in the 1850s during a period of unyielding racial violence in southern California. Some believed that Salomón attempted to assassinate attorney Benjamin Hayes in order to avenge the dishonor he had caused the Lugo family.[36] It is unknown what reaction the Pico brothers had to Salomón's "banditry," as it was called, but it ceased by the mid 1850s, perhaps because of their influence.

Salomón Pico was not the only Mexican American to cause the Yankees grief. Tension continued to rise as men like Joaquín Murrieta terrorized Anglo populations. Pío Pico and Ignacio del Valle gave one hundred horses to a group searching for Murrieta.[37] But the violence continued. By 1856 Mexicans in Los Angeles were outraged and frustrated beyond belief and had nearly lost their patience. After Deputy William Jenkins killed local resident Antonio Ruiz, Mexicanos were on the verge of explosion.[38] Francisco Ramírez, the energetic editor of the pro-Californio newspaper *El Clamor Público*, claimed that Los Angeles was up in arms. Both sides were so tense that revolution seemed inevitable. Ramírez wrote, "For more than six years this city had been a theater of the most atrocious assassinations. The criminals have always escaped."[39] He was right. Although a crowd of Mexicans encircled the jail and demanded justice, an all-white jury found Jenkins innocent.[40] Andrés Pico, along with other prominent officials, attempted to bring calm and order to the situation. Pico led twenty men to track down the leader of the Mexican vigilantes, who was captured and arrested. Although the court eventually released him, mistrust on both sides continued to brew.

While the Mexican community suffered the brunt of the racial violence, the Picos and other rancheros had to maintain a semblance of order in Los Angeles, a city where Mexicans were the majority of the population. As businessmen and regional patróns, they understood the financial burden of social and racial instability. They also understood that without the support of the Anglo community, which was growing in population and importance daily, they would have little chance of maintaining their positions in society. Pico played an important economic role in Los Angeles during the 1850s and for the most part tried to defuse any racial tension. Although he recognized the deep prejudice Anglos had against Mexicans, he refused to let it hurt him financially. Politics and the judicial system became the great equalizing force for Pico's business interests.

Directly following the Ruiz affair, the Republican Party emerged as a hopeful political symbol. For progressive Mexicanos like Francisco P. Ramírez, the upcoming presidential election meant a chance to restore order. More importantly, it could be the way to silence the enemies of California's Latin American population. Ramírez published a glorified account of the fight for Mexican independence, recalling that Mexicans had died to "shake the yoke of oppression and tyranny."[41] Ramírez also reminded his readers that Mexicanos had unalienable rights as citizens, granted by the Treaty of Guadalupe Hidalgo. The adjacent column was a scathing attack on the Democratic presidential candidate James Buchanan. It condemned Buchanan and the Democratic party of California as an anti-Mexican, racist organization that had the audacity to pass the "Greaser Laws."[42] The juxtaposition of one column that glorified Mexican nationalism next to one that condemned the Democrats as racists was classic political maneuvering. Ramírez warned the *hijos del país* that it was time Mexicanos took an active part in electing representatives who would serve their interests.[43] Pío Pico emerged as one of those hopeful representatives.

In an October 1856 edition of *El Clamor Público*, Ramírez published a letter Pico wrote to his cousin Antonio María Pico, urging him to distribute a circular in the north that promoted the positive treatment John Frémont had afforded the Californios during the war. The most prominent Californios in Los Angeles attached their signature to the circular.[44] Addressing the letter to Antonio María was a tactic to reach the Californios and reveal the reasons the *Los Angeles Star*, a pro-Democratic newspaper, had accused Pico of being a deserter during the war. The *Star* countered, urging Angelenos to ignore Pico's circular because his character did not merit their attention. Pico wrote the circular, in fact, in protest to a slandering article the *Star* had published about Frémont, the Republican candidate. Ramírez used the incident to incite Californios against the Democrats. He described Pico as "one of our oldest and most respectable citizens" and accused the editor of the *Star* of orchestrating a smear campaign.[45] Pico came out of this exchange with a renewed sense of political activism. He had demonstrated an incredible amount of energy in helping the Republican Party gain the support of the Mexican population. At the Republican convention in California on October 18, 1856, he was named as a candidate for supervisor of Los Angeles.

For Pico, the Republican Party represented a break from his past with both Mexico and the United States. Although it is difficult to determine exactly what it was about party involvement that appealed to him, the experience made him aware of the issues of slavery and prejudice against his people. Although Frémont and Pico lost their elections, Pico continued his activism in the party for many years.

In November 1860, Pico's brother-in-law José Joaquín Ortega wrote to him about the mounting problems in San Diego County with the upcoming state elections. He told Pico the work was difficult because in San Diego, Democrats seemed to outnumber Republicans four to one.[46] Pico recognized that the Democrats by this time exercised great influence on southern California voters. The Californio population was split on various political issues. But it can be said that many, including Pico, looked to the Republicans for more than just economic gain.

By the end of the decade, Andrés Pico began to rethink his position regarding the Democrats. The chaotic nature of state politics preceding the Civil War, along with the advantages of Republican affiliation, caused Andrés to reconsider the direction of his political future.[47] The Democrats were quickly losing favor in California as the Civil War approached and the issue of slavery dominated the political scene. Finally, near the end of 1860, Andrés abandoned the Democratic Party and switched over to the Republicans. His defection came as a shock to many because he had been elected to the state senate in 1859 as a Democrat. Pío, however, had long-standing ties with the Republicans and was eager to garner the support of his brother for the candidacy of Abraham Lincoln.

CHAPTER 7

The Making of an American Don

After the United States annexed California, Pico was rich in land and cattle but had a relatively small amount of capital. With the arrival of thousands of immigrants and the rise in property values, however, he became an economic sensation almost overnight. Despite the racial and political barriers he faced after his return from exile, he prospered because of his ability to maneuver out of tight political and economic situations. He proved to be one of the most resilient Californio businessmen during the post-annexation period. Pico suffered through years of drought and economic frustration, but unlike most Californios of his class, his economic fortune endured well into the late nineteenth century. His maintenance of traditional sureño networks and the introduction of new business acquaintances spawned his dramatic economic rise during the 1850s. Pico also increased his wealth through the consolidation of his businesses with those of his brother Andrés, a large landowner in his own right, who became one of the outstanding Californio politicians during the early U.S. period. Together, their enormous ranchos brought them a fortune and lasting prosperity. Pico did not follow the typical pattern of "decline" that has characterized the history of nineteenth-century Californios.[1] In fact, Pico protected his financial interests, at times overzealously, by using the newly established California judicial system.

Almost immediately after his return from Mexico, Pico reestablished connections with his former colleagues. He also met with Andrés, and the two began preparing their herds for sale in the northern markets. Andrés's prominence would help offset the negative image California officials had of Pío, allowing him some degree of flexibility in his various endeavors. Pío, however, was less willing to trust the new officials than his brother was. After the U.S. invasion, he was guarded toward them, especially after they had detained him. He had established connections with Mexicanized Anglos whom he counted on to help him with the transition. Hugo Reid, a Scottish immigrant who settled in California during the Mexican period, was a confidant of Pico and helped him as a friend and associate. Pico's compadres J. J. Warner, Henry Delano Fitch, his brother-in-law John Forster, and his friends John Temple and Abel Stearns all became respected citizens during the U.S. period and supported him in many ways. But when it came to land, Pico stood on his own terms and began to profit from his vast holdings. Instead of feeling bewildered by the complexity of racial interactions in California, Pico assumed that he had the upper hand in business and set out to prove it almost immediately.

Pío and Andrés together held over 291,000 acres of land, with disputed claims to many more thousands of acres.[2] Their older brother, José Antonio, was owner of the 26,688-acre Agua Caliente grant issued to him by Governor Alvarado in 1840. He was also contesting a land grant at San Luis Rey. Their enormous landholdings made the brothers immediately wealthy on paper, since property value increased dramatically after U.S. annexation. The Picos wanted more than wealth; they also sought power, prestige, and influence. California's political transformation did not intimidate them in the least. In fact, the Picos were determined to defend their position as landowners even though they spoke little English. Although aware of the racism against Mexicans, they also understood that their wealth set them far ahead economically of almost all the new Anglo settlers. As in the Mexican era, wealth still meant power in California.

Almost immediately, Pico set out to examine the business atmosphere brought about by political change in California. The first thing he did was to hire his brother-in-law José Joaquín Ortega as mayordomo of Rancho Santa Margarita. Ortega, a man in some respects as important as Pico in California affairs, was also the owner of 17,709 acres in Santa Maria in northeast San Diego County. Perhaps Ortega accepted the position because of the pleasant climate or for the salary Pico could afford to pay him, or even because the rancho was ideally situated between San Diego and Los Angeles. It is clear, however, that Ortega rarely soiled his hands with cattle or horses; he had men to do the dirty work for him. In fact, his son Antonio usually handled the typical work of the mayor-domo. Ortega was an influential figure among the Californios despite his advancing age, and he maintained his status after the U.S. invasion. Pico needed an ally in San Diego County, and Ortega proved to be a valuable associate.

Pico wrote to Ortega in 1848, just months after his return from Mexico, concerning the handling and raising of cattle and horses.[3] Pico was trying to reorient his cattle business to the new economy. He knew that people had to be fed and that there were cattle-based products to sell; Ortega hired vaqueros, ranch hands, servants, and farmers; dealt with squatters; served as the main authority in Pico's absence; and most importantly, sold the cattle, horses, and sheep. He could be trusted to protect the family business, garner positive support from the residents, and procure favorable deals in northern markets.

Aside from Ortega, Pico was also working with Andrés and other Mexican ranchers by lending cattle to breed and increase the herds, and moving livestock back and forth between ranches. Although they represented competition to each other, many Mexican ranchers, including Mexicanized Anglos, worked together to their advantage during these years. Many vaqueros preferred to work for a Mexican ranchero rather than be subjected to humiliation, and perhaps violence, from new settlers. As long as there was money to be made, the sureños remained a close-knit group of associates.

José Joaquín Ortega, too, was related to the most prestigious families in California, including the de la Guerras from Santa Barbara. In fact, it was Ortega's influence as a regional patrón that helped sway San Diego voters in the 1863 state election to elect his nephew Pablo de la Guerra as the new judge.[4] The patrón system continued to function after U.S. annexation, giving individuals like Ortega and Pico enormous regional power. From Los Angeles, Pico and many others would often call upon Don Joaquín to assert his influence in San Diego when it came to important political issues. Whether establishing connections, conducting business transactions, or overseeing a vast cattle empire, Ortega administered the ranch with precision.

In 1849, the southern California cattle industry was in the midst of explosive growth. The Gold Rush provided a consumer market that brought sureño rancheros instant wealth. As gold miners poured into California, food became a major concern. Pico wasted no time reorienting his operations toward northern markets. His mayordomos would travel north to procure the most advantageous prices for cattle, which sold for as high as $75 a head until 1856.[5] Before this, the Californios had been lucky to get four dollars a head. The demand for their goods made them far richer than the average forty-niner. Cattle would usually be driven by a group of vaqueros to northern markets such as San Francisco and Sacramento, where merchants would then sell the beef to the miners. Although the Picos staked a claim in the goldfields, and seem to have made some profit, their real gold mine was in feeding the new population.[6] Northern rancheros may have had temporary luck with ranching, but their lands were soon occupied by hordes of squatters. Most of the Anglo population preferred the cool temperatures of the north to the arid desert of the south, temporarily leaving southern rancheros at peace. Pico and his ranchero associates reaped enormous benefits while their relatives in the north suffered.[7]

In 1849 Pico made arrangements to purchase the 8,894-acre Rancho Paso de Bartolo, which he eventually paid for between 1850 and 1852. The $4,642 Pico paid for the land was well worth it.[8] It was situated just east of Los Angeles, next to the San Gabriel River, and had extremely fertile soil. Pico built a lavish twenty-room adobe mansion, a perfect place for a man of his prestige to host important guests. The Ranchito, as Pico affectionately called it, became a primary residence, along with his home on the plaza in Los Angeles, where he conducted much of his business. The river allowed him to grow fruit and vegetables, maintain livestock, and rent parcels of forty acres to various tenants. Pico built a store on the ranch where one could purchase goods, play two games of pool for twenty-five cents, and even buy a shot of *aguardiente,* a fermented beverage, at exaggerated prices.[9] The store carried everything one needed for the household, including cloth, clothing, and paper. He also had a cantina where "dos basitos de liquor" also cost twenty-five cents.[10] Although selling such items at inflated prices to his ranch hands and perhaps to his tenants might seem unfair, Pico was no different than many landowners who took advantage of their good fortune.

Pico's business was never more prosperous than in the early 1850s. The Rancho Santa Margarita had plenty of natural resources and the acreage to graze enormous herds. Pío transferred cattle from Santa Margarita to the Ranchito, and then to San Fernando, where Andrés lived. The brothers often conducted business as a team, using their vast holdings to accommodate an enormous herd. From San Fernando, Pío would have the cattle driven to San Francisco or sold in Los Angeles. The cattle business developed into a more sophisticated enterprise after the U.S. invasion. Pío continued to produce hides, tallow, and suet but in greater amounts than before. The great increase in population also created the need for candles, allowing rancheros to sell tons of suet. The miners who lived in makeshift camps were in constant need of food and *carne seca,* or jerked beef, as the new settlers called it. Carne seca was simple to make and a reliable and easily stored source of protein.

During the 1850s Pío and Andrés put great effort into increasing their fortunes. Both were constantly looking for other ways to capitalize on the new economy. In 1855, for example, Andrés and his eight-year-old son, Rómulo, were removing asphalt by hand in San Fernando when he realized a profit might be made. The Franciscans had used the asphalt, or *brea,* as the Californios called it, to seal rooftops. Andrés took advantage of new technology entering California and used the asphalt to begin what he hoped would become an oil lamp company.[11]

Although nothing came of the venture, Andrés was later involved with the beginnings of the oil industry in California. The discovery of oil came about much like a Hollywood sitcom. In 1865, a man named Ramón Parero was hunting in the San Fernando range when he spotted crude oil. He ran back to town to inform some of the influential men. He also stopped at Andrés's residence, Mission San Fernando, where Dr. Vincent Gelcich, who had married into the northern Pico family, happened to be visiting. Gelcich had come to California from Pennsylvania, where oil deposits had been discovered not long before. Being familiar with the Pennsylvania fields, Gelcich identified the substance that Parero had carried with him in a canteen.[12]

After Parero discovered oil at "Pico Canyon" in San Fernando, Andrés, Sanford Lyon, and other prominent partners founded California's first oil company in 1865; Pío held a small claim in the company. This small operation produced a limited amount of crude oil and shipped it by wagon to Los Angeles. The company later evolved into the Star Oil Company, which had its first big breakthrough in 1876, the year Andrés died. By that time Andrés and Pío had sold their stock in the company because it had seemed to be heading nowhere. Although they had produced a limited number of barrels, the original founders of the claim halted their operation because of lack of expertise. Lyon pushed on, however, and managed to hand-drill the first well in California. Star Oil, which eventually took over the claim, was a predecessor of the Standard Oil Company. The Picos would never see a dime of the millions that were later made. The oil industry was new and almost unknown in California at the time, and unfortunately Andrés and Pío were unlucky in not reorienting their business empire toward oil. Had they, the Pico name might have taken on a whole new meaning in California history.

Instead, Pico maintained his status as a ranchero and landlord. In part because competition grew dramatically across the Southwest, 1856 brought a sudden drop in cattle prices. But Pico's future still looked bright. He made a better living than most California residents did simply by renting his land. The Ranchito was an ideal place for businessmen, families, and ranch hands to live. A forty-acre plot could provide a decent farm for a family. With a temperate climate and the San Gabriel River for irrigation, Pico's Ranchito was ideal for agricultural production and the cultivation of orchards. Pico had an enormous irrigation ditch constructed in the early 1850s, which provided water for cattle as well as Pico's and his tenants' crops. The Ranchito's proximity to Los Angeles also made the location desirable. During this time Pico still maintained the home in the plaza in Los Angeles, that he had acquired in 1845.[13] One could easily make the fifteen-mile trip to the city and have access to all of its conveniences; yet it was removed enough to avoid the violence and the crowds. As late as 1880, Pico was making an enormous amount of money from rent at the Ranchito. He received six dollars per acre during these years, and although there is no precise record of how many tenants he had, it was a profitable number.[14]

But commercial markets began to shift in the late 1850s. Although Pico was able to maintain a comfortable standard of living, simply "getting by" was foreign to his character. As the decade closed, the cattle industry was showing signs of stagnation, and Pico felt the pressure of a sluggish economy. His daring character, evident from the time he entered politics, became a useful political tool for maintaining power. He believed that in order to succeed, one had to take enormous risks, and it was always in his nature to do so. In order to maintain his empire, to pay off some small financial obligations, and to make improvements to his business, in 1855 he secured a mortgage on the Rancho Santa Margarita from the San Francisco firm of Pioche and Bayerque.[15] Sadly, the $25,000 mortgage, which carried an interest rate of 3 percent per month, would haunt him for years. The state's deepening financial crisis and his own increasing legal concerns combined to place him in a tight financial position.

By the late 1850s Pico's financial transactions show that he began to diversify his business strategy. He cosigned many loans, a practice that would net him small sums of money once paid off. For a struggling businessman, or anyone else who needed a loan, Pico was an ideal person to act as security. He had large sums of money at his disposal and was always glad to involve himself in new transactions. One note he signed to Samuel Carpenter, a resident of Los Angeles, backfired, however. In 1856 Carpenter took a loan for $4,058 from John Downey and James McFarland, two prominent businessmen.[16] After Carpenter was unable to repay the loan, Pico was required to put up the money. When Downey and McFarland successfully sued Pico for it, he appealed it all the way to the Supreme Court of California, where he was finally defeated.[17] Carpenter and Pico were required to pay the full amount of the loan, the interest, and $131.15 for the plaintiff's legal fees. For Pico, who most likely paid the entire costs, the case was a business matter. To prove he felt no animosity, he leased a building to Downey and McFarland a few years later.

McFarland and Downey v. Pico offers an ideal example of Pico's complex mix of ambition and recklessness. The case had the potential to be a learning experience. After Pico's appearance before the supreme court, he understood that legal protection at the highest level could be attained for a price he could easily afford. Pico quickly concluded that the court was, in fact, the ideal place to settle business disputes, in part because he had the means to retain the finest legal counsel. For a few hundred dollars, his lawyers could represent him as an honorable citizen and shed any negativity associated with his image. Furthermore, having his own legal team added a sophisticated element to his business life and helped ensure that he could protect his growing empire.

As he became more sophisticated though his legal challenges, Pico demonstrated that a Californio of his caliber was not so easily pushed around. The one hundred thirty dollars he was ordered to pay covered McFarland and Downey's legal fees. This amount was monumental to a man of ordinary means in the 1850s. But for Pico it was a rather small figure, one that allowed McFarland and Downey to hire a lawyer to defend them in court. Pico believed that prejudice would more often than not succumb to cold currency. This observation is what set him apart from other Mexicans in California. His wealth could have bought justice even if it had not been offered as one of his civil rights. In the Los Angeles business world, too, Pico would demand that his presence be felt. When an individual presented a financial challenge, no matter his race or class, Pico would hire a powerful team of lawyers to represent him in court.[18] As Pico became more economically competitive, he relied more and more on the easily accessible legal system to solve his problems.

Although Pico remained financially stable through the eventual fall of the cattle industry, his vast herds dwindled. Drought and the dramatic drop in cattle prices both took their toll. As early as October 1856, Pico was informed that his cattle at Rancho Santa Margarita were sick and hungry.[19] In January 1857 José Joaquín Ortega wrote to him reporting that the Santa Margarita land had finally received some mercy from the drought and crop shortage that had affected all rancheros in the area. During that dreadful winter drought, Pico alone lost 156 animals, which he could have sold for over $5,000.[20] But he was not ready to give up, nor did he feel that environmental conditions merited a change in his ranching-business strategy.

Despite the poor outlook of the cattle industry, Pico still had clients willing to purchase livestock. By then, his cattle sales tended to be to local rancheros or farmers rather than to the northern markets. In March 1857 he sold 230 cows as breeders to a group of Basques.[21] In July he sold an additional 300 head to Juan Serca.[22] Ortega also reported that an additional 700 head had just been branded. With these two sales alone, Pico could have expected to make between $8,400 and $9,500.[23] For that period, even after subtracting his overhead, this was a remarkable amount of money.[24] Pico also had timber, orchards, and land leases that were producing money from the Rancho Santa Margarita. In addition, he still maintained his separate interests at the Ranchito and the Rancho San Fernando, where his other mayordomo, José Antonio Serrano, maintained the employees and supervised the workload.

As the 1850s ended, Pico continued to sell cattle and sheep at a rate that would support his own and his family's operations. Although the cattle business slowed down, Pico remained optimistic about future sales and revenues but seems to have had expenses that equaled or surpassed his intake. Yet in early 1858, when other southern California rancheros were having financial difficulties, Pico was apparently one of few who were able to make sales. Abel Stearns wrote to Cave John Couts, like Sterns a prominent southern California cattle rancher, that "I have only heard of but one sale. Pio Pico sold 1000 . . . all at $15,000."[25] Yet in comparison to the early 1850s, this was a small price for a thousand head. In 1850 Pico could have expected to earn at least $50,000. Antonio Ortega wrote to Pico about the diminishing values: "I regret to tell you that today I contracted all of the livestock at $20 a head because it has been impossible for me to find a better price."[26]

Pico was known to have some of the finest mares in California, many of which he used for racing and breeding. Numerous individuals and businesses purchased Pico's horses, brood mares, and other livestock. One company that did business with Pico was James Birch's Overland Mail Line. In June 1857, at the request of Birch, the Picos sold six mules to J. C. Dunlap, an employee of the company. In October 1857, Dunlap wrote to Andrés Pico about the mules and also mentioned that he had heard Pío had a herd of finely bred mares. Dunlap eventually purchased twenty mares for a total price of $2,900. This sale represents one of many, and clearly indicates another way Pico was able to remain competitive during a time of economic hardship. He did not hesitate to bring suit when his interests were threatened. In fact, by 1858 Birch found that he could not make the payment deadline and agreed to pay the brothers the full amount with interest over a short period. But after Birch died in November 1858, the administrator of the Birch estate refused to pay the debt to Pico, arguing that the claim was invalid. Pico sued for legal costs, the amount of the debt and interest, and eventually won the case in the Los Angeles Superior Court. Stevens, the administrator, protested to the supreme court, which also ruled in Pico's favor.[27] This victory is proof that some Californios found justice in the new legal system.

Despite Pico's successes, he was not without financial problems. In March 1859 Ortega began to worry about how Pico was managing his business. "Cuñado, open your eyes and view the way in which you allow meddling into your business," he wrote.[28] Ortega was referring to Pico's proclivity to trust strangers and to seek the advice of some who were not among his confidants. Pico's nature was to befriend strangers; he allowed them into his home and forged new alliances easily. This was often an unwise choice on the California frontier, which many newcomers viewed as a place where one could become rich overnight; others believed they could prey on the vulnerable Californio ranchers. Pico replied to Ortega but ignored his warning. He seems to have been preoccupied with his business affairs, and he could not deny a friend in need: "Give my friend Ysidro twenty-five head of cattle," he instructed.[29] Ortega's insight concerning the way Pico managed his affairs was an early indication that Pico was partially responsible for his own misfortune. Time after time in the years to come, Pico put trust in people who ended up cheating him.

By 1859 Pico was pressed to repay various debts, including the 1855 loan from Pioche and Bayerque. As noted, Pico secured the loan using Rancho Santa Margarita as collateral. This loan and smaller ones the brothers had begun securing after the fall of the cattle industry were usually at the rate of 3 percent interest per month, a typical interest rate in the second half of the nineteenth century.[30] In many cases, landowners, especially the Californios, drowned in debt because of the need for credit. The Picos were suddenly no exception. Pico's diminishing herds and his increasing debts soon put him in deep financial trouble. It became difficult to maintain his lifestyle and support his less fortunate family members. He asked Ortega to beg God that he would be able to pay his debts and at least have some corn to offer his brothers and sisters.[31] But by the end of March 1859, he seemed to be facing utter ruin: "Dear Cuñado," he wrote to Ortega, "I no longer have hope that Don Andrés will send money from the North so that I may pay my debts . . . today all I desire is that God allows me to pay all that I owe."[32]

It wasn't bankruptcy that worried Pico, however, but that he would lose his reputation as a competitive business- man. Although he owed thousands of dollars, his property could have been sold for much more than he owed, allowing him the means to live the rest of his life as a wealthy man. But to Pío Pico, giving up his land and estates would be a sign of weakness, an indication that he was finished as a man of importance.

The 1860s found Pico pressed to use the courts, often as a defensive measure for retaining his finances. In 1861 he was forced to bring suit against another elite Californio family, the de la Guerras of Santa Barbara. Pico's suit against Pablo de la Guerra, who had served as a California senator along- side Andrés Pico, signaled that the California economy had so expanded that family ties as a means of building wealth hardly mattered anymore.[33]

The outcome of *Pico v. Guerra* reveals how increasing econo- mic frustration pitted some Californios against one another. There is no reason other than financial burden that this case could not have been settled out of court. But patronage and trust in family ties had become a risky business practice. So many extended Californio families had signed promissory notes to each other that it was imperative to recover some of the money they had lost through bad loans. For example, after the magnificent landholding of José del Carmen Lugo became ruinously encumbered, he lamented, "I had the misfortune of putting my signature on the debts of others in whom I had confidence."[34] Pico was no different. He continued to seek and give loans to friends and families. Ignacio del Valle, once a close friend, wrote that Pico's "friendship is the bane of all his acquaintances and would bankrupt a Rothschild or a Vanderbilt. See what it has done for his more noble and generous brother Don Andrés. He has dissipated a colossal fortune, which had Don Andrés not been coerced and despoiled of, would make him one of the richest capitalists in California."[35] This criticism probably resulted from the increasing tension between Pío and his brother-in-law John Forster over Rancho Santa Margarita, tension caused in part because del Valle and Forster were also related through marriage and therefore shared similar interests. From this time on, Pico began to rely more often on outside resources rather than turning to family members. The cutthroat business atmosphere in Los Angeles also forced him to change his business methods. He was now competing against wealthy outsiders along with his former kinsmen.

With the cattle market in disarray, Pico began to focus more on real estate, although he maintained pockets of livestock. He was literally on the move. He maintained ties to northern colleagues, kept animals with his northern cousins, and traveled widely around the state. The Pico brothers were still known throughout California as wealthy and powerful men, but Pío had a new worry in the behavior of his brother. Andrés's inability to restrain his addiction to gambling threatened to bring both brothers to the brink of disaster.

Cards, cockfights, bullfights, and other forms of gambling were always popular among the Californios. Pío was mildly addicted to gambling, using it as a diversion from a hectic life. He was more likely to gamble with enormous business transactions than to risk his fortune at cards or horse racing. He did admire the horses, but his compulsion was mild compared to that of his brother. As a young man, Pío had gambled with priests, friends, and even an American sea captain in Baja California during the U.S.-Mexican War.[36] During the late Mexican period, a gambling house had been built in the plaza of Los Angeles. The house was devoted to monte, a card game that continued to be popular during the early U.S. period.[37] Rancheros including Pico often patronized the monte house in the 1850s and bet hundreds of dollars.

Horse racing was another favorite activity, but during the heyday of the rancheros in the 1850s, it became quite an important spectacle. Men waged enormous stakes, even by today's standards, during a time when the rancheros had more money than they knew what to do with. Yet historians like to exaggerate the amount Pico and other Californios lost through careless gambling.[38] Pico was directly involved with the most famous race of the time. In October 1852 he rode his prize California-bred horse Sarco against José Sepúlveda's Australian mare Black Swan. Sepúlveda won the nine-mile race by seventy-five yards, and Pico lost $1,600 and three hundred head of cattle.[39] Although this bet would be the equivalent of nearly $25,000 today, the loss at the time was not at all beyond his means, considering his tens of thousands of acres and head of cattle. Because of the high stakes, the prestigious horsemen, and the quality of their breeds, the Sarco–Black Swan race was the most memorable event of its kind, attracting people from all over the state. In sum, counting wagers by all spectators, the bets equaled approximately $50,000. Contrary to popular belief, Pico's loss was a small part of this.[40]

During the era of the Gold Rush and the height of the rancheros, free-flowing money and extravagant spending was the norm. Gambling, luxurious clothes, and expensive imported items were part of the ranchero lifestyle. Some rancheros, of course, were more careless with their money than others. As for the Sarco–Black Swan race, this was not the only time Pico stood to win or lose. Although his gambling was an addiction, there is no evidence that it contributed to his downfall. To the contrary, Pico could easily have used his extravagant bets to bolster his image as a high spender—although he had no need to. While his prize horse Sarco had suffered its first defeat in that race, Pico grew in renown after the Black Swan race.

Andrés also had a long history of gambling—with both money and business deals. In 1852 he showed his reckless love of high stakes when he bet $15,000 on a single horse race.[41] Both the northern and southern California press covered these racing events, especially when they involved someone from a famous Californio family. Andrés's bet and others he may have lost during this period were financially damaging, but not sufficient to destroy the Picos' wealth. Yet in the 1860s, when other crises were also upon them, the matter became more critical. Andrés was in a desperate financial situation for many reasons other than gambling.

In 1862 he lost military command over the southern California district.[42] The reason for his dismissal was probably connected to his political defection. Pío had always opposed the Democrats, and in the late 1850s he most likely offered compelling reasons for Andrés to desert the Democratic Party and support the Republican candidacy of Abraham Lincoln. Leland Stanford won the governorship for the Republican Party, and Andrés's past ties to the Democrats may well have influenced the decision to replace him. Andrés was abruptly out of office, had no military command to bring prestige or even an income, and could not secure an appointment within the Republican Party. He now had to rely entirely on his cattle business for financial support. With deepening money problems, high-interest debts, and the uncertain livestock market, the Picos had to maneuver as well as possible to avoid bankruptcy. Although Andrés remained active in local politics, he now had to get back into the business world that Pío had tried to maintain throughout the 1850s.

Unlike the relationship he had with his older brother, José Antonio, Pío had a strong bond of friendship and love with Andrés. At times it seemed that the happiness of his younger brother consumed Pío's thoughts. In 1859, although Pico was beginning to feel the burden of the broken cattle market, he allowed Andrés to choose the best and most beautiful of a group of prized black stallions as "the ultimate proof of love."[43] Even so, Andrés spent money frivolously and was pressed to cover the debts of the family business. Although the brothers held opposing political views until 1860, their bond was never threatened.

Nevertheless, by 1863 Pío came to the realization that Andrés was squandering money shamelessly. Because their business interests were heavily intertwined, Pío was forced to examine his brother's spending. Pío's usual habit was to send his livestock to Rancho San Fernando, where Andrés lived, and from there have it sold. In 1863 alone, Pío sent fifteen hundred head to San Fernando and continued this throughout the 1860s.[44] However, Andrés's behavior had begun to make him cautious. Andrés would sell the cattle at will, often without consulting Pío. He borrowed money indiscriminately and was rarely able to repay it. While these actions did not anger Pío, he finally realized that he should keep an expense account before Andrés broke him financially. Family friend Agustín Olvera made up an account in 1862, which listed Andrés nearly $60,000 in Pío's debt.[45] The debt only grew as Andrés's financial situation further deteriorated. In consideration of what he owed, on May 30 Andrés transferred his cattle brand to Pío, who thereby gained ownership of all the cattle associated with it. The brand, in the shape of a heart, is usually associated with Pío, although the history of how Pío came to have it is little known. Andrés also transferred his interest in the ranchos San Fernando and Encino to Pío as well as some property in the town of San Fernando.[46]

Even as his financial troubles mounted, Andrés could not stop his reckless gambling. In one of many examples, Pío had an enormous sum of money deposited in a San Francisco bank. The money came from Pío's sale of his interest in the immense ex-mission Rancho San Fernando. According to Albert Johnson, Pío's personal aide during these years, Pico had $125,000 on deposit at the bank.[47] Shortly before one of Andrés's disastrous gambling sprees, Pío sold one-half of Rancho San Fernando to Isaak Lankershim for $115,000. The other half of the ranch he kept until he returned it to Andrés in 1874, to help his younger brother financially.[48] "I asked him what he wanted me to give him," Pío recalled. "He said, 'Give me the San Fernando and the Encino, that will be enough;' I said, 'Then go and get the title made.' The same forenoon late he came again with Mr. Norton to my office and brought the deed to me."[49] In 1869, according to Albert Johnson, Andrés made a large withdrawal from Pío's account in San Francisco. Without doubt he took the money to play monte and in the process lost an astounding $60,000.[50] Although Pío had to rush to San Francisco to raise more money for his brother's sake, he seems to have survived the crisis.

Pío experienced a rejuvenation of sorts after the sale of the San Fernando property. He was still heavily burdened with legal battles over his other properties but was now in the position to rekindle his economic prosperity. From 1869 to 1875 he had a chance to settle his financial problems once and for all. The next logical step, in his mind, was to reinvest in real estate. His main goals were to erase the embarrassment of his increasing financial debacle and to build in Los Angeles. Despite its current run-down condition, he believed the plaza area was exactly the right place to do it.

By the late 1860s the plaza had declined into one of the most violent and unsafe places in Los Angeles. Pico and other investors were eager to shed the plaza of this reputation. The idea was that bringing in new businesses would help attract a more reliable and friendly clientele. Pico, city officials, and other businessmen began to invest in the area. Pico, however, had personal motives behind his involvement. He wanted to see a rebirth of the area the Californios had founded. At this point, in many minds, the deteriorated plaza symbolized the debased aspect of Mexican culture. One street, *calle de los negros*, was translated as "Nigger Alley," and for Yankee residents it represented all that was undesirable about nonwhite culture.[51] Los Angeles had begun to spread in many directions, and Pico himself was quickly becoming a relic of the state's Mexican past. But he would not give up on the idea that Los Angeles could become the financial center of California, with the plaza as a reflection of Californio culture.

Pico clearly seems to have thrived on high-risk business deals; the 1870s were a period when the Californios were completely eclipsed by the massive influx of Anglos arriving from all over the country, and there were no guarantees that Pico's new project would succeed. However, despite his advancing age, he continued to pressure his lawyers and associates to invest in a highly competitive market.

He wasted no time in putting his own new finances to use. After a vacation to New York, taking the new transcontinental railroad across the country and back, Pico began to work.[52] He and Andrés concocted a plan to build a luxury hotel in the plaza area. Andrés was perhaps the one who negotiated with contractors to construct the building. In 1869 Pico purchased the Carrillo home on the plaza as a suitable site for his new hotel.[53]

The Carrillo house was destroyed to make way for the hotel. Pico's townhouse, which was adjacent to Carrillo's home, would remain his local residence. The hotel was built in an Italianate style, and Pico certainly spared no expense in furnishing it. Elegant furniture and paintings from different parts of the world adorned the rooms and halls, along with birdcages, flowers, and gaslit lanterns. He hired the Spaniard Antonio Cuyas to run the hotel for him; he also hired well-known French chef Charlie Laugier to serve exquisite meals to the guests. The hotel was convenient for the local business community, which also had access to a Wells Fargo and Company

The Pico House, in Los Angeles, became an important center of commerce during the 1870s. Courtesy of El Pueblo de Los Angeles Historical Monument.

express office, another restaurant, a bar, a billiard room, and a barber shop.[54]

The Pico House, as it would eventually be called, was the pride and joy of the Pico family. For a time no other hotel in California matched it in elegance and quality. The three-story building was also the first of its kind in Los Angeles.

Pico was heavily concentrating his efforts on plaza-area real estate during these years. To his properties he added a building that eventually became the Farmers and Merchants Bank of Los Angeles.[55] In May 1874 he entered into an agreement with William Perry and James Riley, who were going to erect a three-story building partly on Pico's lot for an early supermarket that would sell confectionaries, tobacco, food, fruit, and other assorted goods.[56] The business was eventually known as the Blue Wing. In the same year, Pico purchased a

nearby home from the widow of Francisco Ocampo. It is not
known what he used this property for, but years later he was
in jeopardy of losing it to the Los Angeles businessman
Bernard Cohn.[57]

It was unfortunate that, having overextended himself in real
estate, Pico's assets were soon tied up in the hands of brokers,
lawyers, and moneylenders. The legal battles that followed
would come to dominate his life. He took out numerous mortgages on his properties to satisfy his obligations, but the Pico
House quickly became encumbered. The hotel was an enormous business venture that he may not have been ready for.
Even before it opened, Pico's assistant, Albert Johnson, wrote
to his family, saying "Andrés made a contract for a new hotel
that will cost $80,000 and cannot rent for more than $5,000
a year."[58] Pío was concerned about maintaining the prestige
of the Pico House at this point and most likely believed the
investment would pay off once property values rose. To his
dismay, property values did increase to an all-time high not
even a decade later, just as the Pico House was in danger of
foreclosure. Pico would have been in a prime situation to
profit from his aggressive real estate investments, but instead
of selling the properties to pay off his debts and live the rest
of his life in comfort, if not luxury, he decided to press on
and fight for the full value.

Early in the next decade Pico's fortune seemed to be
collapsing before his eyes. Not only did he have three cases
before the California Supreme Court, in 1873 the *Forster v.
Pico* case began in San Diego. In this battle he lost his prize
possession, the 133,000-acre Rancho Santa Margarita. *Forster v.
Pico* is by far the most famous of Pico's legal battles.[59] In the
case of Santa Margarita, Pico lost the ranch to his brother-in-
law and confidant, John Forster, whom he had had reason to
trust. Upon marrying Pico's sister, Forster had received Pico's
blessing and entered a coveted family network that made

him wealthy beyond his dreams. Nevertheless, as historians agree, Forster acquired the land through fraud.

The land Pico had granted to Forster, including the Potreros de San Juan Capistrano, had over several years developed into a healthy and steadily growing business. At the same time, Pico's own businesses were declining, and so back in 1855 he had used Rancho Santa Margarita as collateral on a $25,000 loan from the firm Pioche and Bayerque. The move was not considered risky in 1855; the cattle market had slowed but had not entirely collapsed, and Pico could have easily paid the debt had the cattle market continued to produce its earlier enormous profits. But by the early 1860s he was unable to pay back the loan, and facing a period of tremendous drought and slowing sales, he was in jeopardy of losing the ranch. For years Pico had attempted to sell a partial interest in the ranch to Forster, and finally, in 1864, Forster accepted. Pico paid off Pioche and Bayerque, and Forster took one-half of the Rancho Santa Margarita, or so Pico thought.

After Pico signed the deed—which was written in English— over to Forster, he soon learned that he had signed away his entire ranch. Forster could not offer a rational explanation for why Pico would sell the enormous rancho to repay the small debt to Pioche and Bayerque. In fact, Pico proved he had been offered $75,000 for the ranch shortly before the transaction. Pico argued that he had intended to sell only half of the ranch; Forster maintained that Pico had sold him the entire property.[60]

There is little doubt that Pico trusted his brother-in-law Forster, and that his trusting nature would continue to hurt him financially and legally. In the end, charlatans were to blame for swindling the old Californio. And while Pico was careless enough to sign the Santa Margarita deed without having one of his many attorneys look at it, he was not entirely to blame for this mess. There was overwhelming evidence to support Pico's position, including the fact that he continued ranch operations with Forster's knowledge. His own lawyers, oddly, failed to recognize this and other readily available proof they could have used to win Pico's cause.[61] Forster cajoled and told half-truths, and in court he eventually won title to the entire ranch.

The loss of Rancho Santa Margarita was a disaster for Pico. But there were others too. Pico also nearly lost the Ranchito. The case *Pico v. Coleman* revealed that Pico had given some land to his mistress, María Martínez. According to Pico, on May 5, 1855, his fifty-fourth birthday and not long after the death of his wife María (Alvarado), he gave Martínez roughly four acres of land.[62] Coleman, the subsequent buyer of that land, however, argued that the entire ranch had been given to Martínez and that he had purchased it from her. Pico argued that for fifteen years Martínez had occupied only those few acres without claim to the entire rancho. She, in fact, had this land enclosed within the Ranchito in 1865, and in 1868 she had only this land surveyed. In 1870, she sold the land (as specified in the deed) to James Coleman and Carlos Olvera, who made up a contract and, according to Pico, changed the wording so it specified the whole ranch. The sale was for $2,000. After the sale was executed, when Coleman and Olvera tried to claim the whole rancho, Pico brought suit against them.[63]

Two trials followed. During the first, Pico's lawyers introduced much evidence that seemed to support his side of the story. María Martínez had never made any claim to any other part of the Ranchito. Moreover, Pico had made improvements to the rest of the land, including the cultivation of 1,600 acres. By this time, too, tenants occupied 800 acres, paying Pico continuous rent. Despite the overwhelming proof that Coleman and Olvera were perpetrating fraud, in December 1872 the court in Los Angeles ruled that the contract from Pico to Martínez specified the entire Ranchito. But because

Pico had made improvements to and had conducted business on the land, 1,800 acres were awarded to him.[64]

The Los Angeles court seems to have been working against Pico during this trial. Coleman's lawyers had little evidence to show why Pico would sell Martínez the entire Ranchito, valued between $50,000 and $80,000 in 1855, for one dollar. The only argument that made any possible sense was that Martínez was Pico's mistress and that he had given the entire rancho to her as a sign of his love. But there was no plausible reason she would sell the ranch for $2,000, unless she meant to be selling only the few acres Pico had given her. The original contract was put before a group of experts of the Spanish language. Coleman and Olvera argued semantics, saying that in Pico's contract was indisputable proof that he meant to give her the entire ranch.[65]

Aside from the possibility of losing the Ranchito, publicity from the court case meant Pico also disgraced the memory of his late wife. For Coleman, apparently, the fact of Pico's illicit affair helped explain the strange set of circumstances surrounding the deed. During the petition for a rehearing, Coleman stated that he "knew of the intimate relations that had long subsisted between Maria Martinez and Pio Pico, and I supposed that, on account of those relations, while he never disputed the account of his conveyance, he believed that he could induce her to return the property to him for some comparatively trifling consideration."[66] Coleman hoped to paint Pico as womanizer who made rash decisions based on lust.

It seems to have been common knowledge that aside from this affair, Pico also had illegitimate children while still married to his wife, although he only recognized them after her death. Pico had had a relationship with Ascención Ávila that produced a child, Griselda, in 1838, only a few years after his marriage to María Alvarado. Not long after, Ascención gave birth to another baby girl, Joaquina. More recently, in 1871, just two years before the Ranchito appeal, Pico's other mistress, Felicita

Romero, gave birth to Alfredo Pico, whose older brother Ranulfo was also Pico's child.[67] Although Coleman's lawyers did not mention this information, by the time of the case, Pico had four children with two different women who were not his wives. The record is unclear about whether he had any children with María Martínez. But characterizing Pico as an immoral and irrational man strengthened Coleman's cause, and public knowledge of the affair must have caused Pico great shame.

Although Pico had a great amount of evidence to support his side of the case, Martínez's involvement in the lawsuit against him may point to a bitter end to their affair. The lawyers for Coleman, Olvera, and Martínez were certain they would win the case once Martínez testified. She seems to have been emotionally affected by having to testify, and to their great surprise, she testified as a witness in favor of Pico. But after twice denying that Pico had conveyed to her the entire Ranchito, the third time she testified in favor of Coleman—most likely against her will. Lawyers for Coleman and Olvera must have somehow persuaded her behind closed doors. Carlos Olvera, speaking about why he believed the deed conveyed the whole rancho, said, "The comparatively small price, which Maria Martinez exacted from us, I attributed to her intimate relations with Pio Pico. She is an ignorant woman, and was then, as she has appeared since, completely under his control."[68] Despite this testimony, Olvera's lawyers were not able to locate Jesús Gyrado, who had created the original deed and had supposedly claimed that the contract conveyed all of the property to Martínez. Even so, the Los Angeles District Court found in favor of Olvera and Coleman, concluding that Pico had conveyed the entire rancho to her. But fortunately for Pico, his appeal to the supreme court was successful. By 1873 he was able to prove his case without much trouble, and the bulk of the Ranchito was judged to be rightfully his.[69]

Despite the harm to Pico's reputation, he did not allow Coleman's attempt to obtain his property to distract him. Free of the trial, he immediately set out to increase the revenue from his hotel. He was meanwhile still troubled by the claim his brother-in-law John Forster made on the Rancho Santa Margarita. That lawsuit began in January 1873, while his appeal on the Coleman case was in process. Pico's financial obligations were mounting again, and it seemed likely he would have to mortgage the Pico House.

After he lost his appeal in the California Supreme Court over the Forster suit, Pico took out a mortgage for more than $30,000 on the Pico House and his bank building from the San Francisco-based Savings and Loan Society.[70] While he was determined to save his empire from crumbling, he was continuously besieged by legal difficulties, including a suit for the water rights of the Ranchito.[71] He also sued Antonio Cuyas, his former manager at the Pico House, for more than $41,000. It seems that their partnership had failed but that Pico had invested thousands in Cuyas's furniture and office space.[72] The Cuyas suit, particularly, signifies Pico's increasing reliance on the courts to solve issues and to scramble for needed revenue.

The loss of Rancho Santa Margarita and the near loss of the Ranchito was a wake-up call to the aging former governor. Pico displayed intense resolve in 1874 by purchasing two lots in Los Angeles for $2,500 total and also suing the Los Angeles Gas Company for disturbing his business.[73] The city gas company was located near the plaza, and according to Pico, the production and burning of chemicals created "noxious, offensive, unwholesome and discoloring gases, odors and smoke" that were disturbing the tenants and businessmen as well as the good name of the Pico House Hotel. He wanted the nuisance to end. He sued for $2,000 in damage.[74] Unfortunately, he was defeated in court and ordered to pay the defendant's legal fees. Pico's decision to take on such an entity was a bold move by a man who had recently lost an enormous portion of his empire, but ultimately the overriding factor in the case was that the Los Angeles Gas Company was affiliated with the city.

The 1870s were certainly a difficult period for Pico and his family. The loss of the Rancho Santa Margarita and other deepening financial problems began to take a toll on him. To make matters worse, the death of Andrés at age sixty-six, in February 1876, had a deep emotional effect on Pío. He and Andrés had been inseparable, and the circumstances of his death were tragic. Andrés fell into a coma for several weeks before his death.[75] He had, by some family members' accounts, been brutally beaten and dumped on his front porch in Los Angeles. As the story goes, Pío spent a small fortune attempting to find the culprit.[76] Ultimately, though, no one was ever convicted of the crime, and it is uncertain what motive existed for his murder.

The following year, perhaps recognizing his own mortality and the fragmentation of a family that had once enjoyed solid ties, he decided to record his life history.[77] As he did so, however, there arose another crisis over his assets.

The family cohesion that had held the old generation together was self-destructing in a public arena for all to see. This time, sadly, Andrés's death was the cause. Shortly after his tragic end, it was discovered that Andrés had left no will. Either it had never been written or it had been misplaced. This simple confusion created the initial controversy. As the last surviving brother, Pío expected—and wanted—to administer the estate, because for him his brother's assets represented a small sign of economic relief he could distribute throughout the family. He hoped to gain exclusive rights to do this.

In February 1876, Rómulo Pico, whom Andrés had raised, petitioned the probate court of Los Angeles County to allow him to act as the administrator of the estate. According to

Rómulo, his father's property was worth $21,600, and included 900 acres at the former Mission San Fernando, one-quarter of Rancho Encino, 100 head of cattle, 100 horses, and one block of real estate in the town of San Fernando.

Pío issued his own petition for administrative duties to the same court on the same day. If he were to be named administrator of the estate, Pío, not Rómulo, would determine the rightful heirs. Pío believed those heirs were the children of his deceased older brother José Antonio Pico and the children of his four sisters, Concepción, Estefana, Tomasa, and Feliciana. Rómulo, he would maintain in court, had no right to any part of the estate. Without a will, as sole surviving next of kin, legally Pío should have had uncontested rights to administer his brother's estate; but having been challenged, he now had to convince the court that Rómulo was no relation to Pío's brother Andrés. The suit, therefore, was about to expose surprising and damaging secrets about the private lives of this once very wealthy and enviable extended Californio family.

In *Pico v. Pico,* Pío brought the suit against Rómulo.[78] The trial was set for early March 1876. When the two appeared in court to present their arguments, each man was determined to protect his interests, no matter the damage. Rómulo claimed that Andrés Pico was his legal father and that he had been granted the right to administer the estate. Pío contended that Rómulo was neither his brother's illegitimate son nor his adopted son. He argued that Rómulo was instead the son of Vicente Moraga and María Antonia Domínguez. His lawyers were able to produce an affidavit from Vicente's son José Moraga, who testified that "Romulo is the fourth born of my brothers." Pío also produced letters from Rómulo to José Moraga in which he addressed José as "dear brother" and signed his name "Rómulo Moraga."

José Moraga also testified, saying that he was in constant contact with his brothers, especially Rómulo, until April 5, 1876.

That was the day—as the trial continued—that Rómulo dropped a bombshell: he exposed his mother's illicit affair with Andrés Pico. The next day José Moraga wrote Rómulo a scathing letter, vowing he would never speak to him again. José accused Rómulo of having been "carried away by vile interest . . . shaming the whole of us and scandalizing [the entire] city."[79] Rómulo replied bitterly, "[I have never] associated with you as a brother—nor do I care one damn [*carajo*], nor did I ever care, to know if you live or die."[80] Pío's defense lawyers used this letter as evidence that Rómulo was willing to throw away a lifetime relationship with his own birth brother for the sake of winning a legal decision.

Rómulo promoted his cause just as aggressively as Pico did his own. He implied that Pío had purposely destroyed the will because it did not list him as executor. Rómulo testified that his father, Andrés, had named him administrator before he had died. Finally, Rómulo forced his mother to take the stand. Under great distress and humiliation, Antonia Domínguez de Moraga testified that she had in fact had an adulterous affair with Andrés Pico, and that through the course of their relationship, Rómulo was born. Pío appealed the court's decision to make Rómulo executor.

For the relatively insignificant value of Andrés's estate, Pío and Rómulo were willing to expose their loved ones to public scrutiny and gossip. It is uncertain what Pío would have gained personally after he distributed the property to his family members. Certainly he wanted to provide for them in time of need. But this case may also reveal strategies Pío's lawyers had begun using to take advantage of the aging ranchero. The defense team exerted a tremendous amount of energy on the case; naturally, the legal fees were excessive. Hoping to further solidify his position, and perhaps at their urging, Pío hired two additional lawyers, Howard and Hazard, to assist his existing team of Glassell, Smith, and Smith. He also hired the professional Spanish translator and interpreter

W. W. Durham. Thus at the age of seventy-five, Pico retained five lawyers and an interpreter to argue a single case.

After all the maneuvering and appeals to the California Supreme Court, Pío and Rómulo lost everything that was left; the property went to lawyer Andrew Glassell through a court order to satisfy his outstanding legal fees.[81] The bad blood between Pío and Rómulo not only disturbed family unity, but resulted in the loss of property that could have benefited the family as a whole. Instead, both men were left with little more than continued financial difficulties and bitter feelings.

To Pico and his lawyers, every case seemed to be driven by a sense of urgency during these years, and time after time, small issues were appealed all the way to the state supreme court. *Pico v. Pico* is a prime example of these dynamics. An elderly Pico's reckless business habits allowed his lawyers to take advantage of his increasingly litigious character. Yet Pico was not simply an innocent victim trying to defend himself against an unscrupulous foe. He sued with the intent of protecting his fortune and to increase it. A perfect example is when he sued Wolf Kalisher and Henry Wartenburg for $5,000.[82] The strange nature of this case was that Pico purchased the right to sue from the victims.

The case came to trial as Pico was facing yet another round of severe legal attacks against his property. Pico needed cash quickly, and any sign of potential relief was part of his greater plan to fix his finances. It was alleged that in 1877 Kalisher and Wartenburg had forcefully taken 2,350 sheep from two poor shepherds. Unable to cover the costs of litigation, the shepherds sought help from Pico, who was still known as an influential man among the Mexican population. He purchased the stolen sheep, and the shepherds granted him the rights to any claims against Kalisher and Wartenburg. Without ever having been harmed by the defendants, Pico took them through a lengthy and costly appeals process. The trial ended in September 1878 with a decision against Pico in the Los Angeles

District Court, demanding he pay $20.50 for the defendant's legal fees. Pico, not surprisingly, appealed to the California Supreme Court, and the decision was reversed in his favor. Although Pico still had other financial resources he could rely on, the funds from such a case helped his economic situation.

By the mid-1870s Pico had rented much of the Ranchito to tenants, hoping to recover lost revenue. The Pico House, as Pío's assistant Albert Johnson had presumed, was not a profitable investment. By 1880, Pico was pressed to pay back the mortgage he had taken out on it. Remarkably, Pico's disposition during this period was positive. Despite all of the loss and sorrows he had experienced, he continued to fight off attacks on his business and character. Perhaps his legal battles revealed signs of a man in an increasingly desperate financial situation. Yet Pico used the courts effectively, despite the fact that he had enemies within the legal establishment itself.

There was more to Pico's financial difficulties than simple racism that may have influenced some rulings against him. He was also often an agent of his own demise. By 1880 he was struggling with many creditors, including, as noted, the Savings and Loan Society of San Francisco. Ultimately, as this decade came to a close, it would determine whether or not Pico would survive as a wealthy landowner. During the mid-1870s Pico's fortunes had shifted, and seemingly his luck had begun to run out; Los Angeles was changing drastically, and Anglos were finally outnumbering the Californios. In the 1880s, however, he faced what would be his most difficult opposition. The city had grown in epic proportions, and Pío Pico was no longer a regional patrón.

CHAPTER 8

"An Occasional Miscarriage of Justice"

Reassessing Pío Pico's Financial Decline

Pico was ninety years old when he lost the remainder of his property in one of California's most unjust legal cases, *Pico v. Cohn.* Had he been able to maneuver his business approach slightly, and had he not been the victim of fraud, Pico would have died with an enormous fortune. Indeed, the *Los Angeles Times* wrote, with a bit of exaggeration, that if Pico "had saved the land that was his when the state was formed he would now be the richest man of California—richer than Stanford and Hearst combined."[1] It is important to understand that Pico did not ultimately fail because of pressure from a racist society. Some Californians, as earlier chapters have noted, perhaps viewed Pico as racially inferior, yet he proved through successful business enterprises and litigation that he could compete in an aggressive economic atmosphere.

Pico's ability to deal with prejudice toward Mexicans indicates that his ruin was more a combination of cunning individuals who wanted to destroy him and his own reckless business practices. His most costly case, *Pico v. Cohn,* was more dramatic than any other he had faced. The case also suggests the extent of fraud that some individuals would commit in order to divest the old ranchero of his estate.

Pico's lawsuit against Bernard Cohn was not only his most costly, it was also his longest and his last. The press described Pico as "prepared to fight it out if it takes the remainder of his life."[2] His troubles began with a mortgage he took from the San Francisco-based Savings and Loan Society in 1874. By 1883 Pico was unable to repay the loan and faced the loss of his remaining property. He had intended to maintain his property until he could secure a profit, but with rising property taxes in southern California, he needed new loans in order to pay his creditors. Pico had known Bernard Cohn for over ten years. Cohn was a local businessman whom Pico trusted. Unfortunately, Pico once again erratically negotiated the contract, which again turned out to be a bill of sale rather than a loan. How can one reconcile Pico's careless behavior? He was one of the most successful businessmen in early California history, yet one who too easily trusted those who befriended him. Pico alleged that the sale had been procured through fraud and that, in fact, the entire case was a sham skillfully created to take what rightfully belonged to him.

By 1880, although the cattle market had declined and Pico's wealth was not what it once was, he still had a net worth of more than $275,000.[3] This amount, however, was Pico's worth on paper. With his assets tied up in myriad legal suits, he was low on cash. Yet despite the fact that his property was in danger of foreclosure and tied up in lawsuits, he was not without options. The sale of his properties would have paid his debts, which totaled approximately $100,000; the remaining $175,000 was still an enormous sum that would have provided for his family. Pico, however, was not ready to "retire." Even at his advanced age—he was then seventy-nine—he continued to thrive on competition. As the Californios were losing political power in Los Angeles, it became crucial for Pico to maintain what he could of his dignity, heritage, and wealth. The sale of his assets was not a realistic option for a man who had risen to the top of society by sheer guile.

After the loss of the enormous Rancho Santa Margarita y Las Flores and the sale of Mission San Fernando, Pico could no longer call himself a rancher. He had also sold more than 50 percent of the Ranchito by 1883. Nevertheless, he was determined to put his finances in order. Unfortunately for his economic future, Pico quickly learned that he was far better at ranching than at managing property. Just four years after the opening of the Pico House, he had been forced to take out mortgages on his properties. Soon he was also desperately searching for funds to satisfy the mortgage on the Ranchito, a debt that had increased with interest since February 1874 to more than $45,000 and was due for repayment.[4] These and his other crises explain his maneuvering for money and his use of legal proceedings as a way to rescue a crumbling empire that verged on disaster. In 1880 alone, he was tied up in four major lawsuits, three in the California Supreme Court.[5]

His public image, ironically, was somewhat positive. The *Los Angeles Times*, perhaps because of its pro-Republican leanings, always depicted Pico as a respected old gentleman who was a friend of many white residents. In 1882 a story appeared that looked back fondly at California's transition to U.S. control. It quoted Pico's 1846 speech to the California Assembly in which he reported on the arrival of Yankee adventurers: "Already have the wagons of that perfidious people scaled the almost inaccessible summits of the Sierra Nevada, crossed the entire continent and penetrated the fruitful valley of the Sacramento. What that astonishing people will next undertake, I cannot say; but in whatever enterprise they embark, they will be successful." The writer went on to call Pico a venerable friend to the "Yankee immigrants."[6] The *Los Angeles Times* portrayed him as no longer a threat to California's changed economic power structure, and even as something of a cherished relic of California's glorious history. The story helped bolster Pico's image during his bitter legal battles. Two years later, the same paper called him an "Ancient Patriarch" and still a lively member of society, "a staunch Republican in politics." Pico, it said, had "an eye undimmed and strength unabated as when the strange Gringo invaded his domains, and wrestled from him his dominion nearly four decades ago."[7] Even if the press portrayed Pico as a noteworthy and capable citizen, his detractors were undeterred.

When Pico could not repay the loan on the Ranchito property, the Savings and Loan Society sued him for the right to claim their debt or to foreclose on the property.[8] Finally, the Superior Court of San Francisco ordered the sale of the Ranchito at public auction. Since the early 1850s the Ranchito had been his home. Although he could not bear the thought of "outsiders" claiming the land he had worked so hard for, the Ranchito was auctioned off at the door of the Los Angeles Court House on October 10, 1882. A Los Angeles man, A. R. Loomis, paid $39,755 for the property. A shrewd businessman, Loomis gave Pico the option to reclaim the property for $45,288.44 in U.S. gold coin by April 10 the next year. Pico was also required to pay some $14,900 in liens against the property from other, separate lawsuits. Altogether he owed about $61,000 on the Ranchito.[9] To make matters worse, the Savings and Loan Society continued to haunt him over disputed mortgages on the Pico House and the Los Angeles bank building, claiming outright ownership since 1880. They also charged that Pico refused to leave the property and asked for $5,000 in damages due to lost revenue.

As the Pico House case unfolded, it came to light that Pico was the victim of a plot to divest him of that property. Although he had in the past claimed fraud—in the case against his brother-in-law Forster—and lost, he once again had overwhelming evidence on his side. For one, the Savings and Loan Society claimed that Pico had foreclosed on a mortgage (the hotel), but he could in fact prove he had paid it. In court, Pico produced a receipt proving payment in full, along with two

View of the Pico House and the Los Angeles Plaza, ca. 1880. Courtesy of El Pueblo de Los Angeles Historical Monument.

witnesses who testified that the Savings and Loan Society had agreed to return Pico's titles to the Pico House and the Los Angeles bank building. One of the witnesses was a notary public from San Francisco who had been present at the transaction.[10] But unfortunately, during his business transaction with the Savings and Loan Society, Pico had unwittingly signed a document that put him $27,000 in debt to the Savings and Loan Society, money they claimed Pico owed outright. Pico's legal team found it impossible to contest the document. Although he had satisfied his debt, the document he signed put him and his property back in the same financial position as before.

During the Savings and Loan trial, and later in the trial with Bernard Cohn, Pico's attorneys argued that he was ignorant of the law and that he was unable to speak the English language.[11] This was a simple defensive strategy to account for the fact that Pico had mistakenly signed deeds of sale when he believed he was signing loan papers. In fact, the Code of Civil Procedure for the State of California protected against fraud and could have effectively barred Pico's damaging mistakes. According to the law, all signatures had to be obtained in good faith; his lawyers only had to prove that Pico did not willingly sign away his fortune. But these tactics did not help Pico because his signature suggested he had knowledge of the transaction.

The case with Bernard Cohn had its roots in the Savings and Loan Society debacle. In searching for money to reclaim the Ranchito from Loomis, Pico had various loan options open to him. Bernard Cohn agreed to loan him $62,000 at 10 percent interest using Ranchito as collateral. Pico agreed to accept if he could not find a better rate. Another option came from his nephews Marcus and Juan Forster, with whom Pico had reestablished relations after the death of their father in 1882.[12] The Forsters had inherited an enormous amount of property from their father, including Rancho Santa Margarita, and had sufficient money to cover Pico's debts. The brothers agreed to lend the money to Pico at 6 percent annual interest. The terms were only that Pico had to use his property as security, with the option to redeem after the debt was paid. It wasn't difficult for Pico to accept his nephew's offer, which was a safe, low-interest loan.

During the legal dispute between them, Pico received an auspicious offer from the Savings and Loan Society. The firm made an agreement with Pico's attorneys and offered to settle his debts with the option to redeem his property under the condition that Pico end his litigation against them.[13] A representative from the Savings and Loan Society met with Pico's attorney George Smith and was prepared to offer Pico a new loan for $62,000 if he dropped the lawsuit. The Savings and Loan Society would also allow Pico to reclaim the bank and Pico House for $45,000 paid back in two months without interest. To everyone's great surprise, Pico declined the offer, stating that he had made a more advantageous arrangement. Though worried that his nephews might not come through for him, must have been unwilling to deal further with the savings and loan people because of their heated suit.

As April 10, 1883, approached, the date A. R. Loomis had set as the deadline to redeem Ranchito, Pico was worried that he would lose his home forever. Pico was yet undecided on the loan. A few days before the deadline, Pico still hadn't heard from Marcus and Juan Forster. Panicked, he went to Bernard Cohn's office to inquire if the loan offer was still available. Cohn had been hoping Pico would borrow the money, and he eagerly began to negotiate the terms. Cohn agreed to lend Pico $62,837 and pay any other debts Pico was liable for. The only stipulations were that Pico must use Ranchito as security and repay Cohn $65,000 before July 1. At that point, Pico believed, Cohn would return his property to him. Instead, Cohn would contest Pico's account of the transaction.

One month after Cohn issued the loan, Pico was ready to repay $65,000 to fulfill the agreement. Cohn refused to accept it and refused to relinquish the titles. As part of the deal, Cohn had paid the Savings and Loan Society $41,000 to redeem the Pico House and the Los Angeles bank building, and upon doing so he received both titles of ownership. Pico wanted to avoid the risk of another long, difficult, and costly legal battle with Cohn, so he wrote to him at the end of May 1883, agreeing to pay $106,000 plus interest to reconvey his titles. "I hereby offer to pay you the sum agreed upon . . . and I demand of you a deed of conveyance of the said properties," his letter said.[14] Cohn replied that he wanted "the sum of one hundred and eighty-five thousand dollars" for the property and only then would he relinquish the titles.[15] Unbelievably, in haste to make the Loomis deadline, Pico again signed away his property without studying Cohn's contract, which, once again, was a deed of sale. Although he agreed to it, Pico was shocked at Cohn's counteroffer and even more bewildered when he learned that Cohn was claiming outright ownership of Ranchito. Pico's attorneys probably understood that their client was again taken by fraud, but a signed deed was difficult to refute.

In the mid-1880s, then, *Pico v. Cohn* became one of southern California's most dramatic legal events. Cohn retained a lawyer named Anson Brunson, who had considerable experience with Pico's legal history. Brunson was a prominent Los Angeles attorney with high political aspirations. Although he had participated in various Republican Party committees with Pico, the two waged a dramatic battle in the California courtrooms that went on for more than a decade.[16]

It is clear that Brunson knew a great deal about Pico. Over the years, many clients went to Brunson to fight Pico in court.[17] Pico was prepared for a battle, however, with his own legal resources. He called his longtime friend Francisco "Pancho" Johnson as one of his main witnesses. Johnson had been his interpreter for many years, including serving as agent and translator during the negotiations with Cohn. Although this led to a falling out, Johnson and Pico had known each other since at least 1835, and Pico never expected Johnson to testify as he did. When Johnson took the stand on behalf of Pico, he said, "I didn't recommend Pío to go to Mr. Cohn at all; I told him Mr. Cohn will give him money enough to get out of his troubles, under that deed of conveyance . . . there was nothing said in the conversation on the morning of the 6th about Mr. Pico having the right to redeem [his titles]."[18]

Pico was shocked at his friend's statement. Pico's lawyers had interviewed Johnson thoroughly before the trial and determined that he was a fit witness.[19] The most likely cause for Johnson's change of heart was the deteriorating relationship between him and Pico over Johnson's help negotiating the transaction with Cohn. Although a friend of Pico, Johnson argued that he did not work for free and expected a payment of four thousand dollars, which he said was the fee for helping negotiate the transaction with Cohn. When Pico did not pay, in November 1883, Johnson filed a lawsuit, *Johnson v. Pico*, over the money.[20]

The use of Johnson as a witness after relations had deteriorated with Pico can be seen as grave negligence on the part of Pico's lawyers, or perhaps something worse. The question remains: Could Pico's legal team have made such an obvious miscalculation, or were they hoping to prolong the trial in order to exact more legal fees from the aging Californio? In fact, Pico's lawyers knew firsthand that Johnson said he would *not* testify for Pico unless he were paid for his help. Pico's lawyers attempted to use this evidence against Johnson and in the process were able to prove he had perjured himself. Johnson denied their allegation that he was trying to spite Pico. His excuse for his testimony was that he simply would not provide further services to Pico because of their disagreement over the fee he was owed.[21] Johnson's testimony was shaky at best, but the most damaging evidence against him was a receipt from Cohn for $250 made out to him just prior to the testimony.[22] Apparently, Cohn had paid him to testify adversely.

In the trial, Cohn hoped to keep his defense simple and uncomplicated. He stated that he had always intended to purchase the hotel and bank properties from Pico. Because of Pico's reputation, Cohn said, "I positively refused to make a loan to him, because making a loan to him means a law suit."[23] He attempted to counter many of Pico's strongest arguments. Cohn stated that Pico had never informed him of the other, more beneficial offers he had been given. Nevertheless, the Cohn defense could never provide a convincing reason for Pico agreeing to sell the property to Cohn for far less than its market value. Cohn claimed that from the beginning Pico was well aware that this was a sale and said that he (Cohn) had been collecting the rents from the Pico House and Los Angeles bank building since the purchase, without Pico's objection. As for the Ranchito, Cohn said Pico occupied the house there as a rental agreement. Apparently Cohn had given all the tenants on Ranchito notice of sale and collected rent from some of them. He had received $60 from Chico Garcia, who rented ten acres at six dollars per acre a month. Aside from what he earned from rent, Cohn had also hired men to care for the ranch and had spent $8,000 on improvements. Cohn said that the property was worth 25 percent more now than it had been when he purchased it. According to Cohn, Pico had never objected to the sale or the liens he paid for him. It was obvious that Cohn's case had many holes in it. Despite his testimony, and that of others who gave damaging statements about Pico's character and lack of honesty, the court ruled against Cohn.[24]

The court found that Pico was the owner of the Pico House and Los Angeles bank building at the time of the deed, but that he did have to meet the demands of the Savings and Loan Society of San Francisco. It also found that Cohn had created the deed as a mortgage and not an actual sale. Therefore, Judge Volney E. Howard on January 23, 1884, ruled in Pico's favor, setting the amount that he owed Cohn at $103,000. Pico was given sixty days to pay, after which he could redeem his properties. Cohn was also ordered to pay Pico any rent received on properties as of December 4, 1883, when the trial began. Furthermore, Pico was to receive the cost of his legal fees from Cohn. The court believed that Cohn had gained the property fraudulently, although he had Pico's signature on the deed.

Pico's argument, that Cohn had refused to issue the loan unless the contract was made without the involvement of lawyers, was what apparently influenced the Los Angeles court.[25] The judge cited a "Doctrine of Equity," whereby the court protects those who are liable because they are "overcome by cunning or artifice or undue influence."[26] He went on to state that inadequacy of price was no excuse to rescind a contract, but when undue influence and intrigue were used to obtain a favorable contract, the court had the right to rescind it. The court also found that F. "Pancho" Johnson, Pico's former friend, although testifying negatively for Pico as his witness, had also committed fraud and had been paid $250 by Cohn for unknown services. "Johnson, in his shuffling reply to questions, says that the $250 was a present from Cohn," the judge stated, "but this is contrary to proof and voucher of Cohn."[27]

A separate incident also suggested that Cohn himself considered Pico the true owner of the property. In April 1883, before the controversy over the loan became public knowledge, Pico had joined Cohn in a suit against Loomis, who had purchased the Ranchito at public auction.[28] Pico and Cohn wanted to reclaim leases worth $5,000 they believed they were entitled to. Pico's lawyers argued that had Cohn not considered Pico the owner of the property, he would have sued Loomis on his own.

Pico felt vindicated. He was more than ready to pay the amount he owed Cohn, and in doing so, he would have had full, unencumbered titles to all of his properties, including the Pico House, the Los Angeles bank building, the Ocampo house, and the Ranchito. Had Pico been able to avoid the force that was mounting against him, he would have retired as the only Californio who had succeeded in avoiding economic disaster. To make this happen, his next step was to take a low-interest loan from his nephews, Marcos and Juan Forster.[29]

Meanwhile, Cohn appealed the decision and was granted a retrial.[30] The court then issued Pico the chance to avoid the new trial on the condition that he pay Cohn $138,000 to return the titles. Pico did not understand why he should pay an additional $35,000, and it remains unknown how or why the court came to this decision. Nevertheless, Pico refused, and worse, he made the mistake of believing that he would find continued justice in court. He appealed to the California Supreme Court on Cohn's right to a new trial, but unfortunately for Pico, when the supreme court met in July 1885, it ruled that the lower court had correctly issued a new trial.

By the time the new trial began in Los Angeles, Pancho Johnson had died. His earlier testimony was all that was left for the plaintiffs to use. Pico's lawyers had believed that they could use the testimony to prove Pancho had been paid to testify against Pico's cause. This proved to be a huge mistake, for the Superior Court of Los Angeles believed Johnson's earlier testimony, which corroborated Cohn's story. The court awarded Cohn full title to the property without giving Pico the option to redeem it.[31] To the great surprise of Pico and his lawyers, he was left with few options but to appeal to the supreme court. Just before the last decision, Pico told the local press that he generally had good relations with the Americanos. "They have always paid for what I have given them, and I wish you to tell the Americans how I feel and how I have been treated so that they will help me and see that justice is done. . . . The matter is in the courts now, and if Americans only understand the truth of it they will not let me be wronged."[32] Pico appealed each decision several more times and was finally defeated in court for the last time in 1891.[33]

Pico quickly found out why his "luck" had changed so drastically. Cohn's lawyer, Anson Brunson, had years of experience dealing with Pico and litigation. He had opposed him in at least seven California Supreme Court cases.[34] He had also represented Pío's sister, Magdalena Pico, during the *Forster v.*

Pío Pico at approximately ninety years of age, as he was beginning the fight, in *Pico vs. Cohn*, to keep his remaining property. Courtesy of the Anaheim Public Library.

Pico case.[35] His court record shows that Brunson was involved in cases that originated in California's three largest cities. He had traveled the whole of California simply to oppose Pico. It is likely that individuals sought him out because he knew Pico's style in court, he knew his legal team, and he may have even harbored ill feelings for Pico. And if his actions are any indication of this, he certainly did.

Pico, in return, had serious issues with Brunson. In fact, another case, *Pico v. Williams,* came about as a result of Brunson's undue influence in Pico's litigation. While serving as Cohn's attorney, Brunson was elected superior court judge of Los Angeles County. The superior court was divided into two departments, one presided over by Brunson and the other by Judge W. A. Cheney. When Cheney took a leave of absence, Judge B. T. Williams replaced him. However, instead of presiding over Cheney's department, Judge Williams was assigned to Brunson's. As a superior court judge, Brunson had become an important figure within an elite group of justices. Before Cheney left, he and Brunson wrote to the California governor, George Stoneman, asking that Williams be allowed to preside over cases in the Los Angeles Superior Court because Cheney would be absent.[36] The governor approved their request. But why Judge Williams then presided within Brunson's, rather than Cheney's, jurisdiction is unknown.

Pico's attorneys claimed that if the trial was held in Brunson's jurisdiction, Brunson would have influence over Williams, who was appointed judge in the *Pico v. Cohn* case; Pico sued to stop the transfer.[37] They also argued that Brunson maintained contact with Cohn in order to procure a favorable decision. The Cheney-Brunson letter to Governor Stoneman proves further that Brunson maintained interest in the case. After his term as superior court justice ended, he once again appeared as lawyer for Julius B. Cohn in Pico's final appeal to the state supreme court in 1891.[38]

While it is difficult to prove that Pico was the victim of a conspiracy because the evidence is no more than circumstantial, Brunson was no friend of Pío Pico. He had faced him many times, had become accustomed to the way he conducted business, and perhaps wanted to see him ruined once and for all. After the 1891 supreme court decision, Pico was tired of fighting and ultimately had no recourse. Despite the fact that the burden of proof had weighed in Pico's favor, the court emphatically stated, with seeming disregard of the evidence, that "endless litigation, in which nothing was ever finally determined, would be worse than occasional miscarriages of justice."[39]

At the age of ninety, one of the last Californio leaders was financially ruined. Looking back at *Pico v. Cohn*, however, it cannot be said that he could not compete in the new Anglo-dominated economy. Nor can it be said that Pico was disillusioned by the complexity of the U.S. legal system, which, in fact, had often decided in his favor. But along the way, Pico also made some unwise and miscalculated business transactions. His ultimate demise was more associated with corrupt and cunning individuals who conspired to destroy the old governor than a systematic process aimed at destroying the Californios.

CHAPTER 9

La Última Palabra (The Last Word)

After the trial, and at ninety years of age, Pico was forced to leave the Ranchito for good. He lived a few more years in his beloved Los Angeles until his death in 1894. Pico fought for his legacy, and had he not been the victim of selfish profiteers and his own poor decisions, he would have left a grand estate to his remaining family. As it was, he left nothing of worth to his children.[1] He had outlived Bernard Cohn, who never saw the end of his trial with Pico. By the time of the appeal, Cohn had probably concluded that he was fighting Pico so that he could leave a fortune to his family. Even Pico's old friend-turned-foe Pancho Johnson had died before the case was settled. Before his death, Johnson, riddled with guilt for ruining and betraying his friend and *paisano*, admitted to perjury in the case of *Pico v. Cohn*.[2] This was part of the tragedy of Pico's later life.

After the trial, Pico was resigned to living his last few years in the homes of his family and friends. He remained active, however, and was often seen in public. Yet it is difficult to judge how Pico felt about all that had transpired in his life. He had been humiliated by the court, and by the fact that he had nothing to leave his family. Perhaps for the first time since the U.S. invasion in 1846, Pico began to reflect on his involvement with American advancement.

In late September 1891, only about two weeks after the fateful Cohn decision, Pico received a letter from a representative of the Mexican government. The lawyer E. Chazan, a high official under Porfirio Díaz, dictator of Mexico at the time, wrote to Pico with urgent business.[3] Chazan was inquiring about the Santa Catalina Islands off the coast of southern California. Santa Catalina had been in dispute for some time after the U.S.-Mexican War, and Porfirio Díaz hoped to restore the island to the Mexican nation. According to Chazan, Mexico had been in uninterrupted possession of the island, and the claims of the United States were unfounded. Chazan requested that the ninety-year-old Pico, as "a faithful son of Mexico," help his fatherland in an international trial to determine which country was the true owner.[4] Pico replied that when he was governor, the political situation of California and the short duration of his tenure had not allowed his cabinet to determine the legal jurisdiction of the territory.[5] He noted that many of the important documents had been destroyed during the U.S. invasion, making the investigation more difficult. He politely declined the request for help, but said that he would happily assist Chazan with any questions he might have. The timing of Pico's reply, typed on the letterhead of a notary public, reveals his continued intentions concerning his properties. It is likely that Pico wanted the record to show that he was not plotting with Mexico to dispossess the United States.

For the most part, the press had a positive view of Pico. The pro-Republican editor at the *Los Angeles Times* seems to have felt great concern for Pico's legal woes. Directly after the final decision of the state supreme court, an outpouring of interest in Pico's well-being and newspaper features about him aroused the public sentiment. The *Los Angeles Herald*, a pro-Democrat newspaper, reported on the *Pico v. Cohn* decision with an article titled "An Old Case at Last Settled."[6] The *Herald* argued that all irregularities were alleged, and that Pico had simply lost the case. The *Los Angeles Times*, on the other hand, responded with a series of articles looking at Pico's life, his legal issues, and his economic misfortune. "Southern Californians, and old-timers generally, will experience a feeling of sorrow when they learn that the venerable Pio Pico, the last native Governor of the State, and a worthy representative of his race, has lost the lawsuit, upon which his fortune depended, and is now absolutely reduced to a state of penury."[7] The reporter went on to say that his problems were caused by an "indiscretion peculiar to his race." Pico's "indiscretion," that he was too trustworthy, kind, and hospitable, was admirable but not cautious according to the reporter. Even so, the article questioned the decision of the court, in which the "principal witness is admittedly a perjurer." He went on to ask, "Is not some measure of relief for the ruined man possible?"

In the same edition, another journalist reported on a visit she made to Pico's house at the Ranchito. The reporter described the land, the ranch hands busy at their work, and the gentle breeze as she approached Pico's adobe. She portrayed Pico as a gentleman of the "old school," writing that "the Governor extended his hand to me with all the courtly grace of a far younger cavalier, and assisted me to the ground."[8] It was clear that the reporter had captured the sentiment of many, that with the defeat of Pico, an era of California history had vanished. She pondered the old California adobes: "And they do not look out of place even in the midst of a new life that is crowding them on every hand; and they ought to be permitted to stay. We shall miss their picturesque charm when they have vanished, and shall regret their destruction."

Even as many Californians felt sympathetic at his loss of property, Pico was planning yet another fight. The *Los Angeles Times* had tried to entice the public to hold a benefit to raise

Pico's adobe at El Ranchito, Whittier, California, is seen here ca. 1895, shortly after Pico lost it in the *Pico v. Cohn* decision. Courtesy of the Whittier Public Library.

money on Pico's behalf. The reporter questioned how Pico could have fallen into such misfortune. "The *caballero muy rico*, the *hidalgo muy gallan*, the grandee *muy generoso* remains, white-haired and penniless, the last relic, forlorn and forsaken amid the changed aspects of his old domain."[9] Pico's lawyer George Smith wrote an editorial stating that the case was not entirely over. Smith noted that by the court's own words, "the adverse judgment against Pico was due exclusively to Johnson's false testimony."[10] Smith went on to reveal that the court had agreed that perjury had been committed, but because this information came after the final disposition was made, it would not grant a new trial. Smith stated that he would file a petition to overturn this decision with a rehearing. Clearly, Pico would need money to pay legal fees, and the *Los Angeles Times* continued asking the public for help. The newspaper noted that certain individuals were planning to ask the California legislature to give Pico a pension as a former public servant.[11] Pico's compadre Juan Warner met with the Los Angeles City Council to convince them of Pico's kindness and importance to state history, and to ask if they could assist him financially.[12]

The news in the press was not all positive, however. The *Los Angeles Herald* argued against his right to a pension, and even went so far as to claim that Pico's nephews granted him a monthly allowance of fifty dollars.[13] The *Herald* clearly did not support the charitable views the *Los Angeles Times* called for. At the same time, an unnamed individual wrote a letter to the editor of the *Times* claiming that the allegations of fraud were untrue and that a new hearing should never take place.[14] The editorial, signed only by the name "FACT," declared that "Our Superior Court is not peculiar in its disregard of Mr. Pico's testimony. His history as a witness is not flattering." The writer declared, "There is no warrant for the statement that Pico was defrauded."

Pico's enemies could not stop the call for relief, even if it shook the core of Pico's elitist sensibilities. His friends sponsored a horse racing benefit that, unfortunately, failed to attract more than six people.[15] Perhaps the most humiliating of the charitable efforts taking place was led by a group of elementary school children who raised a few dollars for Pico in class as they discussed his legacy.[16]

As late as September 1891, Pico was fighting to begin a fourth appeal of *Pico v. Cohn*. His energy and his determination to seek justice had not died even in his advanced age. But his lawyer wrote him with the news that his firm could do nothing more to assist him.[17] Smith suggested that Pico contact the lawyers of Juan Luco, an expert in land litigation, in San Francisco. Pico did just that. He contacted Luco to ask for assistance against Cohn. Luco replied that he had no doubt that his lawyers would "take his cause."[18]

Nothing came of his request to Luco's lawyers, however. Pico moved about the city, living with various friends and relatives. It is certain that he was furious with the outcome of his legal battles. Earlier in his life, he had rarely shown contempt for Anglo settlers, despite the irreversible change he had watched them make. In fact, he had embraced them and allowed them into his family. He was still treated with respect in some ceremonial events. For example, in 1892 he was invited to attend the California State Fair in Sacramento as an honored guest.[19] However, within a year, Pico's feelings toward Anglo society seem to have soured. His reply to an invitation to attend Chicago's world fair reveals how bitter his feelings had become.

In May 1893 the World's Columbian Exhibition opened in Chicago. Months earlier, organizers of the fair invited Pico to the exhibition as representative of the Old West. Pico was thoroughly insulted at the invitation. If he had ever been naïve about his Mexican heritage in a changing world, he was not now. In a reply published in the *Los Angeles Times*, he said, "No, I will not go, for two good reasons. The first is because I am poor, and the second is because I do not intend to go to the big show to be one of the animals on exhibit. If those gringos imagine for a moment that they can take me back there and show me in a side tent at two bits a head they are very much mistaken."[20] Pico's scorching response shows that he believed the organizers had no thought of honoring him but were simply out to make a buck. For him, the invitation was an insult and would have become the final humiliation of the old governor.

Yet Pico was not a simple victim cast aside by a changing society. Having grown up in poverty, he showed again and again that he could succeed without a formal education and as a man of mixed heritage in a race-conscious society. Despite the fact that certain individuals seemed determined to humiliate him, Pico stood among the elite of California society. Removed from his beloved Ranchito, he is said to have lived with friends and relatives, including his compadre J. J. Warner, and in his final years the defeated yet proud Californio don was often seen riding a carriage around the streets of Los Angeles with the swiftness of an energetic young man.[21] It has become commonplace for historians to note that Pico was buried in a pauper's grave after his death on September 11, 1894, certainly a tradition epitomized in the writing of Franciscan historian Zephyrin Englehardt.[22] But the *Los Angeles Times* described his funeral as one fit for someone of Pico's historic legacy: "The funeral services took place at St. Vincent's Church . . . assisted by Bishop Montgomery, in the sanctuary. . . .The casket, in which lay the body of the deceased, was placed in front of the altar, under the light of many candles, and the impressive ceremonies of the Catholic church were performed, solemn high requiem mass being celebrated. The church was filled to its utmost capacity with friends, all the old Spanish families and Californians being present."[23]

Pío de Jesús Pico's life reminds us of the hostile changes California went though during the nineteenth century. The flags of Spain, Mexico, and the United States flew over Los Angeles during his lifetime. California's chaotic environment shaped Pico's nature and his very life. In fact, Pico centered himself in the midst of California's chaos; the overthrow of Governor Victoria and Governor Micheltorena, and Pico's constant battles against his northern rivals, kept him immersed in political intrigue. Brute force, not revolutionary ideals, kept Pico competitive.

It is difficult to understand exactly how Pico maneuvered himself into a position of power, but it had something to do with his incredible drive to succeed. Pico was never afraid to take chances, and it was this trait that brought him to the pinnacle of success in Californio society. As the last governor of California under Mexican rule, Pico naturally represents a link between Mexican and Anglo California. Although his quest to seek funding for the defense of California was in vain, the motive was not. The Californios who fought to protect their country were engaged in an honorable task, despite the great odds against them. Pico viewed men like Juan Bandini, who happened to be his longtime compadre, as traitors. Many Californios in the south held this sentiment, and were not eager to hand themselves over to the United States. Pride, honor, and status were at stake.

Directly after the war with Mexico, Anglos learned to conduct business Mexican style, and vice versa. Yet Anglos who wanted to excel in southern California could also succeed if they were foresightful enough to marry into one of the land-owning Mexican families. In this way, elite patronage continued for approximately two decades after the war. Similarly, after Pico returned to California at the end of the war, it was not so easy to shed a lifetime of beliefs and behaviors based on a system of elite Mexican patronage. He continued to function within this privileged world, adapting when necessary. He grew wealthy beyond his dreams, became an avid supporter of U.S. capitalism, and proved to be a versatile businessman. In the end, however, his major fault was a failure to be skeptical of those who befriended him. Although many of his legal cases were successful, he worked tirelessly to win back what he had signed away. His failed cases, particularly *Pico v. Cohn*, show the severe bias some justices had against the old Californio.

Yet Pico's legacy has far surpassed the expectations of his critics. The distinctive qualities of the Californio dons, their fusion of innocence and arrogance, determination and failure, plentitude and misery, are unequivocally represented in the life of Don Pío Pico. He has become a figure of pride and a symbol of Mexican American self-determination. His building in the old plaza of Los Angeles shines as an example of Californio achievement. On Cinco de Mayo 2001, Los Angeles proudly celebrated its Mexican past and the two hundredth birthday of one of its most prestigious sons—Don Pío Pico. The old plaza at Olvera Street was crowded with celebrants— Aztec dancers, mariachis, local dignitaries, and rock bands, and festivities that filled the plaza from corner to corner. On a far edge of the plaza, an exhibit drew curious individuals to view portraits of the old governor. A large banner with Pico's image proudly adorned the façade of the building and welcomed people to the Pico House Hotel, the pride and joy of the Pico family. After decades of sitting vacant and being used as a storage facility, the Pico House was once again open to the public, not as a place of business, but as a historic landmark. Pico, it seems, had defeated his detractors and had become a symbol of ethnic pride in California's multi-cultural heritage.

Despite his many faults, Pico contributed a great deal to California. His resilience and determination during an unfavorable period for Mexican Americans are personal qualities that will endure. In reevaluating his life, it is evident that Pico's demise was anything but inevitable. With better decisions and fewer enemies, Pico may have died a rich man. Yet, like so many other Californios, he seemed destined to fall by the wayside. His accomplishments, his role in California history, were overshadowed by men like Junípero Serra.

With the death of Pico and others of his generation, Californio culture was a quickly fading element of society. New and younger arrivals from the interior of Mexico had dramatically changed California's Mexican culture. Mexican farmers, miners, and city dwellers, with a different culture and way of expressing themselves, began to change the old Californio traditions. In the late twentieth century, however, Mexican Americans in California began to search for inspirational historical examples of their forebears.

Today, as the demographics of Mexican Americans in California soar to new heights, Pío Pico is a historic figure many look up to as a shining and inspirational example of the Mexican past. Pío Pico's life story reminds us of a unique multicultural legacy in California. Pico's two hundredth birthday celebration in Los Angeles revealed that he has taken on a new role in California's history. Today, Cinco de Mayo is a celebration not only of the Mexican past but also of a Californio past, rich in its Mexican, American Indian, African American, and European roots.

Notes

Abbreviations Used in the Notes

AFP   Archivo de la Familia Pico, Bancroft Library, University of California, Berkeley

AGN   Archivo General de la Nación, Provincias Internas Tomo 1 (Californias), Microfilm Collection, Bancroft Library, University of California, Berkeley

BANC MSS   Bancroft manuscripts, Bancroft Library, University of California, Berkeley

BHC   Benjamin Hayes Collection, Bancroft Library, University of California, Berkeley

BL, UCB   Bancroft Library, University of California, Berkeley

C-A   California archives, Bancroft Library, University of California, Berkeley

C-B   Californians' personal papers, biography, Bancroft Library, University of California, Berkeley

C-C   California church records, Bancroft Library, University of California, Berkeley

CHD   California Historical Documents Collection, Huntington Library, San Marino

GFC   Guerra Family Collection, Santa Barbara Mission-Archive Library, Santa Barbara

WPA   Works Project Administration, Inventory of the Supreme Court of California Records, Office of the Secretary of State, Sacramento

Introduction

1. See for example Monroy, *Thrown Among Strangers*, and Pitt, *Decline of the Californios*. A Californio was a Mexican born in California before its annexation to the United States in 1848.

2. The most impressive study on "decline" is Pitt, *Decline of the Californios*.

Chapter 1. A California Family

1. See Cole's foreword to the English translation of Pico's testimony, in Pico, *Historical Narrative*, 11–17.

2. Robinson, *Life in California*, 12.

3. For an interesting discussion on this topic, see Voss, "From Casta to Californio," 461–74.

4. Bolton, *Font's Complete Diary*, 112.

5. Weber, *The Spanish Frontier in North America*, 261–62.

6. For an excellent study of race and Spanish colonialism on the frontier, see Alonso, *Thread of Blood*.

7. Pico, *Narración Histórica*, MS, Octubre 24, 1877; *Historical Narrative*, 28. Pico recounted that Matilde Carrillo and her son José Antonio Carrillo, later to become his brother-in-law, taught him to read and write. In this biography I use both the original manuscript and the Cole and Welcome (English) edition, translated by Arthur P. Botello. The translation is generally well done and contains useful footnotes. In my notes, the two Pico narratives are identified by their titles, that is, the manuscript in Spanish, the published volume in English.

8. Robinson, *Life in California*, 17–18.

9. Holter, *Pio Pico State Historic Park*, 4. It is unclear in this pamphlet where Holter found his information.

10. Mason, *The Census of 1790*, 85.

11. Ibid., 53.

12. Ibid. This shows how imprecise the listing of castes was. María Eustaquia Gutiérrez was not born in Spain, which was ostensibly the only legitimate way to be listed as a Spaniard. However, by this time in the late colonial period, "español/a" may have simply been used to indicate "white."

13. For an interesting discussion regarding the practice of and desire for racial purity, see Hurtado, *Sex, Gender, and Culture*, 23–27. William

Mason cautions readers to consider the blurring of racial lines in early California, even among those listed as Spaniards, because of the obvious manipulation of racial terms. See Mason, *The Census of 1790*, 46–50.

14. Pico, *Historical Narrative*, 28–29.

15. Pico lists his siblings as José Antonio, Andrés, Concepción, Tomasa, María, Isadora, Estéfana, Jacinta, and Feliciana. See ibid., 20–21.

16. Pablo Vicente de Solá to Don José de la Cruz, 4 June 1817, Provincial State Papers, BANC MSS C-A 13:147.

17. Hackel, "Land, Labor, and Production," 122. Indian neophytes were confined to the missions once baptized and were expected to work for the benefit of the mission.

18. For the relation between the military and the missions in California, see Weber, *The Mexican Frontier*, 62–63.

19. Monroy, *Thrown Among Strangers*, 135.

20. Pico, *Historical Narrative*, 20, n. 4; see also Robinson, *Land in California*, 55–56.

21. Pico, *Historical Narrative*, 19, n. 3. José Dolores was the founder of the northern branch of the Pico family, whose sons Antonio María and José de Jesús became prominent Californios.

22. It is unclear how or why José María Pico was transferred to San Gabriel at this time. Pico, *Historical Narrative*, 21, n. 7. Editors Cole and Welcome do not state that he was at San Gabriel during these years.

23. Neophytes, as Spaniards called them, were Indians baptized into Christianity. They were, in fact, Christians in training, as they were believed still to be in a state of savagery. See Sandos, "Social Control within the Missionary Frontier Society," 266–68.

24. Spanish documents imply that José María could speak the Gabrieleño language. See Lepowsky, "Indian Revolts," 6–12; Sandos, "Toypurina's Revolt," 4–11; Hackel, "Sources of Rebellion," 649; and Castañeda, "Engendering the History of Alta California, 1769–1848," 235–36.

25. Castañeda, "Engendering the History of Alta California," 235–36; Steven Hackel has written an excellent revision of the San Gabriel uprising, dispelling much of the myth and romanticism found in earlier versions of the account. See Hackel, "Sources of Rebellion."

26. For an interesting discussion of the construction of identity in New Spain, see Carrera, *Imagining Identity in New Spain*.

27. The official report, in which the leaders were interrogated, is "Ynterrogatorio sobre la sublevación de San Gabriel, 10 Octubre de 1785," AGN, Provincias Internas Tomo I (Californias): 120.

28. Temple, "Toypurina the Witch and the Indian Uprising," 331. The term "Spaniard" was used loosely by some officials. This is indicated by the fact that José María Pico was born in New Spain (colonial Mexico) and was a mestizo whose mother was mulatto.

29. Miguel Cuevas to Excelentísima Señor, 18 February 1799, AGN, Provincias Internas 6:2.

30. José Antonio de Noriega to José Antonio de la Guerra y Noriega, 31 May 1809, GFC 15:712, Santa Barbara Mission-Archive Library. Napoleon's capture of the Spanish throne created an opportunity for Latin American insurgents to rebel. Guerra y Noriega later became the principal landowner and leading citizen in the Santa Barbara area.

31. Meyer and Sherman, *The Course of Mexican History*, 292. These measures, as well as a formal declaration of independence, were called for at the Congress of Chilpancingo in 1813.

32. José Darío Argüello to unnamed recipient, 20 August 1815, GFC 49:1.

33. Pico, *Historical Narrative*, 23.

34. Ibid., 25.

Chapter 2. California Rebel

1. Juan Bautista Alvarado (1809–1882), a native of Monterey, California, was governor from 1836 to 1842. See Miller, *Juan Alvarado*. A *compadre* is basically a coparent. It is a bonding relationship between parents and godparents that was traditionally sealed with a one-time gift of money or other goods.

2. Although he must have served in lesser capacities before this time, the first record of Pico's political involvement came in 1828, when he won a seat in the state legislature. See "Cuaderno de Actas de Elecciones de Diputados al Congreso General y a la Diputación Territorial, 6 de Octubre de 1828," C-A, Miscellaneous, 1770–1848, 62. Pico also involved himself in politics after early California statehood, but mostly from behind the scenes.

3. This is not to say that they denied their Mexican ancestry. In most parts of Mexico, people from a particular state have a name for themselves that denotes a particular history and subculture.

4. By sovereignty I mean a desire for equal representation within a federal republic.

5. Guedea, "The First Popular Elections in Mexico City," 43. Also known as the Constitution of Cádiz, this document had its roots in the

political ideas of the Enlightenment. It was forged in the absence of the king of Spain, Carlos IV, directly after the Napoleonic invasion, and promulgated in the Cortes of Cádiz in 1812.

6. Weber, *The Mexican Frontier,* 15–16.

7. A territory had less autonomy and less representation than a state. Territories had only a nonvoting member in the Mexican Congress.

8. Anna, *Forging Mexico, 1821–1835,* 5–6.

9. Michael González convincingly argues that especially in Los Angeles, Californios were not opposed to political and cultural ties to Mexico. See González, *This Small City.* González's point is well taken. Pico, for example, an Angeleño himself, fought for greater representation within Mexico. And as we will see in the coming chapter, he worked in the hope that California would someday be the envy of all states within the Mexican Republic.

10. Anna, *Forging Mexico,* 81–82.

11. Brading, *The Origins of Mexican Nationalism,* 66–67.

12. Green, *The Mexican Republic,* 8–9.

13. Ibid., 14.

14. Ibid., 32–33; Lucas Alamán, one of the foremost conservative thinkers, argued that the colonial practice of Indian submission to priests led to a peaceful and harmonious society. Only when given equality did they, according to Alamán, fill with racial hatred and violence toward whites. See Stevens, *Origins of Instability,* 42.

15. From Brading, *The Origins of Mexican Nationalism,* 70. See also Stevens, *Origins of Instability,* 28–29; Green, *The Mexican Republic,* 35–36.

16. Californio politicians were more inclined to oppose federal authority rather than advocate complete separation from Mexico. It is clear that most Californios accepted and even cherished their Mexican heritage. See González, *This Small City,*17.

17. Alvarado, *Historia de California,* 2:34–37, BL, UCB.

18. Pico, *Narración Histórica,* MS, microfilm, C-D 13.

19. Pico, *Historical Narrative,* 32–33. "[M]e sorprendí yo cuando oí á Bringas decirle á Portilla que los paisanos eran el vaso sagrado de la nación, y que los militares no eran otra cosa que criados de la nación, la cual era formado del pueblo y no de los militares." Pico, *Narración Histórica,* 14.

20. Notificación de la ley 20 de Marzo á los RR.PP. misioneros, July 15, 1829, Departmental State Papers, 1821–1846, BANC MSS C-A 27:270.

21. Bancroft, *History of California,* 3:16–17.

22. Rosenus, *General M. G. Vallejo*, 12.

23. Miller, *Juan Alvarado*, 21.

24. One outspoken Mexican observer, Fray Servando Teresa de Mier, believed that unlike the English colonies, Mexico had always been united. The separation of Mexico under the federalist model, according to Mier, would sever a Mexico united under centralist principles. Although Mier believed in a strong central government, he also believed in a weak and dependent federal system. See Di Tella, *National Popular Politics*, 149; Meyer and Sherman, *The Course of Mexican History*, 314. Stevens, *Origins of Instability*, 31.

25. Rodríguez and Jaime, "The Constitution of 1824," 77–80.

26. Sánchez, *Telling Identities*, 99.

27. Quoted in Miller, *Juan Alvarado*, 16.

28. Pío's sister María Casimira Pico married José Joaquín Ortega, a powerful ranchero and politician, in 1821. José Joaquín's grandfather José Francisco de Ortega (known as the first white man to see the San Francisco Bay) was married to María Antonia Victoria Carrillo. Pico, *Historical Narrative*, 21.

29. Ibid., 22.

30. Pío Pico would later marry a relative of Juan Bautista Alvarado; Juan Bautista Alvarado, a nephew of Mariano Vallejo, would later become Pico's compadre; Mariano G. Vallejo married Pico's cousin and was an uncle to Alvarado; José Joaquín Ortega married Pico's sister; Santiago Argüello married Ortega's sister; Antonio María Osio married Argüello's sister; Juan Bandini was Pico's compadre; and Tomás Yorba, also Pico's compadre. Although I have found no reference to it in the archives, in Osio, *History of Alta California*, 5–6, Beebe and Senkewicz argue that Pico's wife, María Ignacia Alvarado, was a distant cousin of Juan Bautista Alvarado. This may have been the case since most of the California Alvarados came from Loreto, Baja California. Pico, *Historical Narrative*, 20, 41.

31. Rancho Petaluma, Documents Pertaining to the Adjudication of Private Land Claims in California, BANC MSS, Land Case Files, 1852–63, no. 321, BL, UCB.

32. Moyer, *Historic Ranchos of San Diego*, 4.

33. Ibid. A *mayordomo*, more specifically, is the overseer of the ranch who answered to no one except the proprietor. During the period, a mayordomo was a highly sought-after and prestigious position.

34. Green, *The Mexican Republic*, 87, 155–65.

35. Ibid., 140–61; Anna, *Forging Mexico*, 196–204. Mexican historian Enrique Krauze defined the York Rite Masons as "anti-Spanish,

radical, pro-American and embryonic liberals." The Yorkinos were founded in Mexico by U.S. Ambassador Joel R. Poinsett. The opposition rite in Mexico was the Scottish Rite Masons, who were pro-English, moderate, and centralists. Together, Krauze argues, their destructive actions actually worked to undermine federalism. See Krauze, *Biography of Power*, 130.

36. Krauze, *Biography of Power*, 130; Green, *The Mexican Republic*, 154–61.

37. Krauze, *Biography of Power*, 223–27; Green, *The Mexican Republic*, 162–70.

38. Echeandía brought the practice of the Yorkino meetings to young Californio politicians, where he was able to entrench radical federalist beliefs among them. See Sánchez, *Telling Identities*, 110–15.

39. Green, *The Mexican Republic*, 198–99.

40. Sánchez, *Telling Identities*, 112–13.

41. Weber, "California in 1831," 1–6.

42. The fact that a single individual held both posts was also a matter of concern for the Californios.

43. Echeandía and many California officials had attempted to break up the power structure of the Church through secularization even before Victoria was appointed governor. However, the first major secularization policy was José María de Echeandía's *Plan para convertir en pueblos las misiones de la alta California, Julio y Agosto de 1830*, box 6, folder 256, GFC.

44. See Pico, *Historical Narrative*, 40.

45. Manuel Victoria, *Manifesto a los habitantes de la alta California*, 21 September 1831, AFP.

46. Ibid.

47. Weber, *The Mexican Frontier*, 29.

48. Pío Pico, *Contestación a la locución del Comandante General y Jefe Político, Don Manuel Victoria*, 15 October 1831, AFP. The contestación was a *bando*, a notice posted in public.

49. Ibid.

50. Many authors, including Cole and Welcome, editors of Pico's narrative, characterize Don Pío as a "revolutionary." See Pico, *Historical Narrative*, 13.

51. Pico, *Contestación*, 15 October 1831.

52. Pico, *Historical Narrative*, 41.

53. Andrés Pico was only twenty-one at the time of this incident. He was a military man during the Mexican period and acted as the last comandante general of Mexican California when José Castro fled to

Mexico. For his bravery and military feats at the Battle of San Pasqual, he became enormously popular during the U.S. period and rose to the level of state senator and was a top military commander during the same period.

54. Pico, *Historical Narrative*, 41.

55. Bancroft, *History of California*, 3:198.

56. Quoted in Bancroft, *History of California*, 3:199. The "booty" Durán referred to was Church land.

57. Ibid.

58. Pico, *Historical Narrative*, 41.

59. Tays, "Revolutionary California," 115.

60. Pico, *Historical Narrative*, 42. Pico recalled that at least seventy men were incarcerated.

61. Ibid., 43.

62. These two goals were the entire focus of the plan. See *Plan de San Diego, 29 de Noviembre 1831*, AFP.

63. Ibid., 45.

64. Bancroft, *History of California*, 3:204.

65. Ibid., 3:201.

66. Pico, *Historical Narrative*, 47.

67. Ibid, 50–51. About the 1831 Battle of Cahuenga, Bancroft wrote, "Pico's narrative of the whole affair is remarkably accurate in every case where its accuracy can be tested, and is therefore worthy of some credit where no such test is possible." Bancroft, *History of California*, 3:205, n. 42. The two soldiers who were killed were Romualdo Pacheco, a prominent military official from Guanajuato, Mexico, and the soldier José María Ávila.

68. Osio, *History of Alta California*, 110–11. The *mazatecos* were Victoria's soldiers.

69. Bancroft, *History of California*, 3:212, n. 57.

70. Ibid., 3:216. Pages 216–18 contain a full account of the assembly proceedings for this day.

71. The politicians of northern and southern California began a regional battle of supremacy over the territory. They fought over many issues, especially the location of the customs house, which the north had the privilege of overseeing.

72. Pico, *Historical Narrative*, 54.

73. Ibid.

74. José María de Echeandía to Pío Pico, 1 February 1832, Departmental State Papers, 1821–1846, BANC MSS C-A 28:40–41.

75. Echeandía to Manuel Domínguez, 6 February 1832, Departmental State Papers, ibid., 28:42.

76. Osio, *History of Alta California,* 111. At the time, Victoria believed he was dying from his wound.

77. Echeandía to Pío Pico, 16 February 1832, Departmental State Papers, 1821–1846, BANC MSS C-A 28:43–44.

78. Bancroft, *History of California,* 3:226.

79. Ibid., 3:232. Carlos Carrillo, brother of José Antonio, was a close associate of his brother-in-law José de la Guerra y Noriega, comandante of the Santa Barbara Presidio. Guerra was also more conservative in his views. Carrillo later changed his mind and supported some liberal issues like secularization of the missions.

Chapter 3. Secularization and Rebellion

1. The laws for secularization had a troubled past. The liberal Spanish courts made a first attempt to fully secularize the missions in 1813. Conservative politicians briefly suspended secularization, but liberals reestablished it in 1821 and finally passed legislation in 1833. See Lozano and Dublan, "Decreto del Congreso Mejicano," II:548–49; Jackson and Castillo, *Indians, Franciscans, and Spanish Colonization,* 88–89.

2. Three recent studies reveal that secularization indeed brought about a revitalized sense of autonomy among the California neophyte population. See Hackel, *Children of Coyote,* 377–80; Sandos, *Converting California,* 108–10; Street, *Beasts of the Field,* 81–85.

3. Missionaries had control over mission temporalities, that is, civil and political control over mission lands and neophytes. Secularization in California took this control away and placed it in the hands of the government, at the same time beginning the process aimed at distributing mission property to Indians.

4. The casta system was a hierarchy of races with Indians and Africans on the bottom and Spaniards on top. Those castas higher up on the scale had more privileges.

5. José María de Echeandía, *Decreto de emancipación a favor de neófitos,* 25 July 1826, in Bancroft, *History of California,* 3:103. Many Californios viewed secularization as a necessary step to comply with

Mexican colonization laws, or the *Ley General de 18 de Agosto, 1824.* See Agustín Zamorano, *Reglamento para la colonización de los territorios de la República, 19 de Noviembre, 1829,* Missions and Colonization, C-A 53 Tomo II, 2–6.

6. Steven Hackel forcefully argues that some ex-neophytes indeed prospered from land grants after secularization. A select few even increased their land holdings above those that secularization reserved for them. However, he makes it clear that the cases he presents were the exception, not the rule. Hackel, *Children of Coyote,* 388–405.

7. This was the plan to convert California's missions to pueblos. Echeandía's decree came under turbulent circumstances, during Anastacio Bustamante's rise to power. Before the overthrow of President Vicente Guerrero, officials named a liberal candidate, Antonio Garcia, to replace Echeandía as governor of California, but the appointment was revoked with the rise of the conservatives. See Bancroft, *History of California,* 3:181–82.

8. Englehardt, *Missions and Missionaries,* 4:337.

9. The vast size of mission property, even after the distribution to the Indians, made it possible for the government to manage and profit from excess lands. The government made profit by continuing some of the mission's economic productivity, such as ranching. The resulting income would contribute to the territories' military, educational, and other unidentified costs.

10. Echeandía, *Ley sobre administración de misiones,* 6 January, 1831, Departmental Records, C-A 49:2, 66–78; Echeandía, *Reglamento de secularización de las misiones, 18 de Noviembre, 1832,* State Papers: Missions and Colonization, BANC MSS C-A 53 Tomo II:59–69. These decrees reinforced or clarified the plan of 1830. Meanwhile, California's representative to the Mexican national Congress, Carlos Carrillo, supported the missionaries. He warned Congress of the devastating effect secularization would have in California. See Bancroft, *History of California,* 3:311.

11. Three major pieces of legislation are Echeandía, *Plan para convertir en pueblos las misiones de la alta California, Julio y Agosto de 1830,* GFC, box 6, folder 256; Lozano and Dublan, "Decreto del Congreso Mejicano"; Figueroa, *Reglamento provisional para la secularización de las Misiones de la Alta California, 9 de Agosto de 1834,* State Papers: Missions and Colonization, BANC MSS C-A 53 Tomo II:166–74.

12. Lucas Alamán to Figueroa, 17 May 1832, State Papers: Missions and Colonization, BANC MSS C-A 53 Tomo II:34–36. See also Figueroa, *Manifesto*, 2–3. Figueroa's manifesto has the distinction of being the first book printed in California.

13. José Figueroa, *Informe en que se opone al proyecto de secularización*, 5 de Octubre de 1833, State Papers: Missions and Colonization, BANC MSS C-A 53 Tomo II:72

14. Ibid.

15. Ibid.

16. José Figueroa, *Prevenciones provisionales para la emancipación de Indios reducidos*, 15 de Julio 1833, in Bancroft, *History of California*, 3:328–29.

17. Ibid.

18. Alamán wanted to prevent an Anglo takeover of Texas. See Green, *The Mexican Republic*, 210–26.

19. Di Tella, *National Popular Politics*, 224.

20. Meyer and Sherman, *The Course of Mexican History*, 326.

21. Ibid.; Figueroa, *Manifesto*, 3. For the translated version of the Mexican secularization law, see *Decreto del Congreso Mejicano secularizando las Misiones*, 17 de Agosto de 1833, in Bancroft, *History of California*, 3:336.

22. Ibid.

23. Fray Francisco García to José Figueroa, 24 September 1833, State Papers: Missions and Colonization, BANC MSS C-A 53 Tomo II:83.

24. Ibid.

25. Ibid.

26. Figueroa, *Reglamento provisional*.

27. The reglamento issued one hundred to four hundred *varas* squared. One square vara is 7.52 square feet. Therefore, according to this reglamento, all heads of household and all adults over the age of twenty should have received at least one hundred by one hundred varas of land. Four hundred varas squared equals 160,000 square varas or 27.62 acres. Thus, one hundred square varas equaled roughly 7 acres. See Pauley, "Weights and Measurements," 114–25. According to the archives, San Luis Rey had a population of only 2,844 in 1834. See Jackson, *Indian Population Decline*, appendix 4, p. 175.

28. Jackson, *Indian Population Decline*, appendix 4, p. 175.

29. Ibid.

30. For example, San Luis Rey spanned from just south of San Juan Capistrano, near Santa Margarita, to San Marcos. This is an area roughly

thirty miles across. Despite the fact that Indian pueblos were created and over a thousand individuals were to be given at least one hundred varas, vast acreage remained.

31. See Jackson, *Indian Population Decline*, 6–7; Monroy, *Thrown Among Strangers*, 86–87.

32. Englehardt, *San Luis Rey Mission*, 52–53.

33. Ibid.

34. Hutchinson, *Frontier Settlement*, 277–78.

35. José María Osuna to Jefe Superior, 5 November 1835, BHC, *Missions*, 1:229.

36. Ibid. By this time Pico had already been appointed comisionado. It is uncertain what Portilla's position was on the matter or why, in fact, he was there.

37. An early study focused on how California natives themselves were partially responsible for the decline of the missions. See Phillips, "Indians and the Breakdown of the Spanish Mission System," *Ethnohistory* 21:4 (Fall 1974). Phillips argues that secularization led to passive resistance, causing neophytes to flee, leading to the financial collapse of California's missions. He doesn't address other forms of resistance, however.

38. Figueroa, *Reglamento provisional.*

39. José Figueroa to Alcalde del Pueblo de Las Flores, 8 May 1835, State Papers: Missions, BANC MSS C-A 51:7, 95.

40. Joaquín de los Rios y Ruiz to unknown, 15 November 1840, State Papers: Missions, BANC MSS C-A 51 Tomo VII:95. Rios y Ruiz notes news from the "Alcalde of Pala," simply named Nepomuceno.

41. For Pico's early political career in San Diego, see *Resultados de elecciones de San Diego, 6 de Octubre, 1828, Cuaderno de Actas de Elecciones de Diputados al Congresso General y á la Diputación Territorial,* Miscellaneous, 1770–1848, BANC MSS C-A 62:330. Pico became a *vocal* of the diputación with three of six votes from appointed electors.

42. Moyer, *Historic Ranchos of San Diego,* 4. Pico later acquired Rancho Santa Margarita, also in the San Diego jurisdiction.

43. Echeandía, *Plan para convertir en pueblos las misiones de la alta California.*

44. Echeandía, *Reglamento para los encargados de justicia y de la policia de las misiones del Departamento de San Diego,* 29 January 1833, State Papers: Missions and Colonization, BANC MSS C-A 53 Tomo II:112–15. This law came about after Echeandía's secularization plans.

45. Ibid.

46. Pío Pico to Santiago Argüello, 24 January 1836, in Hayes, *Missions of Alta California*, BHC, BANC MSS C-C 21, 1:293. In this note, Pico accepts the appointment as *encargado*.

47. Pico, *Historical Narrative*, 91. Pico meant an Indian alcalde since he had no authority to order such a punishment against the so-called *gente de razón* (Hispanic Christians). Although Pico had not yet been elected as encargado de justicia, the laws were in place, giving the comisionado of missions a hand in justice.

48. Pío Pico to Mariano Guadalupe Vallejo, 16 April 1836, Vallejo, *Documentos*, BANC MSS C-B 3:192. Pico was Vallejo's cousin through marriage.

49. Ibid.

50. Ignacio del Valle wrote that Pico sent from San Luis Rey $1,359 "reales, viveres y esquilmos" for the support of the troops. Ignacio del Valle to unknown, 3 August 1836, State Papers: Missions, BANC MSS C-A 51:119. Other than occasional financial support of the troops, little is mentioned in the records.

51. *Inventario*, Mission San Luis Rey, 22 August de 1835, State Papers: Missions, BANC MSS C-A 51:11–12.

52. Ibid.

53. *Inventario*, Mission Santa Ines, 1 August 1836, State Papers: Missions, BANC MSS C-A 51: 27.

54. Receipt signed by Pío Pico, 9 September 1836, San Luis Rey, in Hayes, *Missions of Alta California*, BHC, BANC MSS C-C 21, vol. 1. Unfortunately, it is impossible to tell what happened to this revenue.

55. Pico, *Historical Narrative*, 89.

56. César, *Cosas de Indios*, BL, UCB.

57. See for example a complaint from the pueblo of Las Flores that Pico's cattle were occupying the entire pueblo, eating crops, and destroying their subsistence. Guillermo Hartnell to unknown, 26 August 1840, BANC MSS C-A 51:287–90.

58. Pico, *Historical Narrative*, 98–99.

59. César, *Cosas de Indios*.

60. Ibid.

61. Santiago Argüello to Jefe Politico, 9 June 1836, Departmental State Papers: Benicia, Prefecturas y Juzgados, 1828–1846, BANC MSS C-A 42:263–64.

62. Pico, *Historical Narrative*, 91; Bancroft, *History of California*, 3:624, n. 17. As previously mentioned, in November 1835 a similar delegation formed to protest the actions of administrator Pablo de la Portilla.

63. Santiago Argüello to Jefe Politico, 9 June 1836, Departmental State Papers: Benicia, Prefecturas y Juzgados, 1828–1846, BANC MSS C-A 42:263–64. Although it is unclear who gave Apis permission, the Argüello letter reveals that "emancipated" Indians were still required to obtain official permission to travel, even within San Diego.

64. Ibid.

65. Pico, *Historical Narrative*, 91–93.

66. Ibid.

67. Nicolás Gutiérrez to Alcalde Constitutional de San Diego, 7 June 1836, in Hayes, *Missions of Alta California*, BHC, BANC MSS C-C 21, 1:68.

68. Pablo Apis to José Castro, 7 November 1836, in Vallejo, *Documentos*, BANC MSS C-B 3:236. In this letter, Apis petitioned Castro to return to his home in order to take care of his family and his aging parents. Castro granted his request on 8 November 1836. Apis had served nearly five months.

69. Nicolás Gutiérrez to Comandante General, 9 July 1836, in Hayes, *Missions of Alta California*, BHC, BANC MSS C-C 21, 1:293. Pico had the *comandante militar* of San Diego, Nicolás Gutiérrez, arrest the emancipated neophyte, José Manuel, for undisclosed crimes.

70. Mariano Chico to Alcalde Constitutional de San Diego, 20 June 1836, in ibid. Unfortunately, the document does not describe the attacks.

71. Nicolás Gutiérrez to Alcalde Constitutional de San Diego, 11 July 1836, in ibid.

72. Mariano Chico to Nicolás Gutiérrez, 11 July 1836, in ibid.

73. Pío Pico to Santiago Argüello, 16 September 1836, in ibid. Pico had his eye on Las Flores and would acquire title to it a decade later. A *regidor* was a town councilor.

74. Pío Pico to Santiago Argüello, 6 November 1836, in ibid., 315.

75. Weber, *The Mexican Frontier*, 255–56.

76. The federal government actually appointed Carrillo governor, which Alvarado rejected.

77. Pico was actually arrested on Christmas Eve 1837 in his San Diego home while entertaining many important families. At the time he was playing the devil in a *pastorela*, a religious play in honor of Christ. José Castro had surrounded the house and arrested Pico and some of his guests on the spot. It is unclear if Pico was sentenced right away or if he was required to serve time at a later date. Pico was imprisoned at Santa Barbara in May 1838 but seems to have been released because of illness. Alvarado even honored him by asking him to serve as godfather

to a child, possibly his illegitimate son, although Pico says the boy was the son of Alvarado's relative. See Beebe and Senkewicz, *Testimonios*, 139; Miller, *Juan Alvarado*, 60–61; Pico, *Historical Narrative*, 85–86.

78. Monroy, "The Creation and Re-creation of Californio Society," in Gutierrez and Orsi, *Contested Eden*,191.

79. See Sánchez, *Telling Identities*,143–44. There is a discrepancy in dates. Pico recalls the attack coming during his imprisonment in May 1838, while Bancroft writes the date of May 1837, which seems to be supported by documents that Bancroft calls "contradictory." See Bancroft, *History of California*, 4:68, n. 50.

80. Andrés Pico to Mariano Guadalupe Vallejo, 7 February 1839, in Vallejo, *Documentos*, BANC MSS C-B 6:188.

81. Andrés Pico to José Antonio Estudillo, 19 May 1839, in Hayes, *Missions of Alta California*, BHC, BANC MSS C-C 21, 1:293.

82. José Antonio Pico to M. G. Vallejo, 21 July 1839, in Vallejo, *Documentos*, BANC MSS C-B 7: 393. Although Pico did not say if the *malhechores* were Indian, he did indicate that the people they killed were *gente de razón* (Christians). Given this distinction, the perpetrators were most likely Indians (*sin razón*).

83. José Antonio Pico to M. G. Vallejo, 6 July 1839, in ibid., 7:314.

84. Tiburcio Tapia to Supremo Gobierno, May 1839, in Hayes, *Missions of Alta California*, BHC, BANC MSS C-C 21, 1:293.

85. Pío Pico to José Antonio Pico, 7 June 1839, in Vallejo, *Documentos*, BANC MSS C-B 7: 188.

86. Pico to Guillermo Hartnell, 12 June 1839, in ibid., 206. Dakin, *The Lives of William Hartnell*, 222, 266.

87. Dakin, *The Lives of William Hartnell*, 230. In her biography of Hartnell, Dakin may have intentionally misrepresented Pico by implying that his heavyset frame may have been due to the condition elephantiasis.

88. Bancroft, *History of California*, 4:58. The reglamento was dated 1 March 1840.

89. See Farris, *The Diary and Copybook of William E. P. Hartnell*, 33, 54–55, 123.

90. Joaquín de los Rios y Ruiz to unknown, 15 November 1840, State Papers: Missions, BANC MSS C-A 51 Tomo X:262.

91. Certification—William E. Hartnell, Visitador General de Misiones, August 16 1840, in Pío Pico Papers, Additions, folder 3.

92. "Petition of Señores Pico for Santa Margarita," 12 March 1841, 1:351–52, Los Angeles County Records, Huntington Library. See also Bancroft, *History of California*, 4:621. Rancho Santa Margarita is now

Camp Pendleton military base. This was the largest Mexican land grant approved by the U.S. government after the U.S.-Mexican War.

93. Pío and Andrés Pico to Sub Prefecto y Alvarado, Petition for Rancho Temecula, 2 December 1840, in Pico Papers, Additions, folder 5. For the grant to Apis see Cowan, *Ranchos of California*.

94. Anna, *Forging Mexico*, 256–57.

Chapter 4. The Pivotal Years, 1840–1846

1. "Petition of Señores Pico for Santa Margarita," 12 March 1841, Los Angeles County Records, 1:351–52, Huntington Library. Because Santa Margarita was made up of land belonging to Mission San Luis Rey, such grants to prominent Californios were certainly the fruits of the secularization movement in California.

2. This was a favorable exchange for the inhabitants of Temecula because Pico was no longer trying to control their land. However, Las Flores, which Pico later acquired, adjoined Santa Margarita and had four hundred Indian residents, who were angered that Pico had legal control of the area. The local justice of the peace calmed their anger by appointing three Indian alcaldes to represent them. See Bancroft, *History of California*, 4:628, n. 8.

3. Pico, *Historical Narrative*, 99.

4. Cleland, *Cattle on a Thousand Hills*, 55–56. Cleland quoted Pico as saying, "My Mayordomo is the person who represents my interests at the rancho and is subject only to the proprietor or owner of the ranch. His business is to take care of the cattle and do whatever is demanded, to deliver or sell cattle when he is commanded, and he arranges the laborers of the ranch."

5. For a short but important history of the Los Angeles pueblos, see Robinson, *Los Angeles from the Days of the Pueblo*, 50.

6. Ibid., 53–54.

7. Bancroft lists him as a tithe collector in Los Angeles in 1841. Bancroft, *History of California*, 4:778.

8. Castillo, *The Los Angeles Barrio, 1850–1890*, 13.

9. Moyer, *Historic Ranchos of San Diego*, 25.

10. *Pío Pico, encargado de justicia—Las Flores*, 10 April 1842, Los Angeles County Records, 1:149 A.

11. Moyer, *Historic Ranchos of San Diego*, 28.

12. Miller, *Juan Alvarado*, 92.

13. Bancroft, *History of California*, 4:300–311.

14. Miller, *Juan Alvarado*, 94–95.

15. Bancroft, *History of California*, 4:294. Alvarado made Jimeno Casarín acting governor for the purpose. This way a legitimate transfer of authority could take place. Bancroft argued that the real reason Alvarado sent Casarín was because he did not want to "render the abajeños [the southern California population] spectators of his humiliation."

16. Ibid., 4:369. Micheltorena's decree was entitled *Decreto por el cual devuelve la administración de Misiones á los frailes, 29 de Marzo, 1843.*

17. Ibid., 4:373.

18. Pico, *Historical Narrative*, 100. See also Bancroft, *History of California*, 4:361. John Sutter became a naturalized Mexican citizen, and in 1839 Governor Juan Bautista Alvarado granted him 48,800 acres in the Sacramento Valley. Sutter's New Helvetia compound actually became a friendly stopover for overlanders crossing the Sierra Nevada.

19. Miller, *Juan Alvarado*, 99.

20. Juan Bautista Alvarado, *Historia de California*, 5:20, BL, UCB. Alvarado's historia was completed in 1876.

21. Miller, *Juan Alvarado*, 100.

22. Pico, *Historical Narrative*, 103.

23. Ibid., 104.

24. José Antonio de la Guerra y Noriega to Pío Pico, 9 February 1845, in GFC, folder 475, box 10.

25. Pico to Guerra y Noriega, 12 February 1845, in GFC, folder 768.

26. Pico, *Historical Narrative*, 105.

27. Ibid.

28. Bancroft, *History of California*, 4:499–500, n. 25.

29. Ibid., 502–503.

30. Pico, *Historical Narrative*, 111–12. Pico replied that it was inappropriate to discuss such matters with him, although he admitted that he preferred Vallejo and that he felt the comandancia was his by right.

31. Pico accused Castro of cowardice in the battle against Micheltorena. His exact words were "Castro . . . appeared to be hiding behind a small hill near the culverin. He was wrapped in a serape, and instead of his hat, he had another made of straw such as is made by the Indians." Pico, *Historical Narrative*, 110.

32. Bancroft, *History of California*, 4:555.

33. Ibid., 4:556.

34. Pico even purchased a large house near the plaza of Los Angeles as his headquarters. The move was no surprise to anyone; Pico had always believed that Los Angeles by right should be the capital. Castro and Alvarado understood this when they asked for Pico's help against Micheltorena.

35. Ibid., 4:558.

36. Pico to Juan Bandini, 29 January 1846, in Bandini, *Documentos*, C-B 68:65.

37. Ibid.

38. Bancroft, *History of California*, 4:557–58.

39. Pico to Administrator and Prefect, 15 April 1846, in Pico, *Documentos*, 3:166. See also Bancroft, *History of California*, 5:36.

40. Pico to Alvarado, 18 February 1846, Departmental State Papers, BANC MSS 4:71. See also Bancroft, *History of California*, 5:32, n. 1.

41. Quoted in Billington, *The Far Western Frontier*, 144.

42. Bancroft, *History of California*, 4:519, n. 1.

43. Pico, *Historical Narrative*, 119, n. 162.

44. Ibid., 120.

45. Ibid., 125.

46. John C. Jones to Thomas O. Larkin, 1 May 1845, quoted in Bancroft, *History of California*, 4:523. This letter was written on 1 May 1845. Jones also mentions that he cannot believe that such an undistinguished man as Pico could serve as governor.

47. Bancroft, *History of California*, 4:540.

48. Pico, *Historical Narrative*, 126.

49. Luis Vignes was born in Cadillac, France, and became a Mexican citizen. He is considered the founder of the California wine industry. His ranch was located at present-day Union Station in Los Angeles. See ibid., 71, n. 93; 127.

50. Ibid., 127–28.

51. Ibid., 128–29.

52. Ibid.

53. Pico to Abel Stearns, 7 March 1845, Abel Stearns Collection, box 49.

54. José de la Guerra y Noriega to Andrés Pico, 22 April 1845, CHD, HM 40518, Huntington Library.

55. "Pico a los conciudadanos de California," 27 August 1845, in AFP.

56. Pico, *Historical Narrative*, 122.

57. Pío Pico, *Decreto*, 23 May 1845, in AFP.

58. Bancroft, *History of California*, 4:543.

59. Minister Montes de Oca to Governor of California, 14 November 1845, quoted in Bancroft, *History of California*, 5:560–61, n. 6.

60. Bancroft argued that the friars "were old, worn-out, discouraged men, utterly incompetent to overcome the obstacles that beset their path as administrators." Bancroft, *History of California*, 4:546–47.

61. Pico's entire secularization decree is printed in ibid., 4: 340–41.

62. Ibid., 4:344.

63. Durán to Pico, 26 March 1845, printed and translated in ibid.

64. Englehardt, *Missions and Missionaries*, 4:348.

65. Bancroft, *History of California*, 4:548. A *bando* is a political decree usually circulated to the pueblos.

66. Ibid.

67. Fr. Real to Fr. Ánzar, 2 July 1845, quoted in Englehardt, *Missions and Missionaries*, 4:360.

68. Fr. Durán to Pico, 17 May 1845, quoted in ibid., 4:368.

69. Pico, secularization decree, 28 May 1845, in Pico, *Documentos*.

70. This rule applied to Carmelo, San Juan Bautista, San Juan Capistrano, and San Francisco Solano. See ibid.

71. Pico to Fr. Durán, 2 July 1845, quoted in Englehardt, *Missions and Missionaries*, 4:381.

72. Fr. Durán to Pico, 3 July 1845, quoted in ibid., 4:382–83.

73. Ibid.

74. Pico to Fr. Esténaga, 1–2 July 1845, quoted in ibid., 4:383.

75. Fray Durán to Pico, 10 July 1845, quoted in ibid., 4:384–85.

76. Ibid., 4:433.

77. Pico, "Reglamento para la enagenación y arriendo de las Misiones," 28 October 1845, in Olvera, *Documentos*, C–B 87. The decree is translated and printed in full in Englehardt, *Missions and Missionaries*, 4:445–50.

78. The information concerning the prices paid for the sale and renting of the missions was sent to Fray Durán by Pico, 6 February 1846, quoted in Englehardt, *Missions and Missionaries*, 4:468–69.

79. Pico to Fray Durán, 6 February 1846, quoted in ibid., 4:468–69.

80. The resolution to sell the missions that was introduced by Juan Bandini, after its approval by the assembly, was produced in a circular (bando) by Pico on 4 April 1846.

81. Pico, *Historical Narrative*, 122.

82. Bancroft, *History of California*, 5:560, n. 8. The government sold San Juan Bautista to O. Deleisseques for the price of the mission's debt; Mission San José was sold to Pío's brother Andrés Pico and Juan B.

Alvarado for $12,000; Mission San Luis Rey was sold to Pío's brother José Antonio Pico and José Antonio Cot for $2,437; Antonio Suñol and Pío's cousin Antonio María Pico purchased Mission San Rafael for $8,000; José Arnaz purchased Mission San Buenaventura for $12,000; Santiago Argüello was given title to Mission San Diego for past services to the government; Hugo Reid and William Workman purchased Mission San Gabriel for the prices of its debt; Mission Santa Barbara was sold to Richard Den for $7,500; José María Covarrubias and Joaquín Carrillo purchased Santa Inés for $7,000; Mission San Fernando was sold to Eulogio de Célis for $14,000; and one Soberanes purchased Mission Soledad for $800.

Chapter 5. Governor Pico and War with the United States

1. Castillo, *The Treaty of Guadalupe Hidalgo*, 13–17.
2. John August Sutter was a Swiss immigrant who came to California in 1839. After Sutter became a citizen, Governor Alvarado granted him the 48,800-acre ranch that was known as Nueva Helvetia. Located in the Sacramento Valley, the ranch was a strategic meeting place for Yankees who traversed the Sierra Nevada.
3. Quote by Starr, *California: a History*, 65–66.
4. Walker, *Bear Flag Rising*, 94.
5. Sessions of the Assembly, 2 March 1845, in Agustín Olvera, *Documentos*, BANC MSS C-B 87:13–14.
6. Bancroft, *History of California*, 5:38–39.
7. President Herrera made the official appointment on 3 September 1845. See ibid., 5:40.
8. Ibid., 5:41–42.
9. *Acta de junta militar*, Monterey, 11 April 1846, Departmental State Papers, Monterey, BANC MSS C-A 43:50–51.
10. Bancroft, *History of California*, 5:42.
11. Another possible reason the norteños may have supported Paredes was that his revolt was proclaimed in favor of the propertied classes. See Di Tella, *National Popular Politics*, 245.
12. Meyer and Sherman, *The Course of Mexican History*, 344.
13. Bancroft, *History of California*, 5:42.
14. Pico to Vallejo, 2 May 1846, Vallejo, *Documentos*, BANC MSS C-B 12:204.
15. Vallejo to Pico, 1 July 1846, Vallejo, *Documentos*, BANC MSS C-B 12:219. See also Bancroft, *History of California*, 5:43.

16. Bancroft, *History of California*, 5:61; Monroy, *Thrown Among Strangers*, 176.

17. Bancroft, *History of California*, 5:47.

18. In their histories of California, Vallejo and Alvarado say that Castro convoked the junta in order to displace Pico from power. See ibid., 5:48–49.

19. Haas, "War in California, 1846–1848," in Gutiérrez and Orsi, *Contested Eden* 338–39.

20. Pico to Bandini, 3 June 1846, Bandini, *Documentos*, C-B 68:72. Bandini was absent from the assembly meetings due to illness.

21. Bandini to Pico, 29 June 1846, Bandini, *Documentos*, C-B 68:80.

22. Bancroft, *History of California*, 5:49, n. 40. Pico also sold public lands near Los Angeles for $200.

23. Ibid., 5:53.

24. Castro to Pico, 8 June 1846, Bandini, *Documentos*, C-B 68:73.

25. Ibid.

26. Pico to Larkin, 29 June 1846, reprinted in *Historical Society of Southern California, Publications* 10:129–30.

27. Ibid.

28. Pico, Proclamation, 23 June 1846, Abel Stearns Collection, box 49, Huntington Library. A complete translation is found in Bancroft, *History of California*, 5:138.

29. Ibid.

30. Pico to Figueroa, Requeña, Stearns, Botello, and Gallardo, 27 June 1846, ASC, box 49.

31. Fox, *Macnamara's Irish Colony*, 127.

32. Ibid., 140.

33. Pico, *Historical Narrative*, 123.

34. Dorotea Valdez mentioned that Pico was negotiating a protectorate with English vice consul James Alexander Forbes. Forbes was a naturalized Mexican citizen, married to Californio Ana María Galindo. If true, nothing came of it. Beebe and Senkewicz, *Testimonios*, 40.

35. Ibid, 131. While he was constitutional governor in 1846, Pico issued two separate land grants to José Castro, one for more than 48,000 acres. If Castro was in fact his enemy, Pico was either acting as a diligent public servant in issuing grants or using the grants to make amends. See Hoffmann, *Reports of Land Cases*, app., 77, 89.

36. Pico, Proclamation, 27 July 1846, CHD, HM 40534, Huntington Library.

37. Pico, Proclamation, 16 July 1846, translated in Bancroft, *History of California*, 5:263, n. 9. The proclamation also explains how the draft will be organized.

38. Pico to Sloat, 25 July 1846, ASC, box 49.

39. These would come to be known as Pico's "eleventh hour grants," for which he was accused of fraud. See Pitt, *Decline of the Californios*, 87, 90, 92.

40. Castro, Proclamation on Leaving the Country, 9 August 1846, California File, FAC 96, Huntington Library.

41. Bancroft, *History of California*, 5:275, n. 22.

42. Pico, *Historical Narrative*, 134.

43. Bancroft, *History of California*, 5:271.

44. Quoted in Weber, *Foreigners in Their Native Land*, 118–19.

45. Ibid.

46. Pico, *Historical Narrative*, 140.

47. The war in California is an important subject but has been adequately covered by many historians. For a recent article covering the Californio side of the war, see Haas, "War in California, 1846–1848" in Gutiérrez and Orsi, *Contested Eden*, 331–55.

48. Pico, *Historical Narrative*, 141.

49. Ibid.

50. Ibid.

51. Henry D. Fitch to Archibald Gillespie, September 18, 1846, Archibald H. Gillespie Papers (Collection 133), Department of Special Collections, Charles E. Young Research Library, University of California, Los Angeles.

52. Pico to Minister of Foreign Relations, Interior and Police, Mexico, 27 October 1846, quoted in Tays, "Pio Pico's Correspondence," 114.

53. Ibid.

54. Ibid.

55. Pico to Minister of Interior and Foreign Relations, 15 November 1846, quoted in ibid., 125.

56. Ibid., 126.

57. Ibid., 127.

58. Ibid.

59. Ibid.

60. Antonio Lopez de Santa Anna to 1st Secretary of the Ministry of Foreign Affairs and Interior, 30 December 1846, quoted in ibid., 129.

61. Rosenus, *General M. G. Vallejo*, 169.

62. Pitt, *Decline of the Californios*, 35.

Chapter 6. Pico Reborn

1. Griswold del Castillo, *The Los Angeles Barrio*, 28.

2. Pitt, *Decline of the Californios*, 86.

3. Robinson, *Land in California*, 116.

4. Ibid., 126–27; Pitt, *Decline of the Californios*, 95–96.

5. Hoffmann, *Reports of Land Cases*. It must be noted that all grants were not petitioned before the court, although most of Pico's grants most likely were because they had been issued less than five years before the creation of the land commission.

6. Pico's term in office lasted from February 1845 to July 1846. Eighty-seven grants were issued in seven months of 1846 compared with only fifty-nine issued in eleven months in 1845.

7. Pitt, *Decline of the Californios*, 90.

8. Robinson, *Land in California*, 105.

9. Stevenson to Mason, 26 July 1848, quoted in Bennett, *Reports of Cases*, 1:579.

10. Ibid. His actual words were, "It is believed that he was not in that place between about the middle of June and the latter part of July [1846]."

11. Hoffmann, *Reports of Land Cases*, app., 52. The grant was made on 17 June 1846.

12. Castillo, *The Treaty of Guadalupe Hidalgo*, 72–77.

13. Quoted in Fox, *Macnamara's Irish Colony*, 188.

14. J. D. Stevenson to Governor Richard B. Mason, July 1848, in Bennett, *Reports of Cases*, app., 1.

15. Gray, *Forster vs. Pico*, 67–68.

16. Almaguer, *Racial Fault Lines*, 38.

17. Quoted in Monroy, *Thrown among Strangers*, 163.

18. See Cleland, *Cattle on a Thousand Hills*, 42–43.

19. Bancroft, *History of California*, 5:588.

20. Quoted in ibid., 5:590, n. 16.

21. Ibid.

22. Pitt, *Decline of the Californios*, 155.

23. Ibid., 125–26. The main complaints the protestors had was that they were excluded and had more in common with Washington than the invited Californios.

24. Pico won the 1853 seat on the Los Angeles City Council, although it appears he never served much time.

25. *El Clamor Público*, 10 July 1855.

26. Ibid., 7 August 1855.

27. Ibid., 28 August 1855. Ramirez was stretching the truth. Californios often won decisions in state court.

28. Ibid., 23 October 1855.

29. Ibid.

30. Gray, *Forster vs. Pico*, 96.

31. Pitt, *Decline of the Californios*, 199.

32. Quoted in Cleland, *Cattle on a Thousand Hills*, 42.

33. Pico was also confronted with squatters. He ordered his mayordomo to confront the squatters who were camped somewhere at Rancho Santa Margarita. They were eventually persuaded to leave. See Pico to Ortega, 24 May 1855, Pico Papers, Additions, folder 40.

34. Castillo, *The Los Angeles Barrio*, 106–107.

35. Ibid., 105.

36. Ibid., 107.

37. *Los Angeles Star*, 6 August 1853.

38. Ibid., 7 February 1857. See also Gray, *Forster vs. Pico*, 84–85.

39. *El Clamor Público*, July 26, 1856.

40. Pitt, *Decline of the Californios*, 162–66; Castillo, *The Los Angeles Barrio*, 108–109; *El Clamor Público*, July 26, 1856.

41. *El Clamor Público*, September 27, 1856.

42. Ibid. The California Anti-Vagrancy Act of 1855 was an obvious political attack against Mexicans. It became known as the Greaser Laws, and prohibited the free movement of Mexicans and rejected the state constitutional requirement that laws be translated into Spanish. The law was later repealed.

43. Various issues of *El Clamor Público* during this period use this term to describe the native Mexican inhabitants of California. Although the term *hijos del país* is used throughout Latin America, it is probable that this term as applied to Californios surfaced during these tense struggles between gringos and Mexicanos.

44. *El Clamor Público*, October 4, 1856.

45. Ibid., October 11, 1856.

46. Ortega to Pico, 7 November 1860, Pico Papers, Additions.

47. Gray, *Forster vs. Pico*, 93–94.

Chapter 7. The Making of an American Don

1. Leonard Pitt, who wrote the first important study of economic and political decline among the Californios, correctly argued that "in the south, islands of rancho lands remained intact, at least until the 1870's." Nevertheless, little is said about real estate development. Pitt, *Decline of the Californios*, 250. Douglas Monroy contends that at the same time, generally speaking, "the Californio rancheros had been dispossessed of their land." Monroy, *Thrown Among Strangers*, 228. Like these two, others have written about Mexicans in California as having agency, that is, defending themselves in the face of oppression, yet most focus on political challenges, an emerging social consciousness, or the creation of a racialized, subordinate population. See Castillo, *The Los Angeles Barrio*; Camarillo, *Chicanos in a Changing Society*; and Almaguer, *Racial Fault Lines*.

2. California State Archive, Spanish and Mexican Land Grant Maps, 1855–1875, Sacramento, Calif.

3. Pico to José Joaquín Ortega, 1 October 1848, Pico Papers, Additions, folder 40.

4. Pitt, *Decline of the Californios*. 239. De la Guerra eventually won the state judgeship.

5. Cleland, *Cattle on a Thousand Hills*, 106.

6. Gray, *Forster vs. Pico*, 54–56.

7. Pitt, *Decline of the Californios*, 104–105.

8. Newland and Dallas, *Pio Pico Adobe Restoration*, 24.

9. Pío Pico, receipt book from Rancho Paso de Bartolo, 1874, Mathew Keller Collection, Huntington Library, box 3 (13).

10. Ibid.

11. Ripley, "The San Fernando Pass," Part 14.

12. Ibid.

13. Robinson, *Los Angeles from the Days of the Pueblo*, 45, 48.

14. *Pico v. Cohn et al.*, California State Supreme Court case no. 9665, July 30 1885, California State Archives, Office of the Secretary of State, Sacramento. This document shows that by 1883, Pico personally occupied only fifty of the nearly four thousand acres of the Ranchito that he still owned; the rest was rented to tenants.

15. Gray, *Forster vs. Pico*, 82.

16. Downey would become governor of California in 1861.

17. California Reports, *McFarland and Downey v. Pico*, 8 Cal. 626; 1857 Cal.

18. California Reports, *Pico v. Cohn*, 78 Cal. 384; 20 P. 706; 1889 Cal. At one point, during his most tragic, bitter, and hard-fought suit, *Pico v. Cohn*, he hired four law firms, including eleven lawyers, to aid him. All eleven lawyers were probably not fully involved in the case. Yet it is certain that the four firms were in Pico's employment.

19. José Joaquín Ortega to Pico, 23 October 1856, Pico Papers, Additions, folder 22.

20. José Joaquín Ortega to Pico, 10 March 1857, ibid.

21. José Joaquín Ortega to Pico, 22 March 1857, ibid.

22. José Joaquín Ortega to Pico, 4 July 1857, ibid.

23. This was market price according to Cleland, *Cattle on a Thousand Hills*, 110.

24. Williamson, "Six Ways to Compute," *Measuring Worth*, 2008. Available [online]: www.measuringworth.com [24 August 2008].

25. Abel Stearns to Cave J. Couts, 4 February 1858, Cave J. Couts Collection, Huntington Library, CT 2178. This amount had the purchasing power of nearly $321,000 today.

26. Antonio María Ortega to Pío Pico, 29 October 1858, Pico Papers, Additions, folder 20.

27. *Pico et al v. Stevens*, California Reports, 18 Cal. 376; 1861 Cal.

28. José Joaquín Ortega to Pico, 1 March 1859, Pico Papers, Additions, folder 22. The Spanish term *cuñado* is translated as brother-in-law.

29. Pío Pico to José Joaquín Ortega, 14 March 1859, ibid., folder 40.

30. Gray, *Forster vs. Pico*, 82–83.

31. Pico to Ortega, 14 March 1859, Pico Papers, Additions, folder 40.

32. Pico to Ortega, 29 March 1859, ibid.

33. *Pico v. De la Guerra et al.*, California Reports, 18 Cal. 422; 1861 Cal. The suit concerned a five-thousand-dollar loan Pico made to the family of William Hartnell, the former mission inspector whose reports led to Pico's replacement at Mission San Luis Rey. Hartnell, who married into the de la Guerra family, died in 1854 indebted to Pico. When Pico presented the debt to the Guerra family in the late 1850s, the interest and loan together had amounted to more than $11,000, which Pico was awarded in the lower courts. Unfortunately, under Guerra's 1861 appeal to the California Supreme Court, the defendants were dismissed

from liability due to a technicality; the ten-month period for claims presented against the estate had elapsed when Pico's lawyers filed in 1855. Because Pico's lawyers had filed the claim with the court and not directly to the executors, Pico was technically three days late.

34. Quoted in Monroy, *Thrown among Strangers*, 227.

35. Quoted in Gray, *Forster vs. Pico*, 215.

36. Pico mentioned in his *Historical Narrative* that he encountered an American war frigate and that he won seven thousand dollars from the officers aboard. Pico, *Historical Narrative*, 143–44.

37. Robinson, *Los Angeles from the Days of the Pueblo*, 49.

38. Monroy, *Thrown among Strangers*, 227.

39. Pitt, for instance, felt it worthy to mention that Pablo de la Guerra spent eighty dollars on a chair when he could have used the money to pay legal fees. The Guerra family was among the richest in southern California. See Pitt, *Decline of the Californios*, 128. Pitt did mention, however, that this was a "puritan" view.

40. Pitt argued that the entire sum of bets was $25,000 in cash, the rest in livestock. This amount was divided among the numerous individuals who attended the race. See ibid. As late as December 2001, the *Los Angeles Times* reported that "the race contributed to the downfall of Pico, who lost $25,000 and who, more than four decades later, would die penniless." *Los Angeles Times*, December 23, 2001. This exaggeration has become part of the romantic folklore of the high-spending rancheros of the 1850s. The period between the 1852 race and "four decades later" is totally ignored and characterizes the lack of interest historians have had in Pico's post-1848 life. In fact, it is this same approach that has led historians to conclude that Pico simply returned from Mexico, lost his lands, and came to depend on charity for his living expenses. See, for example, Monroy, *Thrown Among Strangers*, 227. Monroy, of course, was not focusing on Pico's biography in his study.

41. *Los Angeles Star*, 23 October 1852; Gray, *Forster vs. Pico*, 81.

42. Gray, *Forster vs. Pico*, 97.

43. Pico to Ortega, 7 March 1859, folder 40, Pico Papers, Additions.

44. *Pío Pico v. Rómulo Pico*, California Supreme Court, 1880, Case no. 6977, California State Archives, Office of the Secretary of State, Sacramento, Calif.

45. Ibid.

46. Ibid.

47. Ibid. As early as 1859 Pico was considering the sale of his interests in the 122,000-acre rancho due to a deteriorating economic situation. See Pío Pico to José Joaquín Ortega, 7 March 1859, Pico Papers, Additions.

48. *Pico v. Pico*, California Supreme Court, Case no. 6977. In Pico's words, "One day Andres came to my office; I was writing and he told me what he wanted, that he wished that I would give him something in order that he might aid me in my business; he could not help because he had nothing; it was necessary that I should give him something that he could aid me as security."

49. Ibid.

50. Albert Johnson to Mother, Mrs. George Granville Johnson, 8 November 1869, Albert Johnson Letters, Arizona Historical Society, Tucson. Albert Johnson was married to Pico's niece.

51. Robinson, *Los Angeles from the Days of the Pueblo*, 64–65.

52. Gray, *Forster vs. Pico*, 124; See also Albert Johnson to Mrs. George Granville Johnson, 23 September 1869, Albert Johnson Letters. The trip seems to have lasted from July to September 1869.

53. Robinson, *Los Angeles from the Days of the Pueblo*, 73.

54. Ibid., 74–75.

55. Putnam, "Pico's Building: Its Genealogy and Biography," *Historical Society of Southern California* 39 (March 1957): 75. Mariano de Villa deeded the building, located next to the Bella Union Hotel, to Pico in 1859 for an unknown amount. In 1869 William Workman, F. P. F. Temple, and Isaias W. Hellman decided to create a partnership with the purpose of opening a bank in Los Angeles. They contracted with Pico to lease his building for this purpose. The bank was never formally called the Los Angeles Bank, though that name was used on some lawsuits. After passing through various owners and partnerships, it became known as the Farmers and Merchants Bank of Los Angeles, the first incorporated bank in the city.

56. Ibid., 82.

57. *Pico v. Cohn et al.*

58. Albert Johnson to Mrs. George Granville Johnson, 8 November 1869, Albert Johnson Letters.

59. For the legal battle see Stephenson, "Forster v. Pico," and Gray, *Forster vs. Pico*.

60. Gray, *Forster vs. Pico*, 129.

61. Ibid., 205–208. According to Gray, Pico's lawyers pressed Forster about why Pico would sell him the entire ranch for half its value, especially when Pico had been offered $75,000 for it. But they did not see the

importance of a receipt showing that Forster purchased 1,500 head of cattle and 150 horses from Pico for a total of $4,920. Adding this price to the amount of Pico's debt equaled what Forster paid for the ranch, which is roughly half of $75,000. This proves that Forster intended to purchase only half of the ranch.

62. Very little is known about Pico's wife, María Ignacia Alvarado de Pico, aside from information in an obituary, as her name rarely appears in the records.

63. *Pico v. Coleman et al.*, California Reports, 47 Cal. 65; 1873 Cal.

64. Ibid.

65. The original contract is as follows: "Saved todos por estar presentes: que yo Pio Pico del condado de Los Angeles, y Estado de California, por y en consideracion de un peso, en plata a mi pagado en mano, por Maria Martinez del mismo condado y Estado por las presentes confieso haber recibido, he contratado, cedido, vendido y enagenado, y por las presentes contrato, cedo y vendo y enageno a la espresada, Maria Martinez, y sus herederos y suscesores para siempre un pedazo de terreno que contiene de oriente a poniente ochocientas sesenta y cinco varas y de norte a sur doscientas noventa y cuatro, cituado al norte de la casa princi- pal de mi residencia y avitacion: *Cuyo terreno cedo, vendo y enageno con el derecho, titulo, intereses,* pretenciones o demanda, que por las leyes, o por la justicia tengo un posecion o puedo tener en espectacion en y, *a todo aquel terreno cituado y estando en el mencionado* condado de los Angeles, conocido por los nombres de Paso de Bartolo y S. Rafael" (emphasis added). *Pico v. Coleman,* Transcript on Appeal, 1873; 42, WPA no. 3177, California Supreme Court.

66. Ibid.

67. Gray, *Forster vs. Pico,* 61–63.

68. *Pico v. Coleman,* Transcript on Appeal, 1873. Olvera also claimed that because of Pico's litigious character, he was preparing for a suit.

69. Ibid.

70. *Pico v. Cohn et al.,* California Reports, 78 Cal 384; 20 p. 706; 1889 Cal.

71. In the water rights case, Nicolas Colimas, water commissioner for Los Nietos, actually destroyed the dam at the Ranchito. See *Pico v. Colimas et als.,* 32 Cal. 578; 1867 Cal.

72. *Pico v. Cuyas,* California Reports, 47 Cal. 161; 1873 Cal; *Pico v. Cuyas,* California Reports, 48 Cal. 639; 1874.

73. *Pico v. Los Angeles Gas Company,* Transcript on Appeal, 1874, 5, WPA no. 1219, California Supreme Court; *Pico v. Gallardo,* California Reports, 52 Cal. 206; 1877 Cal.

74. *Pico v. Los Angeles Gas Company*, Transcript on Appeal, 5.

75. *San Francisco Chronicle*, 15 February 1876; Gray, *Forster vs. Pico*, 227.

76. Gray, *Forster vs. Pico*, 227; *Los Angeles Times*, 27 November 1895.

77. Pico's testimony was recorded in 1877 by Thomas Savage, an agent of collector and historian Hubert Howe Bancroft. Eighteen seventy-five marked the first twenty-five years of statehood, a period when historians, including Bancroft, were scrambling to set down the state's young American history as well as record its Spanish past. Pico may have been contacted by Bancroft's writer for just this reason. See Pico, *Narración Histórica*, MSS C–D 13. As noted earlier, it was translated and published as Cole and Welcome, *Don Pio Pico's Historical Narrative*.

78. Estate of Andrés Pico, 56 California Reports, Cal. 413; 1880 Cal.; *Pio Pico v. Romulo Pico*, 56 California Reports, Cal. 453; 1880 Cal.

79. Ibid.

80. Ibid.

81. Gray, *Forster vs. Pico*, 229–30.

82. *Pico v. Kalisher*, 55 California Reports, Cal. 153; 1880 Cal.

Chapter 8. "An Occasional Miscarriage of Justice"

1. *Los Angeles Times*, 19 February 1891.

2. Ibid., 9 May 1889.

3. This amount has the same value as nearly $5.7 million today. Samuel H. Williamson, "Six Ways to Compute the Relative Value of a U.S. Dollar Amount, 1790 to Present," *Measuring Worth*, 2008. Available [online]: www.eh.net/ehresources/howmuch/dollarq.php [22 August 2008].

4. *Pico v. Cohn*, Transcript on Appeal, 1884; 7, WPA no. 15997, California Supreme Court. Ranchito was located in modern day Whittier, California. In 1883, the Ranchito contained only 3,785 of the original 8,894 acres. Pico owned an additional 560 acres adjoining the Ranchito.

5. *Pico v. Kalisher*, 55 California Reports, Cal. 153; 1880 Cal.; Estate of Andrés Pico, 56 California Reports, Cal. 413; 1880 Cal.; *Pio Pico v. Romulo Pico*, 56 California Reports, Cal. 453; 1880 Cal.; *Lucas v. Pico*, 55 California Reports, Cal. 126; 1880 Cal.

6. *Los Angeles Times*, 12 July 1882.

7. *Los Angeles Times*, 6 December 1884.

8. *Savings and Loan Society v. Pico et. al.* Printed in *Pico v. Cohn*, Transcript on Appeal, 1884, 311.

9. Ibid.

10. Ibid.

11. The argument that Pío was ignorant of the law was a simple strategy his lawyers used to protect him from his careless actions. Nevertheless, many seem to incorrectly believe that this was a valid characterization of Pío and other Californios.

12. John Forster, Pico's brother-in-law, was awarded the entire Rancho Santa Margarita in the 1873 case *Forster v. Pico*. See Gray, *Forster vs. Pico.*

13. *Savings and Loan Society v. Pico et. al.* in *Pico v. Cohn*, Transcript on Appeal, 1884; 313.

14. Quoted in *Pico v. Cohn*, 1884; 17, WPA no. 15997, California Supreme Court.

15. Quoted in ibid.

16. As late as 1890 the two men were vice presidents on a Republican Party committee to elect Col. H. H. Markham governor of California. *Los Angeles Times*, 24 August 1890. He was also present at Pico's signing of Cohn's loan to Pico; Pico's lawyers suspected that Brunson was aware of Cohn's plot but could never prove it.

17. Brunson served as attorney in opposition to Pico's interests in the following cases: *Savings and Loan Society v. Pico; Pico v. Kalisher; Pico v. Forster; Porter v. Pico; Pico v. Los Angeles Gas Company; Pico v. Cohn*; and surprisingly, *Pico v. Pico.*

18. *Pico v. Cohn*, 1884; 141–42, WPA no. 15997.

19. Ibid., 159.

20. Ibid., 162.

21. Ibid.

22. Ibid., 166.

23. Ibid., 341.

24. One witness was Wolf Kalisher, whom Pío had bitterly defeated in a lawsuit. See ibid., 336.

25. *Pico v. Cohn*, Brief of Appellant, no. 9665; 34, California Supreme Court. 26. *Pico v. Cohn*, 1884; 141–42, WPA no. 15997; 63.

27. Ibid., 58.

28. Cohn demanded the lease revenue as part of his initial agreement to pay Pico's debts. See *Cohn and Pico v. Hubbell and Loomis*, 11 April 1883, printed in ibid., 236. At the time, Pico occupied fifty acres of the Ranchito. The other land had been occupied through leases

and contracts. On that land he had some vines and about a hundred goats. In January of 1884 he leased out the remaining fifty acres.

29. It is uncertain whether the loan from his nephews was a reliable offer. Because Pico was broke, it seems obvious that he would have had to secure a separate loan on his properties to pay Cohn. Although this is hardly an ideal solution, the sale of his commercial property would have been sufficient to repay his nephews. Pico would have also generated a large sum of money on the leases of land on the Ranchito.

30. *Pico v. Cohn*, 67 California Reports, Cal. 258; 7 p. 680; 1885 Cal.

31. *Pico v. Julius B. Cohn*, California Reports Cal. 129; 25 p. 970; 1891.

32. *Los Angeles Times*, 12 February 1891. Although the court had decided on the case the day before this paper was published, the reporter had conducted the interview at an earlier date.

33. Ibid.

34. See note 14.

35. Gray, *Forster vs. Pico*, 138.

36. *Pico v. B. T. Williams*, Answer to Alternative Writ of Prohibition, 1887; 17, WPA no. 8493, California Supreme Court.

37. Ibid.

38. Julius B. Cohn was the son of Bernard Cohn, who had died by the time of the final appeal. See California Reports, *Pico v. Julius Cohn*, California Reports, 1891.

39. Ibid.

Chapter 9. *La Última Palabra*

1. *Estate of Pío Pico*, case number 1010, Los Angeles Superior Court Archives.

2. Gray, *Forster vs. Pico*, 231; see also *Pico v. Cohn*, 91, California Reports, 129 (1891).

3. E. Chazan to Pío Pico, 24 September 1891, Pío Pico Papers, folder 36.

4. Ibid.

5. Pío Pico to E. Chazan, 24 October 1891, ibid., folder 40. Pico's exact words were, "Las circunstancias . . . no dieron timepo á elucidar las dependencias contenidas en el territorio."

6. *Los Angeles Herald*, 12 February 1891.

7. *Los Angeles Times*, 12 February 1899.

8. Ibid.

9. Ibid., 13 February 1891.

10. Ibid.

11. Ibid., 19 and 22 February 1891.

12. Ibid., 6 March 1891.

13. *Los Angeles Herald*, 20 February and March 8 1891. The reporter was referring to the Forster brothers. They even argued that the Forsters had offered Pico a home at Santa Margarita.

14. *Los Angeles Times*, 15 March 1891.

15. Ibid., 13 March 1891.

16. Ibid., 8 and 15 March 1891.

17. George H. Smith to Pío Pico, 17 September 1891, Pío Pico Papers, folder 39.

18. Juan Luco to Pío Pico, 17 October 1891, ibid., folder 37.

19. *Los Angeles Times*, 1 September 1892.

20. Ibid., 7 July 1893.

21. Ibid.

22. Many Catholic historians, especially Zephyrin Englehardt, blame Pico for being the greatest enemy of the mission system. See Englehardt, *Missions and Missionaries*, vol. 4. Pico was later transferred to the mausoleum located at the Homestead Museum near Ranchito. He rests beside his wife, María Ignacia Alvarado.

23. *Los Angeles Times*, 14 September 1894.

Bibliography

Manuscripts and Archives

Abel Stearns Collection. Huntington Library, San Marino.

Albert Johnson Letters. Arizona Historical Society, Tucson.

Alvarado, Juan Bautista. *Historia de California*, 1876, 5 vols. Bancroft Library, University of California, Berkeley.

Archibald H. Gillespie Papers. Department of Special Collections, Charles E. Young Research Library, University of California, Los Angeles.

Archives of California, 1767–1848. Bancroft Library, University of California, Berkeley.

Archivo de la Familia Pico. Bancroft Library, University of California, Berkeley.

Archivo General de la Nación, Provincias Internas Tomo 1 (Californios). Microfilm Collection, Bancroft Library, University of California, Berkeley.

Bandini, Juan. *Documentos para la historia de California*. Bancroft Library, University of California, Berkeley.

The California File. Huntington Library, San Marino.

California Historical Documents Collection. Huntington Library, San Marino.

Cave J. Couts Collection. Huntington Library, San Marino.

César, Julio. *Cosas de Indios*. Bancroft Library, University of California, Berkeley.

Documentos Históricas de California. Bancroft Library, University of California, Berkeley.

Guerra Family Collection. Santa Barbara Mission-Archive Library, Santa
    Barbara.
Hayes, Benjamin. *Materials Concerning the Missions of Alta California*. Ban-
    croft Library, University of California, Berkeley.
Land Case Files, 1852–63. Bancroft Library, University of California, Berkeley.
Los Angeles County Records. Huntington Library, San Marino.
Moreno, José Matias. *Documentos para la história de California*. Bancroft
    Library, University of California, Berkeley.
Olvera, Agustín. *Documentos para la história de California*. Bancroft Library,
    University of California, Berkeley.
Pico, Pío. *Documentos para la história de California*. Bancroft Library, Uni-
    versity of California, Berkeley.
———. *Narración Histórica*. Bancroft Library, University of California,
    Berkeley.
———. *Pío Pico Papers, 1845–1846*. Bancroft Library, University of Cali-
    fornia, Berkeley.
———. *Pío Pico Papers, Additions, 1836–1894*. Bancroft Library, University
    of California, Berkeley.
Vallejo, Mariano Guadalupe. *Documentos para la historia de California*, 36
    vols. Bancroft Library, University of California, Berkeley.

Published Primary Sources

Beebe, Rose Marie, and Robert M. Senkewicz, eds. *Testimonios: Early
    California through the Eyes of Women*. Berkeley: Heyday Books, 2006.
Bennett, Nathaniel. *Reports of Cases Argued and Determined in the Supreme
    Court of the State of California*. San Francisco: Marvin and Hitch-
    cock, 1851.
Figueroa, José. *The Manifesto to the Mexican Republic*. Oakland, Calif.:
    Biobooks, 1952.
———. *Reglamento provisional para la secularizacion de las Misiones de
    la Alta California, 9 de Agosto de 1834*. Archives of California,
    Missions and Colonization, Bancroft Library, University of Cali-
    fornia, Berkeley.
Hoffmann, Hon. Ogden. *Reports of Land Cases Determined in the United
    States District Court for the Northern District of California*. San Fran-
    cisco: Numa Hubert Publisher, 1862.
Lozano, José María, and Manuel Dublan, eds. "Decreto del Congreso
    Mejicano secularizando las Misiones, 17 de Agosto, de 1833," in
    Legislacion mexicana; o, coleccion completa de las disposiciones legislativas

expedidas desde la independencia de la republica. 5 vols. Mexico: Imprenta del Comercio, 1876.

Osio, Antonio María, *The History of Alta California: A Memoir of Mexican California,* trans. and ed., Rose Marie Beebe and Robert M. Senkewiczs. Madison: University of Wisconsin Press, 1996.

Pico, Pío. *Don Pío Pico's Historical Narrative,* trans. Arthur P. Botello and ed. Martin Cole and Henry Welcome. Glendale, Calif.: Arthur H. Clark, 1973.

Published Legal Cases

Estate of Andrés Pico, 56 California Reports 413 (1880).

Estate of Pío Pico, Los Angeles Superior Court Archive case no. 1010 (1894).

Hancock v. Pico, 47 California Reports 161 (1873).

McFarland and Downey v. Pico, 8 California Reports 626 (1857).

Pico v. Cohn, 78 California Reports 384 (1889).

Pico v. Coleman et al., 47 California Reports 65 (1873).

Pico v. Colimas et al., 32 California Reports 578 (1867).

Pico v. Cuyas, 47 California Reports 161 (1873).

Pico v. Cuyas, 48 California Reports 639 (1874).

Pico v. De La Guerra et al., 18 California Reports 422 (1861).

Pico v. Gallardo, 52 California Reports 206 (1877).

Pico v. Julius B. Cohn, 129 California Reports 970 (1891).

Pico v. Kalisher, 55 California Reports 153 (1880).

Pío Pico v. Romulo Pico, 56 California Reports 453 (1880).

Pico v. Stevens, 18 California Reports 376 (1861).

Legal Briefs

Pico v. B. T. Williams, Answer to Alternative Writ of Prohibition, California Supreme Court, WPA no. 8493, State Archives, Office of the Secretary of State, Sacramento (1887).

Pico v. Cohn, Brief of Appellant, California Supreme Court, Case no. 9665, State Archives, Office of the Secretary of State, Sacramento (1885).

Pico v. Cohn, Transcript on Appeal, California Supreme Court, WPA no. 15997, State Archives, Office of the Secretary of State, Sacramento (1884).

Pico v. Cohn et al., California State Supreme Court, case no. 9665, California State Archives, Office of the Secretary of State, Sacramento (1885).

Pico v. Coleman, Transcript on Appeal, California Supreme Court, WPA no. 317, State Archives, Office of the Secretary of State, Sacramento (1873).

Pico v. Los Angeles Gas Company, Transcript on Appeal, California Supreme Court, WPA no. 1219, State Archives, Office of the Secretary of State, Sacramento (1874).

Pico v. Pico, California State Archives, California Supreme Court, Case no. 6977, Office of the Secretary of State, Sacramento (1880).

Books, Articles, and Pamphlets

Almaguer, Tomás. *Racial Fault Lines: The Historical Origins of White Supremacy in California.* Berkeley and Los Angeles: University of California Press, 1994.

Alonso, Ana María. *Thread of Blood: Colonialism, Revolution, and Gender on Mexico's Northern Frontier.* Tucson: University of Arizona Press, 1997.

Anna, Timothy E. *Forging Mexico, 1821–1835.* Lincoln: University of Nebraska Press, 1998.

Bancroft, Hubert Howe. *History of California.* 7 vols. San Francisco, Calif.: The History Company, 1886.

———. *Pioneer Register and Index.* Baltimore, Md.: Regional Publishing, 1964.

Billington, Ray Allen. *The Far Western Frontier, 1830–1860.* Albuquerque: University of New Mexico Press, 1995.

Bolton, Herbert Eugene, ed. *Font's Complete Diary: A Chronicle of the Founding of San Francisco.* Berkeley: University of California Press, 1933.

Borrows, Henry D. "Pio Pico: A Biographical and Character Sketch of the Last Mexican Governor of Alta California." *Annual Publication of the Historical Society of Southern California* (1894).

Brading, D.A. *The Origins of Mexican Nationalism.* Cambridge, U.K.: University of Cambridge, Center of Latin American Studies, 1985.

Camarillo, Albert. *Chicanos in a Changing Society: From Mexican Pueblos to American Barrios in Santa Barbara and Southern California, 1848–1930.* Cambridge, Mass.: Harvard University Press, 1996.

Carrera, Magali M. *Imagining Identity in New Spain: Race, Lineage, and the Colonial Body in Portraiture and Casta Painting.* Austin: University of Texas Press, 2003.

Castañeda, Antonia I. "Engendering the History of Alta California, 1769–1848: Gender, Sexuality, and the Family," in Ramón Gutiérrez and Richard J. Orsi, eds. *Contested Eden: California Before the Gold Rush.* Berkeley: University of California Press, 1998.

Castillo, Edward D., ed. *Native American Perspectives on the Hispanic Colonization of Alta California.* New York and London: Garland Publishing, 1991.

Castillo, Richard Griswold del. *The Los Angeles Barrio, 1850–1890.* Berkeley and Los Angeles: University of California Press, 1979.

———. *The Treaty of Guadalupe Hidalgo: A Legacy of Conflict.* Norman: University of Oklahoma Press, 1990.

Cleland, Robert Glass. *The Cattle on a Thousand Hills: Southern California, 1850–1880.* San Marino, Calif.: Henry E. Huntington Library and Art Gallery, 1941.

Cole, Martin. *Pio Pico Miscellany.* Whittier, Calif.: Governor Pico Mansion Society, 1978.

Cowan, Robert C. *Ranchos of California: A List of Spanish Concessions, 1775–1822, and Mexican Grants, 1822–1846.* Fresno, Calif.: Academy Library Guild, 1956.

Dakin, Susanna Bryant. *The Lives of William Hartnell.* Stanford, Calif.: Stanford University Press, 1949.

Di Tella, Torcuato S. *National Popular Politics in Early Independent Mexico, 1820–1847.* Albuquerque: University of New Mexico Press, 1996.

Englehardt, Zephyrin. *The Missions and Missionaries of California.* 4 vols. San Francisco, Calif.: James H. Barry, 1913.

———. *San Luis Rey Mission.* San Francisco: James H. Barry, 1921.

Etulain, Richard W., ed. *Writing Western History: Essays on Major Western Historians.* Albuquerque: University of New Mexico Press, 1991.

Farris, Glenn J., ed. *The Diary and Copybook of William E. P. Hartnell: Visitador General of the Missions of Alta California in 1839 and 1840.* Santa Clara: California Mission Studies Association, 2004.

Fox, John. *Macnamara's Irish Colony and the United States Taking of California in 1846.* Jefferson, N.C.: McFarland & Company, 2000.

Geary, Gerald J. *The Secularization of the California Missions, 1810–1846.* Washington, D.C.: Catholic University of America, 1934.

González, Michael J. *This Small City Will Be a Mexican Paradise: Exploring the Origins of Mexican Culture in Los Angeles, 1821–1846.* Albuquerque: University of New Mexico Press, 2005.

Gray, Paul Bryan. *Forster vs. Pico: The Struggle for the Rancho Santa Margarita.* Spokane, Wash.: Arthur H. Clark, 1998.

Green, Stanley. C. *The Mexican Republic: The First Decade, 1823–32.* Pittsburgh: University of Pennsylvania Press, 1987.

Guedea, Virginia. "The First Popular Elections in Mexico City, 1812–1813," in Jaime E. Rodríguez O., ed. *The Origin of Mexican National Politics.* Wilmington, Del.: Scholarly Resources Inc., 1997.

Gutiérrez, Ramón, and Richard J. Orsi, eds. *Contested Eden: California before the Gold Rush.* Berkeley and Los Angeles: University of California Press, 1998.

Haas, Lisbeth. *Conquests and Historical Identities in California, 1769–1936.* Berkeley and Los Angeles: University of California Press, 1995.

———. "War in California, 1846-1848," in Ramón Gutiérrez and Richard J. Orsi, eds. *Contested Eden: California before the Gold Rush.* Berkeley and Los Angeles: University of California Press, 1998.

Hackel, Steven W. *Children of Coyote: Indian Spanish Relations in Colonial California, 1769–1850.* Chapel Hill: University of North Carolina Press, 2005.

———. "Land, Labor, and Production: The Colonial Economy of Spanish and Mexican California," in Ramón Gutiérrez and Richard J. Orsi, eds. *Contested Eden: California Before the Gold Rush* (Berkeley: University of California Press, 1998).

———. "Sources of Rebellion: Indian Testimony and the Mission San Gabriel Uprising of 1785." *Ethnohistory* 50 (Fall 2003).

Hale, Charles. *Mexican Liberalism in the Age of Mora.* New Haven, Conn.: Yale University Press, 1968.

Hoffmann, Ogden. *Reports of Land Cases Determined in the United States District Court for the Northern District of California.* San Francisco, Calif.: Numa Hubert Publisher, 1862.

Holter, Howard. *Pio Pico State Historic Park.* Sacramento: California Department of Parks and Recreation, 1986.

Hurtado, Albert. *Sex, Gender, and Culture in Old California.* Albuquerque: University of New Mexico Press, 1999.

Hutchinson, Alan. *Frontier Settlement in Mexican California: The Híjar-Padrés Colony and Its Origins, 1769–1835.* New Haven, Conn.: Yale University Press, 1969.

Jackson, Robert H. *Indian Population Decline: The Missions of Northwestern New Spain, 1687–1840.* Albuquerque: University of New Mexico Press, 1994.

Jackson, Robert H., and Edward Castillo. *Indians, Franciscans, and Spanish Colonization: The Impact of the Mission System on California Indians.* Albuquerque: University of New Mexico Press, 1995.

Krauze, Enrique. *Mexico, Biography of Power: History of Modern Mexico, 1810–1996.* New York: Harper Collins, 1997.

Lepowsky, Maria. "Indian Revolts and Cargo Cults: Ritual Violence and Revitalization in California and New Guinea," in Michael E.

Harkin, ed., *Reassessing Revitalization Movements: Perspectives from North America and the Pacific Islands.* Lincoln: University of Nebraska Press, 2004.

Mason, William Marvin. *The Census of 1790: A Demographic History of Colonial California.* Novato, Calif.: Ballena Press, 1998.

McWilliams, Carey. *North from Mexico: The Spanish-Speaking People of the United States.* Philadelphia, Pa.: J. B. Lippincott, 1949.

Meyer, Michael C., and William L. Sherman. *The Course of Mexican History.* 5th ed. New York: Oxford University Press, 1994.

Miller, Robert R. *Juan Alvarado: Governor of California, 1836–1842.* Norman: University of Oklahoma Press, 1998.

Monroy, Douglas. *Thrown among Strangers: The Making of Mexican Culture in Frontier California.* Berkeley and Los Angeles: University of California Press, 1990.

Moyer, Cecil C. *Historic Ranchos of San Diego.* San Diego, Calif.: Union-Tribune Publishing, 1969.

Pauley, Kenneth. "Weights and Measurements in California's Mission Period: Part II—Area Measurements, in Archaeological Cultural and Historical Perspectives on Alta California." *Proceedings of the 20th Annual Conference of the California Mission Studies Association* (2003).

Phillips, George Harwood. *Chiefs and Challengers: Indian Resistance and Cooperation in Southern California.* Berkeley and Los Angeles: University of California Press, 1975.

————."Indians and the Breakdown of the Spanish Mission System in California." *Ethnohistory* 21:4 (Fall 1974).

Pitt, Leonard. *Decline of the Californios: A Social History of the Spanish-Speaking Californians, 1846–1890.* Berkeley and Los Angeles: University of California Press, 1966.

Putnam, Frank B. "Pico's Building: Its Genealogy and Biography." *Historical Society of Southern California* 39 (1957).

Ripley, Vernette Snyder. "The San Fernando (Newhall) Pass. Part 14, 1865–76: Oil and the San Fernando Pass." *Southern California Quarterly* (1948).

Robinson, Alfred. *Life in California: During a Residence of Several Years in That Territory.* New York: Da Capo Press, 1969.

Robinson, W. W. *Land in California: The Story of Mission Lands, Ranchos, Squatters, Mining Claims, Railroad Grants, Land Script, Homesteads.* Berkeley and Los Angeles: University of California Press, 1948.

————. *Los Angeles from the Days of the Pueblo: A Brief History and Guide to the Plaza Area.* Los Angeles: California Historical Society, 1959.

Rodríguez, O., and E. Jaime "The Constitution of 1824 and the Formation of the Mexican State," in Rodríguez O., Jaime E., ed. *The Origin of Mexican National Politics.* Wilmington, Del.: Scholarly Resources, 1997.

Rosenus, Alan. *General M. G. Vallejo and the Advent of the Americans.* Albuquerque: University of New Mexico Press, 1995.

Sánchez, Rosaura. *Telling Identities: The Californio Testimonios.* Minneapolis: University of Minnesota Press, 1995.

Sandos, James A. *Converting California: Indians and Franciscans in the Missions.* New Haven, Conn.: Yale University Press, 2004.

————. "Social Control within Missionary Frontier Society: Alta California, 1769–1821," in Jesús F. de la Teja and Frank Ross, eds., *Choice, Persuasion, and Coercion: Social Control on Spain's North American Frontiers.* Albuquerque: University of New Mexico Press, 2005.

————. "Toypurina's Revolt: Religious Conflict at Mission San Gabriel in 1785," *Boletín: The Journal of the California Mission Studies Association* 24:2 (2007), 4–11.

Starr, Kevin. *California: A History.* New York: Modern Library, 2005.

Stephenson, Terry E. "Forster v. Pico, a Forgotten California Cause Célèbre." *Historical Society of Southern California Quarterly* (June 1936).

Stevens, Donald Fithian. *Origins of Instability in Early Republican Mexico.* Durham, N.C.: Duke University Press.

Street, Richard Steven. *Beasts of the Field: A Narrative History of California Farmworkers, 1769–1913.* Palo Alto: Stanford University Press, 2004.

Tays, George. "Pio Pico's Correspondence with the Mexican Government, 1846–1848." *California Historical Society Quarterly* 13, no. 3 (1934).

————. "Revolutionary California: The Political History of California during the Mexican Period, 1820–1848." Unpublished Ph.D. dissertation, University of California, Berkeley, 1934.

Temple, Thomas Workman, II. "Toypurina the Witch and the Indian Uprising at San Gabriel." Reprinted in Edward D. Castillo, ed., *Native American Perspectives on the Hispanic Colonization of Alta California.* New York and London: Garland, 1991.

Torres Quintero, Gregorio. *México Hacia El Fin Del Virreinato Español.* México: Consejo para la Cultura y las Artes, 1990.

Voss, Barbara L. "From Casta to Californio: Social Identity and the Archaeology of Culture Contact." *American Anthropologist* 107:3 (Sept. 2005).

Walker, Dale L. *Bear Flag Rising: The Conquest of California, 1846.* New York, N.Y.: Tom Goherty Associates, 1999.

Weber, David J., ed. "California in 1831: Heinrich Virmond to Lucas Alaman." *Journal of San Diego History* 21 (Fall 1975).

————. *Foreigners in Their Native Land: Historic Roots of the Mexican Americans.* Albuquerque: University of New Mexico Press, 1973.

————. *The Mexican Frontier, 1821–1846: The American Southwest under Mexico.* Albuquerque: University of New Mexico Press, 1982.

————. *The Spanish Frontier in North America.* New Haven, Conn.: Yale University Press, 1992.

Newspapers

El Clamor Público (Los Angeles)
Los Angeles Herald
Los Angeles Star
Los Angeles Times
San Francisco Chronicle
San Francisco Herald

Index

Serrano, José Antonio, 135
Sherman, William T., 117
siete leyes, 61
Sinaloa, 12–13
Sloat, John, 100–101, 113
Smith, George, 163, 175–76
Solá, Vicente (governor), 16
Sonoma, 98, 100, 106
Sonora, Mexico, 13, 107–108, 120
Spain, 6, 10, 12–13, 17
Spanish constitution, 1812, 23, 25.
    See also Constitution of Cádiz
Standard Oil Company, 132
Stanford, Leland, 141
Star Oil Company, 132
Stearns, Abel, 35, 37, 39, 77, 103,
    118, 121, 127, 136
Stevenson, J. D., 113–14
Stockton, Robert F., 102–103
Stoneman, George (governor),
    170
Superior Court of San Francisco,
    160
Supreme Court of California, 134
Sureños, 37, 61, 69, 71, 80,
    95–99, 104
Sutter, John, 73, 199n18
Sutter's Fort, 93

Tejanos, 72
Temecula, 57–59, 64–68
Temple, John, 127
Texas, 5, 49, 71, 79, 83–84
Tongva (Indians), 18. *See also*
    Luiseños
Toypurina (Indian leader), 18
Treaty of Cahuenga, 107, 111
Treaty of Guadalupe Hidalgo,
    108, 112, 115, 117, 119, 123

Treaty of Las Flores, 61
Treaty of Santa Teresa, 73

United States: citizens of, 6, 91–92,
    96, 99; legal system of, 8, 28. *See
    also* Americanos; Anglo-Americans
U.S.-Mexican War, 4–8, 71, 76,
    79, 84–85, 91, 98, 100–102,
    104, 107, 139, 173

Valdez, Dorotea, 203n34
Vallejo, Mariano Guadalupe, 26,
    28, 31, 41, 55–56, 63–64, 75,
    82, 91, 96–98, 108, 111
Varela, Hilario, 81–82
Varela, Sérbulo, 81
Vastida (Pico), María Jacinta
    (grandmother), 15
Verdugo, José María, 18–19
Victoria, Guadalupe, 25, 31
Victoria, Manuel (governor), 4,
    33–43, 47, 178
Vignes, Luis, 81, 200n49
Virmond, Heinrich, 33

Warner, J. J., 127, 176, 178
Wartenburg, Henry, 155
Wells Fargo and Company, 144
Williams, B. T., 170
World's Columbian Exhibition
    (1893), 177

Yankees, 93, 110, 112, 116, 122, 159
Yerba Buena, 79
Yorkinos, 31, 33, 188n35, 189n38
Yorba, Teodosio, 104
Yorba, Tomás, 30, 41

Zamorano, Agustín, 42
Zúñiga, Ignacio, 20